The city's countryside

The city's countryside

Land and its management in the rural–urban fringe

C. R. Bryant
L. H. Russwurm
A. G. McLellan

University of Waterloo

Longman London and New York

Longman Group Limited
Longman House
Burnt Mill, Harlow, Essex, England
and Associated Companies throughout the world.

Published in the United States of America
by Longman Inc., New York

First published 1982

British Library Cataloguing in Publication Data

Bryant, C. R.
The city's countryside
1. City planning
I. Title II. Russwurm, L. H. III. McLellan, A. G.
333.77 HT166

ISBN 0-582-30045-2

Library of Congress Cataloging in Publication Data

Bryant, C. R., 1945-
The city's countryside.

Bibliography: p.
Includes index.
1. Land use-Management. 2. Regional planning.
I. Russwurm, Lorne H. II. McLellan, A. G. III. Title.
HD111.B75 307.7'2 81-17136
ISBN 0-582-30045-2 (pbk.) AACR2

Printed in Singapore by
Singapore National Printers (Pte) Ltd.

Contents

List of figures

List of tables

Preface

It may seem strange that three people with such apparently divergent interests have collaborated in producing this book. Russwurm has a long-standing interest in urban systems, Bryant in agricultural and rural development and urbanization, while McLellan is a geomorphologist by training with a particular interest in land rehabilitation. Similarly, the geographic focus of our personal research covers a wide area, including Canada, the US, Scotland and France. This diversity of interests has, however, found a common focus in the processes of change and the issues associated with the urban fringe and, more generally, the city's countryside, a microcosm of the land use, social and economic issues of our society. While we have naturally drawn heavily upon our own research experiences, we have concentrated more on providing a series of conceptual frameworks around which the literature we have surveyed has been organized; our hope is that other researchers will find these conceptual frameworks especially useful.

The initial idea for this book goes back almost a decade during the course of which our ideas have evolved through interchange between ourselves, with our colleagues and with our students. In any joint effort, it is sometimes difficult to say who is responsible for which sections and in some instances a section was truly jointly written. However, it is appropriate to identify the overall division of responsibilities for writing this text if for no other reason than to direct the many questions to which we hope our book will give rise. Part I, in which we develop our general approach and the key conceptual frameworks, was a joint effort by Bryant and Russwurm. In Part II, dealing with the activities of the city's countryside, Bryant was responsible for writing Chapters 4 (Land ownership and land conversion), 6 (Agriculture), 7 (Industry and commerce) and 9 (Infrastructure and institutions); Russwurm undertook the writing of Chapter 5 (Country residential development); and McLellan assembled the information for the aggregate industry in Chapter 7 and was responsible for writing Chapter 8 (Recreational activities). In Part III, on land management, Bryant was responsible for writing Chapter 10 (Land use, function and open space in the city's countryside), and the second half of Chapter 12 (The tools and concerns of land-use management) on the open countryside; Russwurm was responsible for writing Chapter 11 (The geography of land management) and the first half of Chapter 12. Finally, Russwurm and Bryant together collaborated on Chapter 13 (Overview and future directions) and compiled the major part of the bibliography, while Bryant undertook the task of integration and editing.

In addition to our own efforts, several other people deserve credit. Karen Steinfieldt, Susan Friesen, Jackie Rugwell, Joan MacLean, and Jackie Forabosco all put their shoulders to the wheel in typing the manuscript and seeing it through its various stages. Our colleague and friend, Richard Preston, proved invaluable as a sounding board for ideas at various times and, last but not least, our families helped us relax when we needed it most.

C. R. Bryant
L. H. Russwurm
A. G. McLellan
University of Waterloo
May 1981.

Acknowledgements

We are grateful to the following for permission to reproduce copyright material: Department of Geography, University of Waterloo: for our tables 4.1 and 4.2 and our fig. 4.1 from *The Rural Real Estate Market*, Publication Series, 1982, by C. R. Bryant; for our table 11.1 and our fig. 2.2 by Russwurm from *Essays on Canadian Urban Process and Form II*, Publication Series 15, 1980, edited by R. E. Preston and L. H. Russwurm; for our fig. 3.1 by Russwurm from *Essays in Canadian Urban Process and Form I*, Publication Series 10, 1977, edited by L. H. Russwurm, R. E. Preston and L. R. G. Martin; for our fig. 8.2 by Greer and Wall from *Recreational Land Use in Southern Ontario*, Publication Series 14, 1979, edited by G. Wall; and for our figs. 12.1 and 12.2 by Russwurm from *Essays on Canadian Urban Process and Form II*, Publication Series 15, 1980, edited by R.E. Preston and L. H. Russwurm; Department of Geography, University of Western Ontario, for our fig. 4.4 by Bryant from *Ontario Geography*, No. 10 (1976); University of Kentucky for our fig. 5.2 by Phillips from *Exurban Commuters in the Kentucky Bluegrass Region*, Monograph 5, Centre for Real Estate and Land Use Analysis, p. 31 (1977); The Canadian Association of Geographers for our fig. 6.2b by Bryant from *The Canadian Geographer*, Vol. 21 (1981); the Institut d'Aménagement et d'Urbanisme de la Région d'Ile-de-France for our figs. 10.1 and 10.2 by Latarjet in the *Cahiers de l'Institut d'Aménagement et d'Urbanisme de la Région d'Ile-de-France*, No. 27 (1972).

I *The structure and problems of the city's countryside*

1 Urbanization and the countryside

The countryside surrounding urban areas is one of the most critical areas of the human ecumene. Within it are resources vital for human society, both for present and future generations. Many urban centres are located in regions endowed with excellent agricultural resources; aggregate resources such as sand and gravel are most valuable when found close to the major markets, the cities, because of transportation costs; groundwater resources in such zones may sometimes prove significant in determining levels of urban growth; the landscape possesses amenity value and constitutes a major recreational resource for urban populations; and, of course, the vast bulk of the developable land needed to support expanding urban populations, economic activities and infrastructure will be found in the countryside currently surrounding cities in most countries.

It is not so much the extent of the resource base contained in the countryside around cities that makes it critical to society, but rather the fact that the land and resources therein are subject to competing, often conflicting, demands. The countryside around cities or, as we prefer to refer to it, the city's countryside, has been placed under pressure increasingly as it has been integrated progressively into a particular form of settlement organization characteristic of the post-industrial age – *the regional city*. The evolution of this broad functional organization of economic, social and, latterly, even political space, has multiplied the demands placed on land and its resources, has created conflicts and stresses, and has stimulated various adaptations of human activities.

The regional city can be thought of as a system that has been expanding into, and becoming integrated with countryside, so that the countryside is an integral part of this settlement form. The city's countryside can also be thought of as an *environment*, itself a complex system, comprising various dimensions – natural, economic, cultural, social and political. Each dimension may involve different components of the total environment system; what is more critical, however, is that the same component may have different values associated with it, depending upon the particular dimension and perspective. Land contains, for example, economic, social and natural environment values which may conflict and which are certainly complex. How these different values are translated into priorities by society in the city's countryside will play a major role in shaping the quality of life for future generations.

Our purpose is therefore to consider the various processes of change in land use occurring around cities, focusing on the Western world and experience. Our primary examples are taken from four countries, the US, the UK, France and Canada, which represent a range of government and cultural structures and with which we are most familiar, though reference is also made to other countries. Our interest is on investigating the stresses and adaptations of various human endeavours in the city's countryside, and on evaluating the collective response to the many land-use issues that have arisen. Throughout, two principal organizing themes are used, viz. the *regional city* form and the *environment as a system*. Furthermore, two other themes are given considerable attention. First, the importance of land ownership considerations is stressed particularly in the discussion of how conflicts arise and of the difficulties they present for conflict resolution. Second, the past and continuing roles of public planning involvement are emphasized because of our concern with the management of the problems and conflicts.

In the remainder of this introductory chapter, we shall consider:

1. the nature of the forces of change affecting the city's countryside, emphasizing the role of urbanization;
2. the types of countrysides developing around cities in relation to the *regional city* framework;
3. the specific forces underlying the evolution of this settlement form.

In the remainder of Part I, the environment of the city's countryside is discussed from a system's perspective, in which the various dimensions of the environment and their associated values are used as a vehicle for understanding the problems in the city's countryside. In Part II, the focus is on each of the principal activities contributing to, or being affected by, land-use pressures – agriculture, sand and gravel extraction, industry, recreation and residential development. Emphasis is placed on the actual processes of change and the identification of the problems created. A discussion of open space at the outset of Part III provides the link between our consideration of land-use activities and the management of land-use functions. In relation to land-use management, various issues are addressed – who is involved? Who should be involved? Why is it necessary? What has been the experience? We conclude by focusing on future directions and challenges in the development of land-use controls and management techniques.

The countryside, the city and urbanization

The countryside has long had special relationships with urban areas. For instance, agricultural development in areas such as the Canadian Prairies fostered the development of many small service centres whose prime function was to provide goods and services to a dispersed agricultural population (Zimmerman and Moneo 1972); in contrast, in mediaeval Europe under the feudal system, the countryside played a more subservient role to the town and city. The roles and positions of the countryside and the city *vis-à-vis* each other have varied from time to time and place to place. Within large parts of Western economies, agricultural service centres have declined in recent decades as agricultural population levels have decreased and it has become more efficient to serve rural areas from a smaller number of centres (Hodge 1965). Within the orbit of metropolitan centres, however, other rural centres have increased in importance following the influx of non-farm inhabitants into the countryside.

Despite such varying relationships, one point remains clear: whatever the exact relationship between countryside and city, and whether the countryside's main function is providing food, a place to live or a place to 'play', city and countryside are integral parts of the same social and economic system (Jung 1971). Thus, changes in city and countryside are interdependent. Since the Second World War, the pace of change in the countryside in Western society has quickened enormously. In the general process of *economic development*, agriculture has experienced a far-reaching revolution in terms of technological development and forms of economic production. Since agriculture is a major user of land around most cities, the impact of these changes on the landscape has been considerable. Intimately connected with the processes of economic development and growth has been another major force that has brought marked changes to the countryside – *urbanization*.

Urbanization, in its most general sense, refers to the complex set of processes by which the proportion of a country's population concentrated in urban areas increases over time (Tisdale 1942; Hauser and Schnore 1965). As an example, using the respective national census definitions of 'urban', the urban population of France increased from 24.6 per cent of the total population in 1846 to 56.2 per cent in 1968 (Bryant 1980), that of the US went from approximately 17 per cent in 1850 to about 73 per cent in 1970 (Clawson and Hall 1973; Bryant 1980), that of England and Wales went from about 50 per cent in 1850 to almost 80 per cent in 1970 (Clawson and Hall 1973) and that of Canada from 19.6 per cent in 1871 to 76.1 per cent in 1971. The process is intimately related to development within the primary sectors, especially agriculture. One result has been a reduction in the primary labour force necessary to satisfy given levels of demand; at the same time, the increasing emphasis on manufacturing and other non-primary activities in the economy has favoured concentration of economic activity in the major urban areas of the country.

Given the post-1945 trends, however, it is probably no longer appropriate to measure level of urbanization simply by the proportion of the population in urban areas. Several factors have contributed to the spread of essentially urban-oriented populations into the city's countryside (Lewis and Maund 1976). A more appropriate measure of urbanization might be the proportion of the population living in broader-functioning urban regions. These regions have been variously termed 'city regions', 'urban fields', 'daily urban systems', 'commuting zones' and 'regional cities'. Whatever the terminology used, the idea is basically the same, i.e. that the geographic elements of such a region are tied together by a common orientation to one or more urban centres. When viewed in this light, levels of urbanization appear even higher. For example, the 243 *Standard Metropolitan Statistical Areas* (SMSAs) alone accounted for 68 per cent of the US population in 1968, compared with the 59 per cent contained in the 168 SMSAs of 1950 (Clawson and Hall 1973). In Canada, the 22 *Census Metropolitan Areas* (CMAs) alone accounted for 55 per cent of national population in 1971, up from 50 per cent in 1961, while analysis of census data (Bryant and Russwurm 1981) shows that census subdivisions falling within 50 km of urban centres with a minimum 1976 population of 40,000 (60 km for CMAs over one million), contained 65 per cent of the national population in 1941 and 76 per cent in 1976. Similarly, in France, the generously defined *Zone de peuplement industriel ou urbain* (ZPIU) accounted for 79 per cent in 1975 (INSEE 1976). These areas are characterized generally by a high proportion of non-farm inhabitants, who have originated partly from migration into the city regions from other regions – a centripetal movement – and partly from a movement of population from the urban areas – a centrifugal movement. The type of region that has been developing can be aptly described by the term 'dispersed city' (Philbrick 1961), *la ville éparpillée* (Bauer and Roux 1976) or 'regional city' (Owen 1972).

The term 'urbanization' has often been used, quite naturally, to describe this process of infiltration of the countryside by non-farm elements, and has been frequently used synonymously with non-agricultural land-use development. In this book, we shall use 'urbanization' rather to refer to the general process outlined above, because urbanization is more than simply a demand for additional land. Indeed, we can view urbanization as creating a range of pressures that can effect changes in the countryside (see Fig. 1.1)

In the Western world, urbanization representing the geographic manifestation of economic development and growth has been associated with higher material living standards, more leisure time and higher income. The higher incomes associated with the concentrated *urban markets* produce *demands for certain goods* produced in the countryside. Specialty agricultural crops have been particularly affected, e.g. greenhouses, nursery products and sod farms, The often-observed difference in living standards between rural and urban areas has been partly responsible for the movement of populations into urban regions, and this in turn can be related to *the demand for labour* in the major urban areas. These population movements have had significant effects both in terms of the original rural population and the new communities evolving subsequent to the spread of non-farm populations in urban regions. And of course, *a demand for land* for various urban-oriented functions exists, which is heightened in the urban region. It is this demand and the ensuing competition for land in the countryside that has sparked most interest and research. The effects of this demand on the countryside are the most obvious and spectacular of all the effects of urbanization on the countryside, including the loss of agricultural land, land speculation and sterilization of land

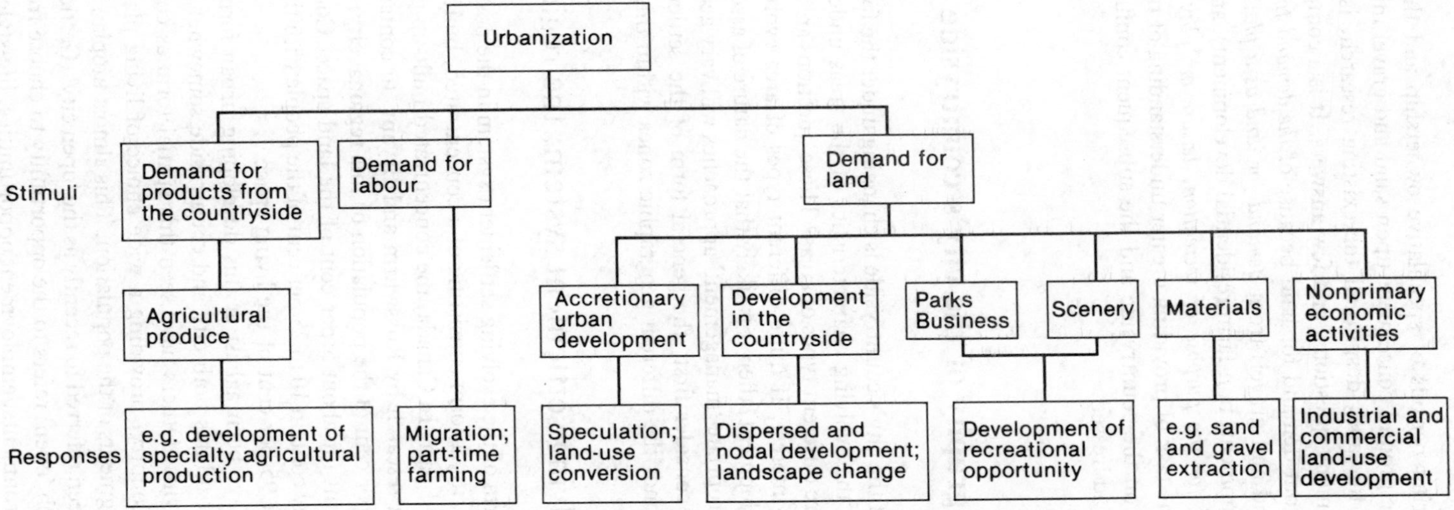

Figure 1.1 Forces of urbanization and the countryside. (Source: adapted from Bryant 1970).

productivity during periods of speculative ownership and the creation of huge holes in the ground consequent upon sand and gravel mining.

This demand for land, despite all the existing research, is still an area where there are many questions, and few answers. It is a complex demand; we can separate out demand for land because of *the demand for an economic resource* (e.g. sand and gravel) from *demand for land as a place to live* (e.g. residential development, non-farm residential development), and again from *demand for land for the purpose of recreation, leisure or 'play'* (Russwurm 1977a). It is to the task of providing greater understanding of these different demands placed on the countryside and the subsequent conflicts produced that our book is addressed.

The geography of the city's countryside

The geography of the city's countryside is changing under the forces outlined above. What are the evolving characteristics of the areas undergoing these changes? Are there different types of areas? These questions are of more than purely academic interest. If quite different types of area evolve under the pressures of development, then it is likely that the nature of associated problems and the appropriate 'management' approaches will vary geographically. Hence, we shall consider first, the general form of the settlement system evolving and second, the different geographic zones within this system.

The evolving settlement system: the regional city

The dominant form of the evolving settlement system in the post-war era has been the *regional city*, a form consisting of a concentrated, built-up part and an open, dispersed part. In Canada, the concentrated built-up part has been found in ongoing research by Russwurm and Bryant, to contain characteristically 75 to 90 per cent of the population of this regional city, even though it may only account for about 5 per cent of the land space. Conversely, the dispersed part may contain 10 to 25 per cent of the people with their activities spread over about 95 per cent of the living space.

Some people have been aghast at this developing urban form (Mumford 1961). To them it dilutes both city and countryside somewhat like pouring water into good wine. Others have seen this spatial form as combining the best of city and country, providing a wide choice of living places and life-styles for many segments of the population. This almost utopian 'best of both worlds' city has been referred to recently as the 'open city' (Gertler and Crowley 1977), in which 'open' refers to the opportunity to choose from a diverse mix of living environments, employment opportunities, life-styles and spatial surroundings. A key characteristic of this settlement form seems to be a scattering of natural environment areas in the built-up city and of urban-related functions in the open environment of the countryside.

We shall refer to this post-industrial settlement form as the 'regional city', a form which has reached its apogee in many parts of North America. Others have referred to it as an 'urban field' (Friedmann 1973a; Hodge 1974) or as an 'urban ecological field' (Gertler 1972). Our own preference is to use the term 'urban field' only for the dispersed part of the regional city. When several regional cities begin to merge or when one regional city becomes so extensive and complex that a single central concentrated core that animates the whole region is no longer clearly identifiable, then we have moved from the regional city to the broader megalopolitan structure (Gottman 1961).

The term 'regional city' is an appropriate one in the sense that a large area is included. The typical life space of such a system would be 80 to 100 km for cities of a million people or more, e.g. Montréal, Vancouver, London, Paris, San Francisco; a radius of 80 km provides a living area of over 20,000 sq. km in extent. In some respects, a regional city based on a large metropolitan area extends even further to include the weekend and seasonal 'play' space of the urban populations, e.g. the cottage developments in the Muskokas north of Toronto, much of Normandy to the west of Paris, and the Rockies for Denver. For smaller cities, say those under 100,000, a life-space radius of 40 to 80 km is more appropriate.

What are the other key characteristics of this regional city? Four aspects seem important. First, there is the mix of nodes of intensive land use and human activity scattered amidst farmland, woodland and sometimes swampland. Smaller cities, towns, villages, new communities, country estate subdivisions, and ribbon, crossroad and isolated developments, all occur. Second, there is a wide choice of possible living environments. Existing small cities, towns and villages, farmlands, forests, land abutting lakes and streams, and hillsides – all are possible living spaces.

The other two attributes concern the movement of people and goods. One is the pattern of flows that develops. The largest flows are still oriented towards the built-up city core, to its downtown as well as to its industrial, shopping and educational activity nodes often located on the edge of the built-up area. At the same time, a complex pattern of cross-directional movement occurs oriented to the activity nodes, both small and large, within the dispersed part of the regional city, and goods and people flow out of the city to outside activity nodes.

Finally, closely linked to these complex patterns of movement are the overlapping life spaces involved for different life functions. The 'work space' may be in one direction, the 'play space' in another, and the 'shopping' and 'social spaces' in yet other directions from the home or 'shelter space'.

Such highly diversified movements are basic to the functioning of our society and economy. They are possible only because of the highly developed networks for transportation, communication and transmission that we possess. The networks in the regional city may be so dense that they could be viewed as random route networks (Stone 1971) through which accessibility is equally possible in all directions. The regional city as a settlement form is possible only because of the density of links that are available.

Regional cities are post-industrial cities (Bell 1973). Increased mobility, better communication technology, wider leisure possibilities and greater environmental concerns have accompanied the shift in employment structure in Western economies from primary and manufacturing activities towards service, administrative, and more recently environmentally oriented activities. While industrial cities were dominated by concentrating, economizing modes of human activity, regional cities as post-industrial cities are additionally being characterized by dispersing, sociologizing modes, to use Bell's ponderous terms. How can we attempt to understand this complex regional city? A systems approach provides a helpful organizing framework.

The term 'system' implies an entity whose component parts are linked together by a series of interactions based on essential animating processes (Chapman 1978). People engage in complex activities at, and betweeen, particular places. These activities are accompanied by movements of people, goods, services, money transactions and messages. Complex patterns of flows which vary with function occur, based on activities carried out in daily, weekly and seasonal life spaces.

The concepts of form, function and structure are important aspects of a systems approach (Wurster 1963; Odum 1972). *Form* refers to the locational aspects of urban systems, or the physical pattern of land-use activities, population distribution and the networks linking them. *Function* refers to the activity itself and the flows necessary for that activity. For instance, the gravel pit operation functions to provide road and building material which has to be moved from one place to another. In systems terminology, *structure* refers to the combination of form and function, the total picture formed by the interlocking parts in their various locations and interrelationships, and in the whys and hows of the flows of people, goods, services, money transactions and messages between the parts.

Real human activity systems in which the natural environment is used for economic and cultural purposes generate the *form* and *function* of the regional city. Environments which are largely man-made, such as the built-up city, represent expressions of these activity systems. These activity systems themselves result from the interactions of the elemental human decision-making units, viz. individuals, households, firms and institutions. *Households* are the basic entity of human living. *Firms* provide goods and services to households and institutions for a profit. *Institutions*, however, do not necessarily demand a profit for their efforts. Institutions can usefully be divided into governmental and non governmental units. Together, they provide goods and services that are best provided collectively or are not being provided by profit-motivated firms.

Since our focus is on the dispersed component of the regional city, the city's countryside, we need to consider certain aspects of its *form* which can be accomplished by examining the different patterns of intensity of development within the dispersed part of the regional city.

Internal structure of the city's countryside

It is probably no surprise to find little agreement between academics and planners over definitions or the appropriate terminology to describe the variety of environments that have evolved within the city's countryside. Different terms such as 'fringe', 'inner fringe', 'rural–urban fringe', 'urban shadow', the 'exurban zone', even 'rurban fringe', are used sometimes interchangeably, sometimes to identify quite separate areas, but usually overlapping to some degree (Martin 1975a). A consensus exists, however, over the broad conceptual notion underlying the immediate countryside of our cities. As Wehrwein noted (1942: 218), over 30 years ago, the 'fringe' is: 'the area of transition, between well recognized urban land uses and the area devoted to agriculture.' A more precise, but equally generally acceptable statement is given by Pryor (1968: 206) who states that it: 'is the zone of transition in land use, social and demographic characteristics, lying between (a) the continuously built-up urban and suburban areas of the central city, and (b) the rural hinterland, characterized by the almost complete absence of non-farm dwellings, occupations and land use, . . .' The notion of 'transition' or a mixture of uses is explicit; however, we should not be led into assuming that this area is ephemeral – quite the contrary, for it is clear that such areas have become a permanent feature of the landscape around many cities, even though their inner and outer boundaries may be dynamic. It is only in the inner fringe of perhaps 10 km radius that much of the land will ultimately be transferred to continuous urban uses. The real definitional problem lies in the exact interpretation of this notion of transition, and in the choice of indicators with which to measure the extent of the 'fringe'.

The problem is easily identified but not so easily resolved. One can think of a continuum from urban to agricultural areas, characterized by changing relationships between a whole series of indicators (property structure, land use, agricultural structure, and social and community structure). Furthermore, the environment in which these areas of transition develop may vary significantly between different cities – contrast the prosperous agricultural areas surrounding most southern Ontario cities in which few engineering difficulties are encountered for construction, with the harsh physical environment around Halifax, Nova Scotia, where severe restrictions are placed by the physical environment on both agricultural investment and construction, or with the constrained locations of such cities as Vancouver, Marseilles and Auckland.

It is useful to portray the variety of situations schematically (Fig. 1.2). This structure, based partly on Russwurm (1975b, 1977a) and Bryant

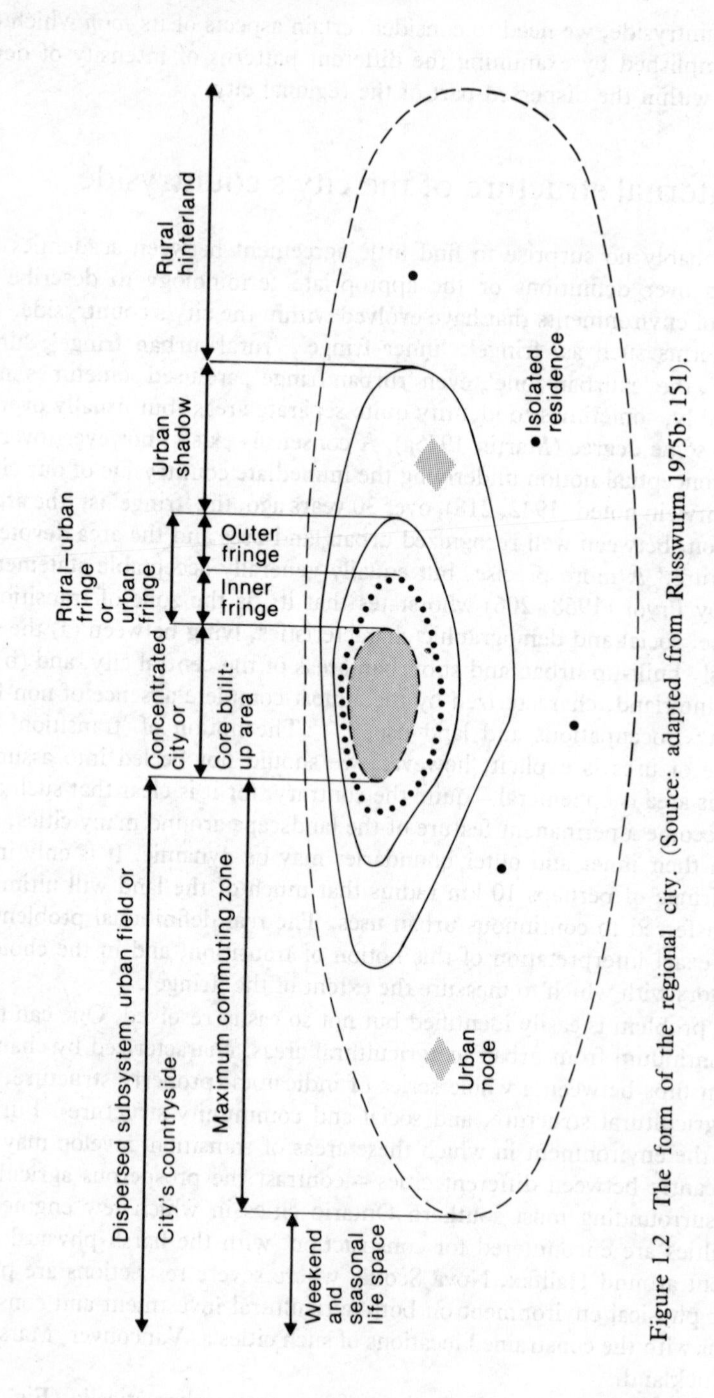

Figure 1.2 The form of the regional city. (Source: adapted from Russwurm 1975b: 151).

(1982), is particularly helpful since it stresses the notion of a continuum between urban area and rural hinterland. It illustrates graphically how we view the various terms and how they will be used in this book. The *inner fringe* is characterized by land in the advanced stages of transition from rural to urban uses – land under construction, land for which subdivision plans have been approved – in short, land where there is little doubt over much of its area about its urban-oriented function and ultimate conversion to urban uses. The *outer fringe* which, together with the inner fringe, forms the rural –urban fringe (sometimes called *urban fringe*) is an area where although rural land uses dominate the landscape, the infiltration of urban-oriented elements is clear. Often single-family dwellings on relatively small lots line the major highways into the city. Surrey, in the Greater Vancouver Regional District, British Columbia, contains classic examples of this type of development which has come to be known as 'ribbon development' or 'bits' of city scattered in the countryside (Hardwick 1974). Both inner fringe and outer fringes contain uses such as cemeteries, auto-wrecking yards and stock yards which are naturally attracted to the urban periphery because of their large space requirements and because of its cheaper land costs, as well as being repelled in a sense by the urban area because of their inherent 'nuisance' characteristics. It is perhaps because of these types of uses that Firey, writing in the 1940s (Firey 1946), could state that one of the characteristics of the 'rurban' (rural–urban) fringes of North American cities was that land use tended to gravitate to low-value uses. Firey's statement was made before the automobile had become truly widespread, permitting a virtual 'explosion' of the city.

In addition to the clearly visible land uses, the rural–urban fringe is characterized by many other changes much more difficult to perceive directly in the landscape. At the inner edge of this zone we would expect many properties to be in the hands of non-farm people, property owners who may have acquired land in expectation of future development. We are dealing with a dynamic situation. What today is rural and within the rural – urban fringe, may tomorrow be entering the final phases of the development process. Small lots may be bought up by people hoping to build their own home one day. Even more subtle is what can happen to farmland owned by farmers, who, anticipating some future development opportunity, may decide not to maintain the same level of investment in their land or to 'mine' the fertility of their soil.

Further out still, there may be an area of 'urban shadow', an area where physical evidence of urban influences on the landscape is minimal, but where the urban or metropolitan presence is felt in terms of some non-farm ownership of land, a scattering of non-farm residences, country estates, and the commuting patterns that develop from these and the outlying small communities and towns (Gertler and Hind-Smith 1962). And finally, the 'urban shadow' merges into the rural hinterland; even there, metropolitan and urban influences do not stop – urbanites may still own properties for weekend retreats and cottages, and the rural people themselves certainly cannot help but be influenced by urban values and ideas that are transmitted through the media. In the final analysis, we have to admit that we live today in a very urbanized society, and that there are not many parts of the Western world that remain unaffected by it.

The key to understanding these various zones is that they are simply different parts of a continuum, and that they are the results of a very complex and dynamic set of processes. Since each may merge into the other, any specific geographic definition must remain subjective. Definitions based on single criteria are subject to most debate, e.g. degree of mixing of land uses, level of non-farm ownership of land, the ratio of farm to non-farm population and commuting zones. Definitions relying upon several variables are likely to gain wider acceptability, but all definitions result eventually in the identification of threshold values and hence in boundaries drawn on maps. It is perhaps best to accept the various approaches to delimiting the rural–urban fringe – for as long as the criteria are made explicit in each study, we can at least evaluate them for what they are.

The structure represented in Fig. 1.2, is, of course, an 'idealized' one. The full sequence of types does not occur around all centres or even in all directions. Sometimes an abrupt change may occur from fringe to rural hinterland – for example, on the south bank of the Montréal region, the Richelieu River provides a distinct barrier to movement along parts of its length so that metropolitan influences are significantly reduced to the south-east of the river (INRS 1973). Sometimes, particularly strict planning controls may have the same effect, e.g. in the industrialized Ruhr area of West Germany where it is common to see cultivated fields immediately adjacent to factories. Similarly, cities in the Great Plains of the US and Canada often have much more distinct edges because of the land-tenure patterns of large square survey sections.

In fact, the rural–urban fringe is often a discontinuous spatial phenomenon around most cities. The existence of a 'fringe' at all is dependent upon pressures for growth, and these are certainly not equal in all directions. Growth often follows major access routes, or concentrates in areas with other features attractive for development. The fact that many studies have not developed these ideas is partly because the information is analysed at a general geographic level which precludes investigating the geography of the 'fringe' at a finer scale. Ferguson (1975), for instance, studied the internal geographic structure of Waterloo Township, which formerly surrounded the cities of Waterloo and Kitchener, Ontario. In Russwurm's study (Russwurm 1970), the whole of this township was identified as forming part of the rural – urban fringe of the two cities. However, Ferguson produced evidence based on real-estate transactions to show that significant parts of the township had not been materially affected by 'fringe processes'. Such differences in empirical findings show the importance of the spatial scale of data collection and analysis which is utilized in a given study.

One final point deserves attention: the question of land ownership. Most discussions of *definitional issues* in the 'fringe' revolve around land use, type and intermixture. While there are a few examples of studies where property structure and ownership have been included, such as non-farm ownership of land (e.g. Russwurm 1970), such studies are most notable for their relative scarcity. Yet, there is little doubt that a basic phenomenon underlying land-use change in the regional city is to be found in changes in the land ownership structure and the real-estate market. Indeed, changes in land ownership usually precede land use changes. In view of the growing body of literature on land development (e.g. Martin 1974; Spurr 1976) and land speculation (e.g. Clawson 1971), it would seem appropriate to investigate the extent of the fringe not only on the basis of a *picture* of the countryside at one particular time but also on the basis of the land market structure over a period of time.

Illustrative of the importance of land ownership structure is a study of 'rural' properties in the Niagara Fruit Belt (Ontario Department of Treasury and Economics 1972), in which a classification was produced with properties arranged along a continuum with 'true' agricultural properties at one end of the scale and 'true' urban (residential) properties at the other. Five so-called 'rurban' properties were identified ranging from the residential holding, a property with a residential local tax assessment, larger than 2 ha and whose owner had an urban occupation, to the part-time farm, a property with a farm assessment and a resident owner who was also a part-time farmer. The five types of 'rurban' properties together occupied almost 21,000 ha in the Niagara Fruit Belt, with two-thirds of them located in the core fruit-growing townships of Saltfleet, Pelham, Niagara and Thorold. Clearly, in order to identify urban and metropolitan influence, it is not sufficient to focus just on land use. Only by investigating land ownership structure and change is it possible to appreciate the magnitude or extent of metropolitan influence in the countryside; hence the importance of land ownership characteristics – social origin, income, motivation for land ownership – will be a recurring theme throughout this book.

The forces underlying the regional city form

Given that the countryside has been subject to the pressures of urbanization which have produced changes in the landscape, the following questions must be posed. Why have the rural–urban fringe and the urban shadow zones, developed the specific characteristics and form that they have? Why the 'sprawled' and dispersed regional city form?

Obviously, *urban population growth* constitutes a first condition. Without such growth, there would be little incentive to move resources, especially labour and land, out of their rural function into an urban-oriented function. However, pressure on resources, particularly land, is not sufficient in itself to account for the geographic configuration of the zones.

A major factor contributing towards the increasing extent of the fringe and shadow has been *the increased mobility of populations* over the last three decades. Probably the most significant component has been increased car ownership, which has increased the household's range of locational choice for a residence. In the US, for example, car-owning families increased from 59 per cent of all families in 1950 to 79 per cent in 1969 (US Bureau of the Census 1970). Workplace and place of residence have become increasingly separated as a result. Commuting distances of 100 km are not uncommon around cities of the Western world. Increased car ownership is in itself a feature of our urbanized and industrialized society, since car ownership has become accessible to most income classes, partly due to mass-production techniques in industry. And public investment in roads and associated infrastructure has certainly not impeded mobility by car. Public transit has also played a role in increasingly mobility, although overall probably less so in North America than in Western Europe. The development of regional public transit systems in many regions has contributed to a significant expansion of 'dormitory' functions for previously rural settlements, e.g. the Paris region with its intra-regional train system, the suburban railways of the London metropolitan area and even the commuter 'Go' trains of the Toronto region. Availability in the countryside of telephone, television and the same energy networks as exist in the city adds further to the potential for dispersion. Whether increasing energy costs will reduce the mobility effects remains to be seen.

While the changing conditions surrounding accessibility have played a significant permissive role in relation to the expansion of the area over which urban influences have spread, other economic, social and cultural factors have fuelled the process and have been important in determining the specific structures that develop. *Economic* factors certainly included considerations of accessibility and thereby the costs of transportation – 'ribbon' or 'strip' development along the major highways into our cities is testimony to the importance of this factor. But there are other costs such as the cost of land and housing, local taxes and the level of services. For the US, Raup (1975) adds post–Second World War housing policies to the list of economic factors; the policies made it easier to own single-family homes, as well as allowing the deductibility of taxes and interest on mortgages from taxable income. The final decision to locate somewhere represents a trade-off between all of these costs as well as the balancing of social and cultural factors. In terms of land costs, the combination of a search for cheap land and the land owner's attempt to realize the capital gains in the value of land has been largely responsible for 'leapfrogging' (Archer 1973), where development, instead of occurring adjacent to already existing urban areas, 'jumps' over large tracts of land which are being held speculatively by their owners, to less accessible land which is cheaper.

To understand fully the configuration and characteristics of fringe and shadow areas, we must also consider *individual rights and desires* (Gertler and

Crowley 1977). Already we have noted that land owners, in an attempt to reap high values from their land, can contribute to a dispersal of different land-use activities, especially residential ones, within the regional city. Furthermore, while some people may seek a home in the countryside because they perceive living costs to be cheaper, many others have been motivated by a desire for 'country' living or for a 'return to nature' (McQuinn 1978; Russwurm 1977b). It has been found, for instance, that hobby farmers have been attracted into the countryside on to farms from their former urban residences by a desire to bring up their families in a 'clean' environment where crime and drugs were perceived to be less in evidence (McKay 1976). *Changing life-styles* are thus an essential ingredient.

The intermixture of uses and functions in these areas can thus be related to the fact that the utility, and value, of these locations converge for many different functions and uses. There is no clearly identifiable boundary that separates areas with markedly different values and utilities for specific uses, a phenomenon accentuated by the greater mobility and flexibility afforded by the transportation developments noted above. This interpretation of the intermixture of uses and functions in fringe and shadow zones is consistent with Firey's (1946) quasi-Thunian analysis of the 'rurban' fringe (Fig. 1.3), in which he argued that the 'utility' of different locations declines differentially for different uses from the central city; at the location of intersection of the utility schedules, both uses possess the same utility and so intermixing occurs.

Finally, while the above factors have contributed to, and permitted, the development of fringe and shadow areas as they exist today, public policy or lack of it has allowed the phenomenon to flourish (Clawson and Hall 1973).

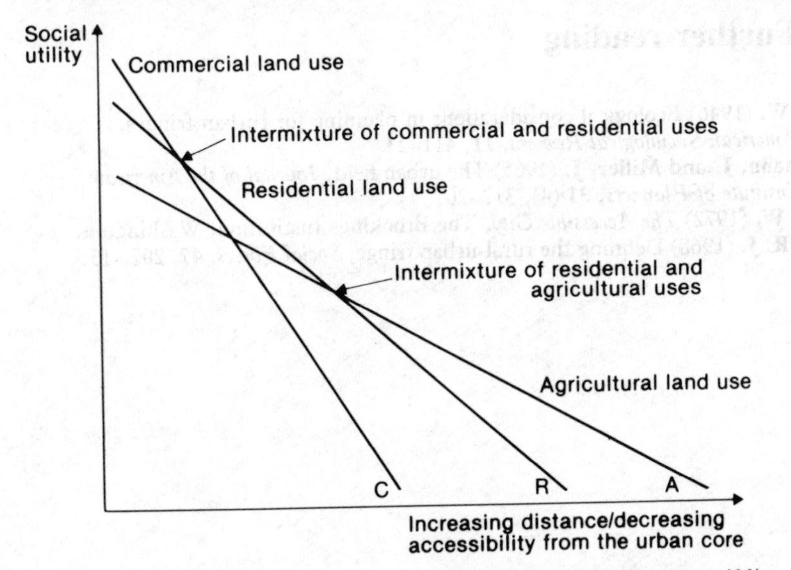

Figure 1.3 Firey's framework. (Source: after Firey 1946: Fig. 1, p. 411).

We should certainly not be surprised at the development of fringes and their associated land use and community problems; they are but the natural outcome of our society and institutions. In the area of public policy, planning controls have rarely been aimed at a scale commensurate with the problems. Municipalities have even contributed to the problems by openly competing for certain types of development. Control has largely been the domain of the individual municipality, despite the fact that the phenomenon itself has developed at a regional level. The development of regionally – based planning mechanisms in parts of Canada, of state-wide programmes in some US states and other forms of regionally structured intervention in many West European countries constitute essential moves towards solving part of the problem.

It is well to reiterate the fact that the countryside around our cities has experienced a quickening in the pace of change in the last three decades. So far, we have focused upon the types of pressures and resulting landscapes being produced by the process of urbanization, especially forces that relate to the demand for land for various functions. But, as noted earlier, these are not the only pressures our countryside is responding to. There are also potent forces related to economic development which have affected different economic activities such as agriculture, mineral extraction and manufacturing. Consequently, our treatment in later chapters will of necessity broaden to consider these as well.

In the next chapter, the city's countryside is discussed as a segment of the regional city comprising three overlapping environments or dimensions, the natural, economic and cultural environments.

Further reading

Firey, W. (1946) Ecological considerations in planning for rurban fringes, *American Sociological Review*, **11**, 411–23.
Friedmann, J. and Miller, J. (1965) The urban field, *Journal of the American Institute of Planners*, **31** (4), 312–20.
Owen, W. (1972) *The Accessible City*, The Brookings Institution, Washington.
Pryor, R. J. (1968) Defining the rural-urban fringe, *Social Forces*, **47**, 202–15.

2 Environments of the city's countryside

The city's countryside, part of the regional city system, can be viewed as comprising three overlapping environments: natural, economic and cultural. The natural environment provides the support systems for life – food, air, water and other resources; the economic environment contains the activities through which natural resources and human resources are used to provide for human needs; and the cultural environment, including social and political subsystems, consists of those activities primarily undertaken for motives other than profit or making a living. Involved in the cultural environment are cumulative group interactions, individual human interactions, group-individual interactions and subsystem interactions of the cultural environment with the economic and natural environments (Fig. 2.1). Values, beliefs, attitudes and perceptions of people are the generating forces of the cultural environment.

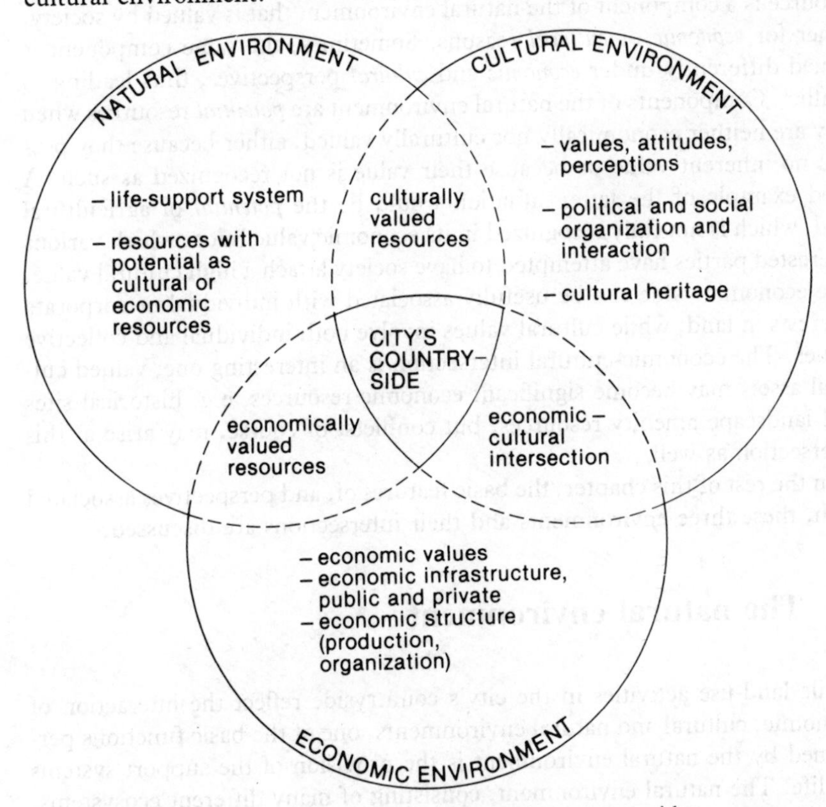

Figure 2.1 Intersection of environments in the city's countryside.

The environments: a conceptual framework

The identification of the three basic environments can be related to Firey's (1960) framework for viewing man-land relationships. The importance of these environments for the city's countryside lies in the different ways in which they intersect (Fig. 2.1). Such a framework can, of course, be utilized to structure thinking about any type of geographic area. For the city's countryside, it highlights how conflict arises because of the divergent values and perspectives associated with the different environments, and helps emphasize the phenomenon of regional variation in the total structure of the city's countryside.

In Chapter 1, our emphasis was on the regional city, suggested as the common form of settlement evolution in the Western world in the post-1945 period. However, we must expect differences in the final structure of the regional city depending upon the particular combination and content of the three basic environments present in a given region.

The natural environment contains the basic life-support systems for human society, as well as resources, both actual and potential. An *actual* resource is a component of the natural environment that is valued by society, either for *economic* or *cultural* reasons. Sometimes, the same component is valued differently under *economic* and *cultural* perspectives, thus leading to conflict. Components of the natural environment are *potential* resources when they are neither economically nor culturally valued, either because they possess no inherent value or because their value is not recognized as such. A good example of the latter situation would be the *potential* of agricultural land, which is not fully recognized in its economic value but to which various interested parties have attempted to have society attach a high cultural value. The economic value can be usefully associated with individual or corporate interests in land, while cultural values involve both individual and collective values. The economic-cultural intersection is an interesting one; valued cultural assets may become significant economic resources, e.g. historical sites and landscape amenity resources, but conflicts, of course, may arise at this intersection as well.

In the rest of this chapter, the basic features of, and perspectives associated with, these three environments and their intersections are discussed.

The natural environment

While land-use activities in the city's countryside reflect the interaction of economic, cultural and natural environments, one of the basic functions performed by the natural environment is the provision of the support systems for life. The natural environment, consisting of many different ecosystems, provides the resources used by man (Fig. 2.2).

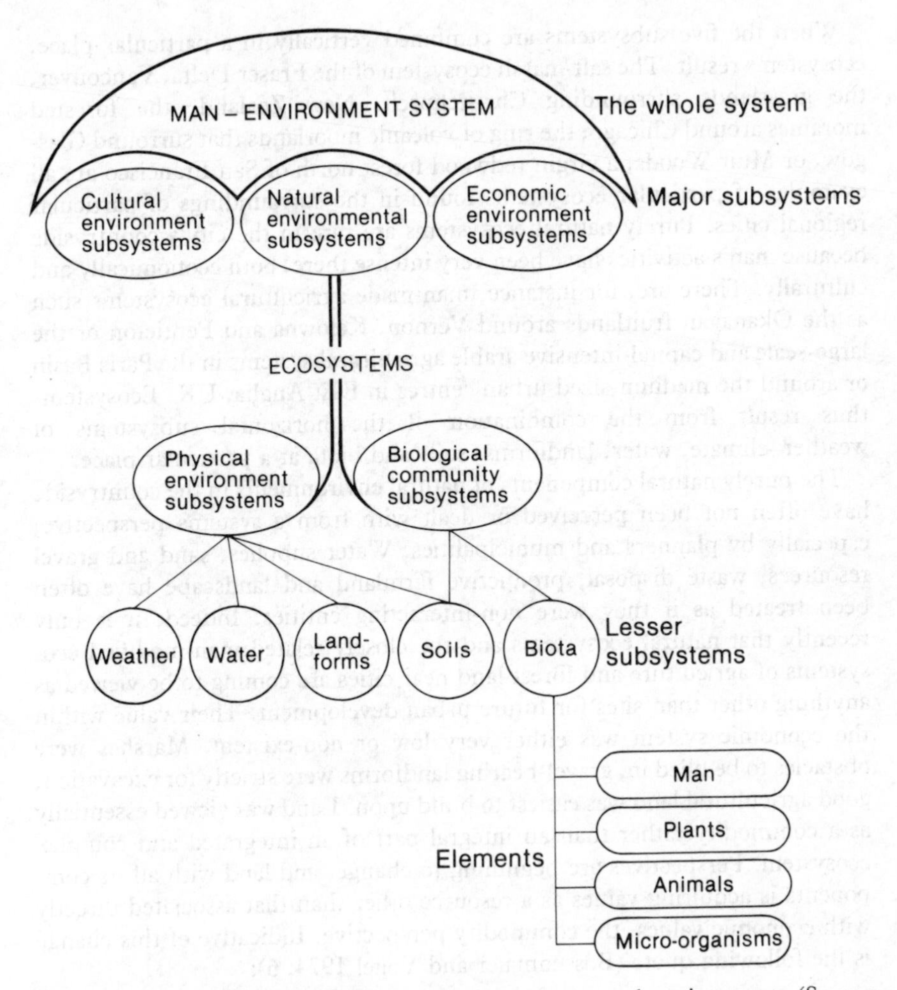

Figure 2.2 The basic life-support systems of the natural environment. (Source: from Russwurm 1980a: 461).

Ecosystems: the structure of the natural environment

Subsystems of the natural environment can be analysed as either horizontal or vertical systems. Viewed horizontally, five subsystems comprise the natural environment: weather–climate, water, landforms, soils and biota (Russwurm and Sommerville 1974). These range from non-living to living subsystems. Soils constitute the interfacing subsystem linking the non-living physical environment consisting of weather and climate, water and landforms with the living biological community.

When the five subsystems are combined vertically in a particular place, ecosystems result. The salt-marsh ecosystem of the Fraser Delta, Vancouver, the grasslands surrounding Christchurch, New Zealand, the forested moraines around Chicago, the ring of volcanic moorlands that surround Glasgow, or Muir Woods, a virgin redwood forest north of San Francisco are all examples of particular ecosystems found in the surroundings of particular regional cities. Purely natural ecosystems are rare in the city's countryside because man's activities have been very intense there, both economically and culturally. There are, for instance, man-made agricultural ecosystems such as the Okanagan fruitlands around Vernon, Kelowna and Penticton or the large-scale and capital-intensive arable agricultural systems in the Paris Basin or around the medium-sized urban centres in East Anglia, UK. Ecosystems thus result from the combination of the horizontal subsystems of weather–climate, water, landforms, soils and biota at a particular place.

The purely natural components of natural environments in the countryside have often not been perceived or dealt with from a systems perspective, especially by planners and municipalities. Water supplies, sand and gravel resources, waste disposal, productive farmland and landscape have often been treated as if they were non-interacting entities. Indeed, it is only recently that natural ecosystems and the closely related man-modified ecosystems of agriculture and forest land near cities are coming to be viewed as anything other than sites for future urban development. Their value within the economic system was either very low or non-existent. Marshes were obstacles to be filled in, gravel-bearing landforms were strictly for excavation, good agricultural land was easiest to build upon. Land was viewed essentially as a commodity rather than an integral part of an integrated and complex ecosystem. Perspectives are beginning to change, and land with all its components is acquiring values as a resource other than that associated directly with economic values, the commodity perspective. Indicative of this change is the following quote (Bossenmaier and Vogel 1974: 6):

> Our understanding and appreciation of natural systems, food webs and energy cycles are expanding. Animals that once were ignored or considered useless or nuisances, such as insects, toads, snakes, sparrows, and wolves, are suddenly assuming roles of importance in the minds of more people. There is far more to this change in attitude than mere 'love of nature'. We are beginning to see clearly a connection between the survival of the human race and the survival of other animals, plants, and whole ecosystems.

The resource and the commodity perspectives of land

Land as a resource and a commodity fulfils four basic functions: place, protection, production and play (Russwurm 1975a). As a 'place' land provides a site on which to locate activities. From an economic standpoint, accessibility to particular nodes is of major importance in determining the relative commodity value of land. Land is sold and bought for the location of houses, factories, businesses or institutions. The other three basic functions are primarily resource-oriented: natural environment based recreational resources for play; soil, mineral and biological resources for production; and biological resources for ecological protection. Land for the production and play functions varies in value as a commodity according to its combined resource capability and accessibility. Sometimes land for production and play commands a direct commodity value, e.g. current value of agricultural land and the urbanite's willingness to pay a premium for a weekend retreat or a second residence; and sometimes, there is a resource component to the value of the land, e.g. the *potential* of agricultural land and the amenity value of landscape. Finally, land for ecological protection is dominantly a resource and cannot be viewed as a market commodity. Such resource values are intrinsically complex and are most easily seen as falling into the cultural–natural environment intersection. Because of the complexity of the values involved, however, it is almost inevitable that different groups of people will place different priorities on the same basic element. Such is the stuff of land-use planning and management!

It is near cities where such conflicts concerning land as a resource or commodity are most severe. The key to developing a more efficient use of land in the city's countryside lies in establishing priorities for the land needed to fulfil these four basic functions, which means that due consideration must be given to the resource value of land as well as its commodity value. We shall provide a synthesis of the various functions of land in Chapter 10, when we discuss the roles and functions of open space, and the importance of determining priorities for open space in planning for the city's countryside. Next we turn briefly to expanding the contention of our introductory paragraph, that the city's countryside is perhaps the most critical zone of the human ecumene.

Criticality of land in the city's countryside

It is in the urban field of regional cities that conflicts between the major functions of land are most acute, and this is accentuated in the rural-urban fringe. Essentially the overall problem is one of a divergence between short-term market values ('land as a commodity') and longer-term resource values ('land as a resource'). The divergence between commodity and resource perspectives involves many questions such as: Where should the new subdivisions or new satellite communities go? What recreational, water supply or sand and gravel land should be set aside for future use? In what areas and in what quantities should agricultural land be preserved? Should environmentally sensitive areas of land be protected in land-use plans?

Most of the land needs of the future must be met from the supply of land in the urban field. Land in the urban field is, almost by definition, the most accessible land to the bulk of a country's population. The bulk of the land necessary to support housing and the associated infrastructure of roads, commercial land uses, industry, and educational, recreational and social facilities will be met in all likelihood within 10 km of the existing built-up edge of cities in the next 50 to 100 years. Even in Great Britain with its advanced new town programme, no more than 5 per cent of the land needs for urban dwellers will be met by such new town developments (Champion 1972). In any case, most of the British New Towns are located in urban-field locations, i.e. within 40 km of an existing built-up area; similarly, the five new towns developed since 1965 in the Paris region are in many ways but extensions of the Paris agglomeration, all being within the daily urban system of Paris (Délégation Générale au District de la Région de Paris 1966).

What is critical is the fact that the urban field which contains so much of the land required for urban development purposes also includes some of the best land for agriculture in many countries (Vining, Plaut and Bieri 1977). It also contains land with considerable recreational resources such as the Laurentian Mountains north of Québec City and Montréal, the California coastal lands, the varied landscapes in the London Green Belt, and parts of the Alps near Lyons. Around some cities, it also contains land underlain by glacial parent materials which provide the raw materials for roads and buildings. It is also the zone from which come the water supplies, both surface and underground, of many cities. Finally, then, it also contains the land that bears the brunt of the detrimental environmental impacts resulting from the development of urban-oriented activities, impacts which affect ecological resources, pollution, landscape amenities, and potential for future uses (Russwurm 1977a).

These detrimental environmental impacts themselves involve complex sets of processes and are associated with many values and perspectives. Ecological impacts include changes wrought upon those land characteristics necessary for the maintenance of air, water, landform, soil, vegetation and wildlife; areas especially sensitive to disturbance include water supply sources, groundwater recharge areas, floodplains, easily erodible slopes, and unusual natural ecosystems including wildlife breeding areas. Close interrelationships exist between pollution impacts and the need for ecological protection. Pollution outputs from urban activities by and large end up in the water, soil and air of the urban fields of regional cities, and agricultural operations also tend to be more intensive near cities, thus contributing to soil and water pollution. No doubt, wilderness areas hold much of their importance to us because of our carelessness with the natural environment near cities. However, because of the accessibility of natural environment areas in the urban field, their value potentially is so much greater than the remoter wilderness areas. Similarly, what is 'rural' to most people is the landscape near cities, again because of accessibility. The amenity value of landscape represents a perceived synthesis of natural, economic and cultural environments. The degradation of landscape amenity is thus a difficult impact to grasp because landscape means different things to different groups. Finally, the development of urban-oriented activities has an impact on the potential of land for future uses. Since some land can be utilized for a wider variety of functions than other areas of land, physical development may reduce unnecessarily the future options available if land with a narrower range of possible functions could have been developed instead; and, of course, pollution and ecological degradation themselves restrict the flexibility of choice of future generations.

Planning and management approaches in which an attempt is made to weigh and assess simultaneously the potential of land for the protection, production, play and place functions are aptly referred to as ecological planning (McHarg 1969; Kitchen 1976). The challenge for management is to work with the land rather than against it, to view it as offering a renewable potential within which economic exploitation and resource maintenance can coexist. How far we advance successfully with this approach depends on the economic and cultural environments of our society.

The economic environment

Two types of resource-use activities are found within the city's countryside: one involves the physical movement of either the resource materials or the products derived from them into the city and elsewhere; the other involves direct use at the site. The export type of resource use entails mainly production functions such as agricultural, mineral and forest production, the products of which are shipped to the city and beyond. Water is a fourth resource exported but often does not involve an economic, i.e. profit, motive. Overall, however, such export resource use is intimately tied to the economic environment. The on-site type of resource use, on the other hand, entails mainly protection and play functions. Residential use of scenic sites, outdoor recreation involving the use of lakes and streams, environmental experiences dependent on hiking, scenery and wildlife viewing, illustrate on-site resource-use activities. These activities have their roots in attitudes, values and perceptions engendered by our cultural environment. While some of these on-site activities are certainly part of the economic environment, such as campsites and recreational complexes, many other activities are not part of the economic production environment. Many of the conflicts that exist in the city's countryside arise because of the divergent values associated with the production-oriented economic environment and the non-economic, non-production-oriented cultural environment.

Production and conflict

The use of land for production in the city's countryside is thus at the heart of land-use activity conflicts, and underlying this are basic issues relating to the nature of interests in land. On the one hand, production involves actually making use of the potential resources in the natural environment, e.g. well-drained and fertile agricultural soils or sand and gravel associated with glacial, lacustrine, alluvial or marine deposits. On the other hand, the same land may be desired for its place function, e.g. for residential or industrial development. Conflicts occur between users interested in the production function of land as well as between such users and others interested in the place or play function.

Such conflicts can therefore occur even when the commodity view of land is all-prevailing. The market allocation process theoretically solves these conflicts by a process in which land is devoted to the use able to generate the highest net return (Gardner 1977). The muddle of land uses still characteristic of the inner urban fringe around many cities, however, reflects the market allocation process and individualism at its worst, because this market allocation process does not take account automatically of the externalities of land development. It is true that externalities, positive and negative, can be accommodated by the market process but first an economic value must be placed on them and this occurs only after a lag period during which society starts to recognize the particular externalities, e.g. pollution effects.

Conflicts over land also reflect individual versus collective, and economic versus ecological and cultural views. Time perspectives involving present–present, present–future and future–future conflicts or trade-offs over land are also part and parcel of the problem. The conflicts that have arisen over the building of any major airport such as Mirabel near Montréal or proposed airports such as those for London or Miami show clearly the whole range of these conflicts.

Land is increasingly viewed today as a resource having ecological, economic, and cultural dimensions. In terms of Fig. 2.1, more of the components of the natural environment are finding their way into the cultural–natural environment or the economic–natural environment intersections, or both. Spillover effects from one parcel of land to another, or the externalities of land development, are recognized by more and more people; whether the land is privately or publicly owned, people are increasingly concerned about what happens to each other's land. As Marion Clawson concludes in one of his books (1972: 158):

> We are likely to see increasing public controls over private land use; the externality relationship will increase in importance and will demand more concern for the general public not directly involved in an existing land use or in a proposed change in land use. The private market will still remain important, although increasingly conditioned by public controls and public incentives. The political process (using this term in a very broad sense) will determine or at least strongly influence many land use decisions.

Particular areas of conflict involving production functions include urban development and good agricultural land; country residential development and agricultural operations; sand and gravel operations and residential uses; sand and gravel operations and natural ecosystems; groundwater removal and agriculture; and agricultural development and landscape amenity.

The extent of such conflicts varies regionally. Specific combinations of the three environments may mean that certain types of conflict are unlikely to be significant in some regions. Where agricultural resources are poor and agriculturally uncompetitive, e.g. around Canadian cities in the Maritime Provinces or Toulouse or Marseilles in France, agriculture–urban development conflicts are not likely to be severe. And conflicts with sand and gravel deposits largely depend upon the resource being found in the urban field, as around many southern Ontario cities.

Market allocation problems

The market allocation process can be regarded as a set of processes whereby land as a commodity is converted to that use which places the highest money value on land (Barlowe 1978). This process is increasingly being moderated by longer-run approaches involving resource views and culturally assigned values. Figure 2.3 shows the general pattern of value around cities that results from market allocation. The place function of land for residential uses has a much higher value than does the production function of agriculture.

The market allocates land on a short-term basis according to demand–supply interactions occurring at a particular place at a particular time. Thus, the potential of the land in the longer term is lost sight of as the market gives land to the highest bidder who views land in terms of a partic-

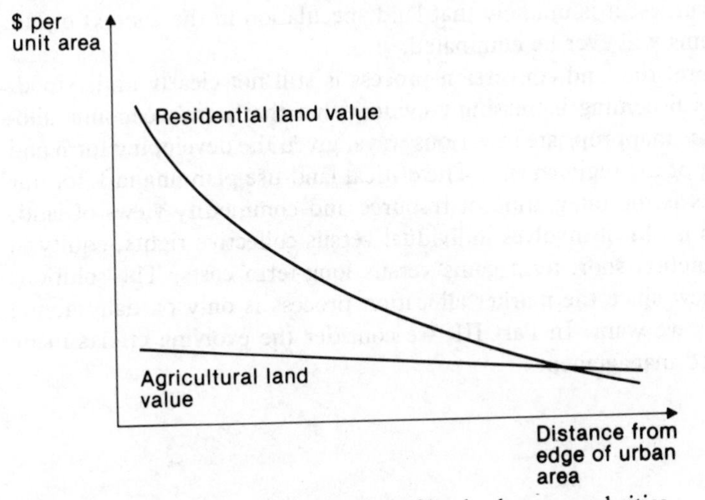

Figure 2.3 Schematic representation of land values around cities.

ular use returning profit to him. Agricultural and forest land as well as the natural environment have commonly been associated with very low priorities under this system. Features of land allocation which reflect the short-term nature of the economic allocation system are seen in:

1. the mixture of sometimes incompatible land-use activities especially in the inner urban fringe, reflecting the lack of consideration of externalities in the short-term;
2. land speculation with its short-term profit goal;
3. the use of land for short-term individual benefits at the expense of longer-term benefits to all, e.g. the development of large residential lots in scenic areas, restricting public access to such resources;
4. perhaps most critical of all, the rising cost of land.

Part of the rising cost of land is related to general inflation, but as well, stocks and land are competitors for investment, with land generally seen as a hedge against inflation. High land values in the urban field from this perspective are thus seen as arising naturally from market forces but may push agricultural land beyond the reach of many farmers while increasing the cost of land for housing. Since all of these problems reflect the lack of consideration of collective values, it is to the public body that we must turn in order to develop a process by which such externalities and resource values can be incorporated into a land-resource allocation system.

Thus, the demands of land for different uses and functions need to be clearly spelled out and set in a framework of land as a resource, not just a commodity. The realistic estimation of land conversion needs would reduce uncertainties in the real-estate market, thereby reducing the speculative motive. Then, for example, the large-scale developers who build our subdivisions and housing estates would not need to maintain large stocks of land as part of their business enterprise. However, we should not underestimate the difficulties in developing such projections of land needs; indeed, because of such difficulties, it is unlikely that land speculation in the context of our societal systems will ever be eliminated.

Furthermore, the land conversion process is still not clearly understood, although it is becoming increasingly evident that the 'pure' economic allocation model is inappropriate in various ways, given the developing form and spatial extent of the regional city. The critical land-use planning task for our regional cities is the integration of resource and commodity views of land. The problem is old: it involves individual versus collective rights, equity in costs and benefits, short-term gains versus long-term costs. The solutions need to be new since the market allocation process is only partially giving us the results we want. In Part III, we consider the evolving efforts made for better land management.

The cultural environment

Many aspects of the cultural environment affect what happens in the city's countryside. How is the countryside perceived? What planning approaches are prevalent and what ideologies underlie them? What individual property rights are accepted as inviolable? What socioeconomic groups live side by side? What are the municipal administrative units involved? What are the most evident interactions with economic and natural environments? These are but some of the questions involved in appreciating the role of the cultural environment in the urban field. To begin with, let us turn to the most concrete expression of the changing cultural environment in the city's countryside, the increasing number of urbanites living in the countryside.

Country urbanites

To a limited degree before, but especially since the Second World War, the countryside around Western cities has been recolonized by urbanites moving out from the built-up city. Thus, today, certainly within 50 km but even within 100 km or more of our cities, there are often more non-farm residences than farm residences. Farmers and urbanites following different lifestyles occupy land space side by side. The regional city spreads its boundaries far and wide. Though these urbanites live in the country, including the small villages and towns, they belong mostly to the city. Often they are called 'exurbanites'. We use this term to refer to people living beyond the city limits but remaining part of the city in most other ways (Punter 1974). At the same time, however, more country urbanites are becoming part-time or hobby farmers, while more farmers are becoming part-time urbanites by working in the city, so the distinction between the two groups becomes blurred.

Research into the phenomenon of the urban recolonization of the countryside in Canada, for example, identified it initially as a cultural phenomenon. The wealthiest families, in most cities, had their country estate (Punter 1974) at an earlier date. Then for a period after the Second World War, economic factors of cheaper land and building one's own home led to a rapid increase in the number of dispersed country residential units. As soon as it became evident that such modest houses were requiring more services than they paid in taxes, planning regulations led to increasing restrictions, often involving (e.g. in Ontario) high minimum lot sizes and minimum floor areas. Consequently, by the 1970s once again only the wealthier urbanite could afford easily to live in the country. The exurbanite process had run a full cycle.

Prior to the completion of the cycle, however, many urbanite households had relocated to the country for cultural reasons. The reasons were many: to be near nature; to have more private space; to keep horses, dogs and other animals; to have a better environment for raising children (Russwurm 1977b; Manitoba Municipal Planning Branch and University of Manitoba 1974). Economic and cultural reasons are often entwined, however.

This phenomenon of increasing numbers of country urbanites is implicit in the regional city form. However, we might expect levelling off in the near future in industrialized countries for three reasons:

1. because of more and more restrictive planning controls making it very difficult to obtain a country lot;
2. because it seems reasonable to assume that only a certain proportion of the urban population is ever desirous of becoming an exurbanite;
3. because of the increasing cost of commuting as petrol prices continue to rise.

The landscape of the countryside is clearly changing. The increasing number and variety of non-farm residences create change, as do the technological changes within farming. As a lived-in environment, the dispersed part of the regional city is partly urban, partly rural, and at least four types of people who live there are distinguishable: farmers, part-time farmers (farmer-urbanites), exurbanites, and second-home urbanites. The interaction of these four groups results in a changing cultural landscape whose artefacts include in North America the pick-up truck, the huge tractor with the enclosed cab, the steel barn and silo, the swimming pool, the station wagon and the white picket fence. In other countries, the specific artefacts may vary, for instance the omnipresent white villa in the French countryside (Bauer and Roux 1976), but everywhere the message is clear: the landscape changes to reflect a different mix of cultural values. This new cultural landscape, neither traditional city nor traditional country, is part of the developing post-industrial society.

Land ownership considerations

With private property one of the bastions of Western society, changing land ownership structures in the city's countryside reflect both cultural and economic values. The motives involved in non-farm ownership of land in the city's countryside are several. They arise from deeply engraved cultural attitudes to land. But cultural reasons such as wanting a home, a cottage or a farm in the countryside, or a deep-seated value that one should own land, are intertwined with economic reasons of investment and speculation. However, what we can do with land we own in the city or the city's countryside is increasingly circumscribed by governmental regulations as the externalities associated with different types of land-use change are appreciated. Nevertheless, the increasing spread of non-farm ownership still characterizes urban fringe and urban shadow areas.

Generally, information on non-farm land ownership is sparse. In Canada real-estate transactions are not combined with assessment; land registry and assessment offices are separate. Land ownership information is even more difficult to come by in many other countries, e.g. the UK (Munton 1976a, b). One is hard put to find research evidence of the spatial pattern of non-farm ownership around our cities, and even less so of the relative importance of different motives for owning land. We need to be concerned about the lack of easily accessible public information on land ownership around our cities because such a lack creates uncertainty and encourages speculation.

Of course, how land is treated from a planning or management perspective also reflects the cultural attitudes and values of a given country. In our private-enterprise societies, the economic place function of land still tends to be of major importance. Increasingly, however, cultural forces are gaining strength, reflected in greater efforts being devoted to planning and management.

Some sociopolitical considerations

Finally, with the increasing influx of urbanites into the city's countryside and the appearance of problems related to the intersection of the natural, economic and cultural environments, sociopolitical issues arise. These issues are themselves part of the cultural environment and reflect the changing mix of residents. Four such issues are:

1. the relationships with and effects on the rural community;
2. the equity issues over taxes paid and services received;
3. the effects on pre-existing settlements, usually agricultural service centres;
4. the ramifications of leisure and recreation pursuits by urbanites.

It was indicated earlier that within the 50 km band around our cities, exurbanites generally equal or exceed the number of farmers today. While the social networks of the exurbanites are more closely linked to the city than to the rural community, links to the rural community increase with length of residence (Walker 1976, 1977). Their children may attend the local school and take part in local activities; the household depends on local garbage collection and road maintenance services; and some countryside churches have seen a resurgence based on more and more exurbanites becoming members.

As farm populations decline with increasing farm size, various rural community services sometimes become difficult to maintain because of the fewer people available, and the decline in farm population has been a major trend in agriculture in industrialized countries. As an example, in the London regional city, southern Ontario (Russwurm 1976), the farm population declined from 122,000 in 1951 to 80,000 in 1971. However, this loss of 42,000 was more than offset by an increase in the scattered non-farm population from 25,000 to 77,000. Therefore, some benefits to the rural community from the influx of exurbanites result simply from the addition of more people. School bussing routes can also become more cost efficient as most exurbanite households have children. On the other hand, additional costs to the rural community can result as more servicing is needed. The *per capita* cost may go down but the absolute cost goes up.

One of the long-standing issues here is that of who pays the taxes versus who receives the services. In North America, the problem has revolved around whether or not farmers are subsidizing urbanites living in the country. In the built-up city, commercial and industrial properties pay more in taxes than they receive in services while the reverse holds for the residential properties. This problem for the countryside was identified shortly after the Second World War; a review of the research in this area has been given by Russwurm (1977a, b). Recent studies (Alberta Land Use Forum 1974; Morgan 1978) indicate that the problem still exists.

The question of taxation and services can obviously lead to conflict of values between farmers and non-farmers. Should the numbers of exurbanite property holders exceed that of farmers, they may be able to 'stack' the local council and thus institute the level of services desired. Such a move means increased taxes for all but, given the subsidy by farmers, they would continue to be hardest hit. Such conflicts appear to surface more readily when a rapid influx of exurbanites occurs over a short period. Somewhat similar conflicts can arise when a subdivision is thrust upon a small agricultural service centre (Wibberley 1974). The newcomers in the subdivision may exceed in numbers the prior residents. Schools and services have to be expanded; water and sewage have to be expanded. In fact the developer may offer to provide such services as a carrot to induce the local council to permit development (Harrison 1976).

In a somewhat larger village, the newcomers may wish to halt 'progress' in the form of apartment buildings while the locals may see such a development as 'growth' (e.g. Sinclair and Westhues 1975). Typically, a small number of centres become the 'status villages' for exurbanites moving out of a particular city. Such phenomena clearly reflect cultural perceptions, attitudes and values.

With increasing time available for leisure, more is given over to outdoor recreation pursuits. The land surrounding our cities is a prime focus of this increased demand. More hunters, fishermen, cross-country skiers, snowmobilers and hikers all can generate trespass problems for farmers. The result is increasing numbers of 'no trespassing' signs (Conservation Council of Ontario 1976). As the number of posted properties increase, pressures increase on unposted ones.

Having now discussed generally the city's countryside as a system consisting of three overlapping environments and some of the broad perspectives associated with them, in the next chapter we adopt a problem approach to bring another viewpoint to bear on the city's countryside. The problem areas to be discussed arise out of interactions of people and land in the overlapping natural, economic and cultural environments.

Further reading

Barlowe, R. (1978) *Land Resource Economics: the Economics of Real Estate* (3rd edn), Prentice-Hall, Englewood Cliffs, N. J.

Clawson, M. (1972) *America's Land and its Use*, The Johns Hopkins Press, Baltimore.

Russwurm, L. H. and Sommerville, E. (eds) (1974) *Man's Natural Environment: a System's Approach*, Duxbury Press, North Scituate, Mass.

Wibberley, G. P. (1972) Conflicts in the countryside, *Town and Country Planning*, **40**, 259–64.

Wibberley, G. P. (1974) Development in the countryside, *Journal of Environmental Management*, **2**, 199–214.

3 Problems of land and people in the city's countryside

The viewpoint in this chapter shifts from the broad level of major environmental subsystems and their associated values and perspectives to focus on problem areas affecting land and people which arise from the activities of people in the natural, economic and cultural environments.

Four broad types of problems are identified. Land use and land conversion conflicts are treated first; this is appropriate because the land conversion conflicts relate directly to changing patterns of land ownership and it is largely through the medium of the real-estate market that evolving economic and cultural values become translated into land use. The ownership structure and the configuration of proprietary interests in land thus constitute an investment 'landscape', one that is hidden from view but full of portent for future functional change. Many of these conflicts are centred on the economic–cultural environment intersection (Fig. 2.1). A second set of problems involve impacts of urbanization on the resource base, impacts that arise primarily from both the cultural–natural environment intersection and the economic–natural environment intersection (Fig. 2.1). Third, another set of problems relates to social issues, which stem largely from interactions both within the cultural environment and between the cultural and economic environments. Finally, all these problems provide the grist for a fourth set of problems, political-management difficulties. With the exception of problems related to the natural environment, our treatment of the problems in this chapter is synoptic since problems related to specific activities are treated in detail in Part II and the political-management difficulties are developed in Part III.

Land use and conversion conflicts

A greater number of different land uses occur in the city's countryside than anywhere else. Cities spread out into the countryside like an advancing wave on a beach, and land in the inner fringe, be it farmland, grassland or forest, is converted to urban use. But there is more than just the advance of the built-up edge. Like a wave breaking on a rocky shore, irregular patches of urban and urban-associated land uses develop well beyond the built-up edge with ribbons of development, at least in the early stages of development of the regional city form, advancing along the highways and roads leading out from our cities. It is this ribbon and scattered development that can best be labelled 'urban sprawl' and which generates most *land-use* conflicts, while it is the wavelike spread of continuous subdivision at the edge of our cities which is associated primarily with *land conversion difficulties*.

Land-use issues

In the first two decades of the post–Second World War period, in North America, and in the interwar period in Britain, it was the haphazard mixing of uses in ribbon development and sprawl which rightly attracted attention. Figure 3.1 provides a specific example of the intermixture of uses around a North American city: motels, service stations, houses, schools, restaurants, farms, and several other uses are haphazardly intermixed. While the specific land-use mix varies around different cities, the theme of mixing of land uses is general. This type of development reflected a situation where land owners possessed the maximum freedom to do with their property as they wished. Such developments also were greatest in those municipalities unprepared for the rapid urban growth emanating from the nearby city. Problems with traffic (Wolfe 1964) and with incompatible uses occurring cheek by jowl plagued councils and planners increasingly, although gradually planning regulations halted much of this haphazard development.

Of course, this pattern of events is grossly schematized chronologically; Great Britain, for example, was significantly in advance of North America in the development of a physical planning system from 1947 onwards (Strachan 1974). Even within countries significant differences have existed. For instance, in Canada, urban sprawl problems surfaced early in Ontario and were largely under control by the early 1970s. The Prairie Provinces, possibly from a deep-rooted feeling that cities should be kept in their place, launched early controls (Winnipeg City Planning Division 1973). However, British Columbia, Québec and the Atlantic Provinces never learned from the Ontario experience and repeated the Ontario problems of the 1940s and 1950s during the 1960s. In British Columbia, a US flavour was added as shopping centres became part of long outward-extending commercial ribbons, e.g. Cranbrook, Kelowna and Penticton, while in Québec and the Atlantic Provinces the historical settlement pattern included ribbons partly because of physical landscape characteristics and partly for cultural reasons such as the long-lot farm layout of Québec. In these provinces much of the ribbon development has involved infilling of the historical pattern. In Nova Scotia, where new highways parallel the old ribbon highways, such infilling may be a good planning solution. But amidst the good farmland of the Saint John Valley and on Prince Edward Island, developing ribbons, mostly residential, are of dubious merit.

While the ribbon development was intensifying and then being controlled, the dispersal of urban (e.g. country residence, industrial and commercial uses) and urban-associated uses (e.g. gravel pits, campgrounds) proliferated.

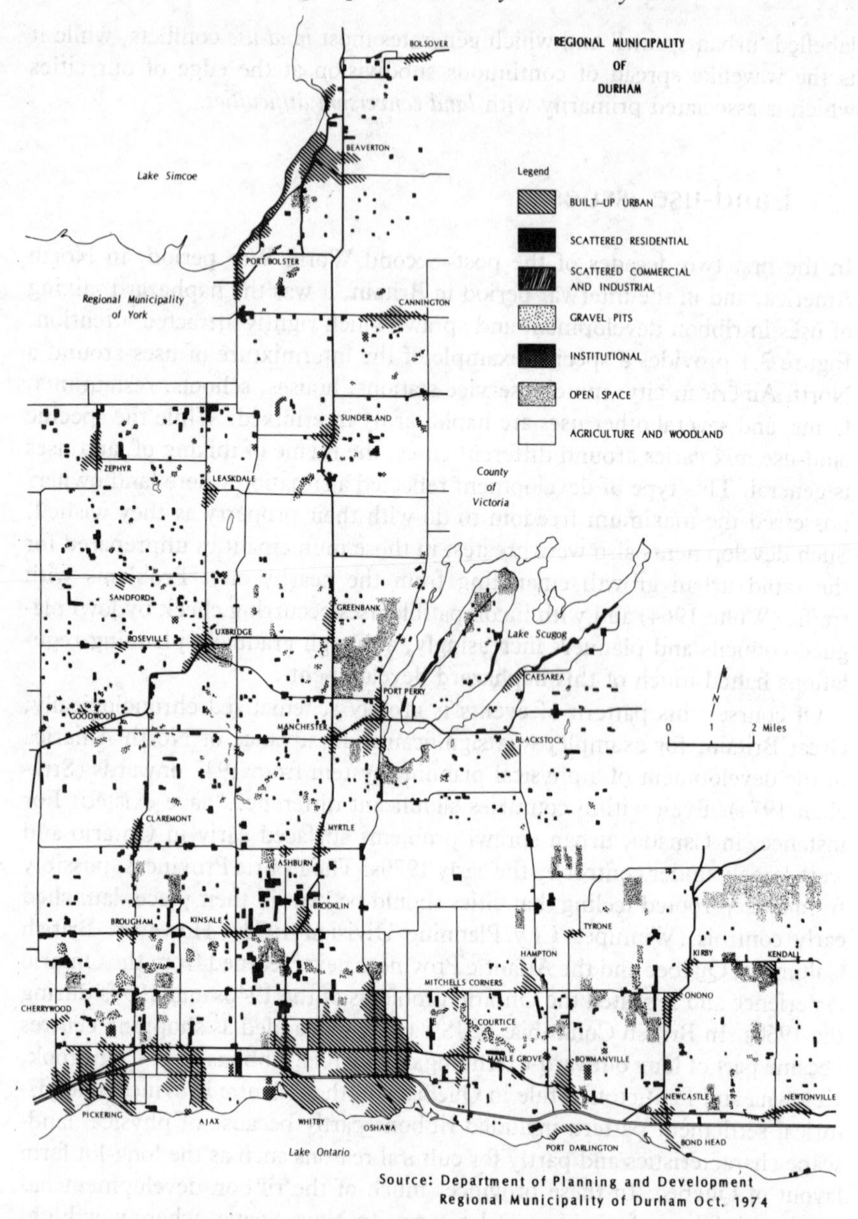

Figure 3.1 Intermixture of land uses beyond the built-up area: a typical example. (Source: Russwurm 1977b: 190. Originally compiled from plans of the Department of Planning and Development, Regional Municipality of Durham, October 1974).

The farm, the hobby farm, the country residence, the gravel pit, the industry unwanted in the built-up city, the space-using industry, the highway-oriented business, the outdoor recreation facility, the waste disposal site, the electricity transformer station – all exist more often than not side by side. The potential for unhappy neighbours and incompatibilities between land uses is high.

Such land-use conflicts are related to what Friedmann (1973b) calls the collective phenomenon, or what economists refer to as externalities or spill-over effects, by which the land-use activity on one property affects other people on neighbouring or nearby properties. Thus, the costs or diseconomies associated with a particular development are spread out beyond the property or activity which benefits. Typical examples of such negative externalities include gravel trucks roaring past country residences, non-farm people using and causing damage to a farmer's property, and the extra taxes required to have the road network maintained where recreational traffic is high. The term 'externalities' is appropriate because not all the costs involved in the act or activity are incurred by the user or the person(s) responsible for that activity. Rather, the general public, or some specific groups or other individuals bear some of the cost while gaining few, if any, of the benefits. Externalities can be positive as well as negative; for instance, good developments may raise land values of surrounding properties.

In a summary way, the various land-use conflicts can be categorized as individual versus societal, present versus future uses, and economic versus noneconomic (e.g. aesthetic, ecological). To complicate matters, conflicts within each of these six categories can be expected. Thus individuals may conflict (e.g. farmer and trespassing urbanite), present uses may conflict (e.g. asphalt plant and country residences) or different economic activities may conflict (e.g. agriculture and gravel pits).

Some land-use conflicts are not immutable and notions of sequential land use and multiple land use are of significance for the city's countryside as a means of reducing conflict and making better use of land. For example, land from which the sand, gravel or stone has been removed with ecological care may be rehabilitated for recreation, residences, industry, agriculture or forestry, while much of the land held on large-lot estates could later be used for farming, forestry or recreation should the need arise. Furthermore, the multiple use of land is a possibility, although in the city's countryside it is primarily a matter of using other people's land (mostly farmers') for recreational and leisure-oriented pursuits. Where the multiple-purpose use of land is not feasible, solutions may involve determining priorities of use, the implication being that the incompatibilities are more than a simple 'misunderstanding' between users and that the market allocation process cannot handle the resource allocation process equitably.

Cultural attitudes are important both in terms of defining the extent of such land-use conflicts and incompatibilities, and in terms of providing solutions. In North America, a strong land ethic has made little headway. In Norway, by contrast, private land is classed as either *inmark* or *utmark*; the former is land over which public passage would disturb the owner, while the latter is land where passage would not directly disturb the owner and is consequently deemed open to the public (Conservation Council of Ontario 1976). In the UK, the footpath system is a well-entrenched historical and cultural fact, and despite inevitable difficulties, represents a considerable resource for the Countryside Commission in its work. The importance of cultural values in land-use conflicts is illustrated further by the existence of groups whose aim it is to bring the public to a better understanding of the countryside and of agriculture in particular, such as the long-standing Association of Agriculture based in London and its more recent counterpart in France, the Association Ville–Campagne (1975).

Land conversion issues

Related closely to land-use conflicts in the city's countryside are land conversion issues. While land-use conflicts occur throughout the urban field, land conversion issues relate primarily to land within a few kilometres of the built-up edge of cities, and will be discussed in detail in Chapter 4. Concern over land conversion centres on the efficiency of the process, and includes increasing land values and the role of 'proper' planning. The conversion process is based on competition, but this is modified by planning and public intervention generally. One might postulate that the greater the degree of acceptance of land-use planning in a country, the less accepted is the economic market place as an efficient allocator of land. On this criterion Canada would occupy a middle position between the US and Western Europe.

Since 1950 the nature of land conversion from rural to urban uses has altered fundamentally in some respects. While conversion of land still occurs dominantly in the inner fringe, and while the actors involved have remained fundamentally similar since 1950, the scale of the development industry at least in North America has changed drastically (Martin 1974; Spurr 1976).The concomitant impact is consequently different. From many small builder-developers in the 1950s, the process has shifted to fewer, larger developers. From the municipality providing minimal services the process frequently has become one where the collectivity provides many services. From minimal planning controls the process has shifted to a plethora of regulations administered by many agencies. Differences, however, occur both between countries and within a given country, e.g. in Canada, small-scale developers are still fairly prominent in Vancouver, Montréal and the Atlantic Provinces (Martin 1977a, b). On the other hand, some of the largest development companies have become so large that their interests are international in scope, e.g. Cadillac-Fairview, Daon, Wimpey.

What, then, are the difficulties that ensue in the land conversion process from rural to urban uses? Obviously one concerns rising land values and their effect on housing costs. Large-scale developers are at times accused of exerting too much influence on prices. The general evidence, however, indicates that they have not been able to distort land prices significantly (Greenspan

1978; US National Academy of Sciences and National Academy of Engineering 1972). Nevertheless, such companies often hold large areas of land, purchased at relatively low prices, which are later worth several times the original purchase price. This appreciation in land value has helped a number of development companies to grow considerably as profits from land were ploughed back into the company (Spurr 1976).

However, factors other than any oligopolistic influences on land costs must be recognized as contributing to the rapid rise in housing costs that was experienced in many countries in the 1970s, e.g. the UK and Canada. An increased demand with higher incomes, a somewhat restricted supply arising out of the implementation of stricter planning regulations added to previous regulations over a short time period (Kearns 1974), general inflation, and expectations of continued rising prices (Munton 1976a) were all factors of considerable importance. Bourne (1977) has categorized the reasons for the rapid rise in housing and land prices into five schools of thought: conspiracy, demand-pull, multiple bottleneck, cost-push, and institutional or neo-Marxian.

Closely related to rising land values are difficulties arising from land speculation and property fragmentation. Much disagreement exists about the phenomenon of land speculation. Clearly it is part of the competition for land in the urban fringe and reflects a commodity view of land. In economic terms, speculation can be viewed as a means of moving land from lower value to higher value uses (Baxter 1975). The person dealing in land makes the land available for willing buyers; in its most precise definition speculation can only be said to occur when the land dealer holds land out of the market in order to gain a price increase (Martin 1977b).

With rapidly rising prices, more people try to speculate. Usually as little money as possible is invested. However, when land markets level off, investors may be left with properties with various financial and legal encumbrances on them causing difficulties (Lindeman 1976). A classic example is the process that left many prairie cities in Canada with a supply of subdivided land following the boom of the early 1900s. Consequently, during the period before the Second World War many parcels of land reverted to the prairie cities as tax-delinquent lands. During such a process, some people benefit considerably from unearned increments in land values, but many others lose.

While there is considerable controversy over the real effects of land speculation, the crux of the issue seems to be that while the public regulates development, the land which is the basis of development is left in private hands. Among the solutions to this problem are:

1. residential land banking, i.e. removing the land part of the conversion process from the hands of the private sector:
2. recapturing the unearned increment in value, as suggested by the recommendations of the 1976 UN Conference on Human Settlements (Gertler 1978). Certainly, when housing prices rise rapidly, developers and land dealers holding land in the right places can make excessive profits;

3. letting the market process have free play and thereby maximizing competition.

A final issue identified as part of the difficulties of land conversion is fragmentation of the property structure. Four specific disadvantages are identifiable:

1. Fragmentation helps drive up land values since smaller parcels are worth more per unit area.
2. It increases the number of owners who have to be dealt with by the municipality.
3. It makes future large-scale land assemblies difficult.
4. When fragmentation becomes too great, farming may be affected by the concomitant higher land prices, by too many country residents, by increasing expectations of appreciating land values, and perhaps above all, by the uncertainty generated about the future of farming in the area.

Land-use conflicts and land conversion difficulties are therefore linked closely with urban impacts on the resource base of the land around our cities.

Urban impacts on the resource base

The basic land resource activities around our cities, as elsewhere, consist of farming, mining and forestry. In addition, the water supply source for many cities is a nearby river, lake, reservoir or groundwater aquifer. Given the accessibility of the city's countryside to many people, recreational use of such land is also significant. And as noted earlier, the importance of the natural environment must never be forgotten since it is our life-support system. Since much of Part II of this book is devoted to specific resource-use activities such as agriculture, recreation and mineral extraction, only a brief catalogue of the issues is given here. However, the impact on the natural environment, which provides the support for the resource activities, is discussed in more detail.

The agricultural resource base

The resource activity near cities which has been of most concern is farming, particularly because many cities are located amidst the best farmland (Vining, Plaut and Bieri 1977). Such a situation is hardly surprising since many cities developed in a symbiotic relationship with their surrounding agricultural hinterlands and grew more or less in accordance with the prosperity of their hinterland. Hence, while some loss of prime farmland is inevitable and may not be serious in the short term, the real concern in many countries has centred around the long-term availability of top-quality agricultural land.

Several types of urban interaction with the agricultural resource base can be identified, each of which presents a particular set of problems for the agricultural resource base, and for agriculture in general, viz. land conversion involved in expanding the built-up city edge outward, country residential development or scattered non-farm development, part-time and hobby farming, recreation, and other urban-associated uses. Land conversion problems related to the agricultural industry in the inner fringe include the issue of the loss of top-quality agricultural land and how inevitable this is and the efficiency of the process of land conversion, e.g. how important is the phenomenon of idling of land and how is it related to land speculation?

Country residential impacts include the question of how much land is really taken by such development, how incompatible is it with development of the agricultural resource base, and how much of the land in such development is really permanently lost from agricultural production. Part of phenomenon of part-time farming, especially hobby farming, is intimately related to country residential development, but a number of issues concerning the agricultural resource base are specific to the part-time farming phenomenon, e.g. does part-time farming maintain the quality of the resource base? Are there significant differences in this respect between different types of part-time farmers? Recreational uses also interact with agriculture and thereby the agricultural resource base and again, several issues arise. For example, how significant is the use of private land (and thus farmland) by the public for fishing, hunting, hiking or simply viewing and what are the implications of these activities for the resource base?

Finally, the urban-associated uses consist largely of land-use activities dependent upon the land as physical resource or site, e.g. the extraction of construction minerals, the removal of water and the building of reservoirs, the use of land for waste disposal, and the use of land for transportation and communications facilities, and commercial and industrial development. All of these types of urban-associated uses hinge on the acquisition of rights over, under or on farmland (or other rural land); all generate heated citizen participation and all occur with greatest frequency and intensity in the surroundings of our cities.

Impacts on the natural environment

Four areas of urban impact in the city's countryside involving our life-support systems were already alluded to in Chapter 2: ecological protection, pollution impacts, landscape amenities and potential for future use. The concern is with both specific areas of natural environment remnants and the natural ecosystem in general. Generally, while agricultural landscapes are man-made and managed, they continue to depend on the continuous biological, chemical and physical processes of the natural environment, as do our other renewable resources, viz. the forest, the water and the air around us.

Thus, any impacts on the natural environment have considerable significance for the support of various economic activities.

Most cities have some remnant natural areas in their surroundings. Sometimes, such remnant areas may be unique in a particular country, e.g. the Niagara Escarpment in southern Ontario. However, even non-unique resources may be of tremendous regional significance owing to considerations of accessibility, e.g. Epping Forest in the London, England, region. Such remnant areas may be sensitive areas subject to deterioration or to the development of hazards if not protected or carefully managed in regard to man's activities. Snowmobiles and all-terrain vehicles damage tree seedlings and delicate swamplands; drainage for agricultural purposes may affect water-recharge areas or destroy nesting sites for waterfowl. Interaction between man's activities and the natural environment areas remaining near our cities are often intense. Where good agricultural land exists, pressures for greater efficiency in farming continually threaten such areas. Two of the most immediate consequences of such pressure are reduced landscape amenities and reduced wildlife habitats.

What are some critical functions that remnant natural areas provide near our cities and why might they be protected? First, they show us the original fabric of the landscape, the natural heritage. They provide habitat for animal species while showing us the diversity of land form and vegetation communities. They may include the only remnant habitat for an orchid, lizard, snake, deer, or be a vestige of virgin forest or swamp. Furthermore, they perform functions of hydrologic value as they are often significant in the cycling, storage and recharging of water supplies. Finally, of course, such areas can be of major aesthetic and recreational value, as they become incorporated into the cultural–natural environment intersection (Fig. 2.1).

An overriding problem has been the lack of overall integration of such areas into land-use planning schemes around cities. This is related to the fact that around most of our cities private ownership of land is the rule and such resources possess little, if any, individual economic value. This situation is gradually changing, and the inclusion of hazard areas and natural areas for protection in land-use plans is becoming more common, reflecting a greater cultural value being placed on the natural environment, e.g. the environmentally sensitive areas that have appeared in the official plans of several Ontario regional municipalities or the specific environment areas designated in the *zones naturelles d'équilibre* in the Paris region (Préfecture de la Région d'Ile-de-France 1976a, b), and, at a broader level the efforts of the International Biological Programme in identifying specific sites worth protecting as species habitat and gene pools. The types of remnant natural environment areas are many, including marshes, swamps, estuaries, shorelines, flood-plains, erodible slopes, unusual natural ecosystems, wildlife breeding areas, landslide areas, watershed supply sources and groundwater recharge areas.

Pollution impacts on the natural environment are, of course, closely related to the theme of ecological protection. Areas near our cities have to absorb most of the pollution resulting from concentration of people and their activities. Industrial air pollution, the chemicals from oil refineries and chemical plants, the sewage that ends up in the streams or lakes, the pesticide, fertilizer or animal waste runoff from intensive farm operations are all part of the pollution impacts around our cities. Yet because of their accessibility to many people, it is the streams and lakes in and near our cities that are probably the most valuable, certainly from a recreational perspective, and therefore deserving of greater attention in terms of conservation. It is not without significance that the Countryside Commission of the UK has a keen interest in urban fringe areas.

In the same vein the landscape amenities of rural landscapes in the city's countryside are of considerable cultural value simply because this is the area that is most accessible to a majority of the population. Whatever the particular regional context, the landscape of the city's countryside reflects a mix of natural and economic environments (Fig. 2.1). But what we prize as important, what we wish to preserve, what we wish to restore or improve, reflects also our cultural environment. As such amenities have become more valued, maintenance of rural character and aspects of landscape have become more prominent in planning documents. However, as this has occurred, some of the other changes that have been part of the 'traditional' rural scene, such as enlargement of field sizes, have come increasingly into conflict with amenity values (Davidson and Wibberley 1977; Préfecture de la Région d'Ile-de-France 1976a, b). Many difficult questions are posed – can we and should we do anything about such changes in a dynamic agricultural landscape? Whose rights are at stake? Who benefits most? Who pays the costs involved in preserving landscape amenities?

Finally, closely related to the issues of ecological protection, pollution impacts and landscape amenity, is the need to assess the land space around our cities for its potential for different types of use and for different intensities of various uses. It is the land around our cities that we tend to treat more as a commodity, but yet it is our most valuable land as a resource because of its accessibility to many people and because of its potential for many functions and uses (see Ch. 10). The natural environment provides the potential, but how we make use of that potential is determined by our economic motives and cultural attitudes working through societal rules and political decisions.

Social issues

Dispersed and widespread urban fringes and even more so, urban shadow zones, developed around our cities with the onslaught of the automobile and its supporting dense road network. Much of the original concern with this phenomenon, as noted earlier, was related to physical issues such as traffic flows and physical land-use incompatibilities. Attention, largely academic, was given slowly, however, to the sociological aspects of this dispersed settlement zone. In the sociologically oriented literature, the rural–urban fringe (e.g. Martin 1953) was seen as a region separate from city and country in both demographic and social terms. Its characteristics were deemed to be intermediate on a continuum between urban and rural and could thus be viewed as a permanent interface between urban and rural. The extent of the real difference between urban and rural, particularly in the major metropolitan regions of Western countries, is certainly debatable but it is clear that the phenomenon of the recolonization of the countryside around many cities brings groups of people together who are different, initially at least, in terms of occupations, origins and life-styles (Walker 1976; Lewis and Maund 1976).

As a result of the juxtaposition of such different groups, stresses and adaptations are inevitable. Two broad social issues are most widespread. First, who benefits and who really pays for the costs involved in exurban development. Closely interwoven with this are planning practices which tend often to be exclusionary and which threaten to make the countryside the preserve of the city rich. The other issue centres upon the influx of newcomers into pre-existing rural agricultural communities and often small settlements which had evolved to provide the goods and services to the rural community. This influx has accompanying benefits and costs which are just beginning to be seriously considered.

The services–taxation issue

In a nutshell, the services–taxation inequity issue as it has developed in North America in the city's countryside is similar to that of the built-up city. Residential units, despite great concern about rising property taxes, do not pay for the services they are accustomed to receive. In the city, commercial and industrial units take up the slack; in the countryside few of these units exist. Consequently, the burden falls on the farmer as the dominant property owner. This issue, already documented during the 1950s (e.g. Krueger 1957), is still not resolved.

Attempts at improving the services–taxation equity problems have been directed both at reducing tax costs to the farmer and increasing tax returns from the exurbanite units. In many jurisdictions, the tax burden on the farmer has been lessened by reduced rate (preferential) assessment or by tax rebates. In Ontario, Canada, for instance, a 50 per cent tax rebate in 1981 was given to farmers having a minimum gross sales of $5000. Furthermore, tax returns from exurbanite units have often been increased by fiscal zoning for both land and buildings, i.e. planning regulations which demand larger lots and larger houses thereby leading to higher assessments and higher tax returns.

An unfortunate but inevitable result of such fiscal zoning practices is exclusionary zoning, because only the wealthier will be able to afford the large lot and large home required. An ethical question is at issue: should country residences be permitted only for those who can pay their way, should they be available to all, or should they be available for none? It is generally accepted in some countries such as Canada, the US and Australia (Australian Department of Urban and Regional Development 1975) that country living is a life-style that some proportion of the population desires and is entitled to. Obviously costs of service provision for households of similar characteristics are cheaper for compact development than for dispersed development. To some degree, both the ethical and practical aspects of this problem have been partially recognized via planning approaches involving small lot sizes, subdivision estates, clustering, and by designating specific areas where country residential development can be located. The planning emphasis, thus, is increasingly directed at more efficient patterns of development designed to reduce cost of services and lessen impacts on the countryside (Smith and Morganti 1980).

A related housing issue concerns the role of mobile homes, particularly in North America, which can provide reasonable housing at reasonable costs with minimal upkeep. In Canada, many more such developments occur in Québec and the Atlantic Provinces than elsewhere. In his study of the Windsor–Quebec axis, Yeates (1975) reports that this wealthy axis has 55 per cent of Canada's housing units, but only 13 per cent of Canada's mobile homes. This difference reflects three things outside Ontario and the Prairie Provinces: a less exclusionary zoning approach, less stringent planning controls, and a greater need for lower-income housing in Québec and the Atlantic Provinces. Yet some excellent examples of mobile-home developments exist in Canada and the US. Especially worthy of recognition is the retirement mobile-home development in a rural setting which could consist of mixed populations of rural and exurbanite people.

Exurban development

Such a suggested integration of rural and urban people in a particular setting brings us to the second major social issue, that of the influx of newcomers into the existing rural agricultural communities and their rural service centres, especially those smaller than about 2500 people. The city's countryside in much of the Western world is no longer mainly the preserve of farm people.

In the broad zone extending 40 to 100 km beyond the built-up edge of our cities, especially where physical planning systems have not been restrictive, a majority of the population living outside settlement nodes is exurbanite. Few of these 'newcomers' have lived there for any length of time. What is happening, then, is an invasion, a recolonization of the countryside, so that two major groups, farmers and exurbanite, are now living side by side. Farmers use the land mainly for its production function, while exurbanites use it for its place and play function. While rural and urban attitudes are both conditioned by the mass media, there are still differences in outlook and attitude (Walker 1976; Council on Rural Development Canada 1979). Clearly a situation exists where social and other conflicts can arise.

Briefly, the issues at the most specific level revolve around complaints by country residents about the noise, dust and odours of adjacent farm operations on the one hand, and by farmers about trespass, litter, gate openings, fence damages, livestock bothering and theft on the other. At a more general level, the issues concern the services–taxation inequity problems just discussed and the increasing political influence on elected councils and planning agencies exerted by exurbanites.

There are also, however, beneficial aspects to the increasing number of country residents. They tend to be more concerned about open space and rural landscape amenities and often provide citizen leadership on issues such as pipelines, the routing of electricity transmission corridors and new highway routes. They provide added human resources for lagging rural social institutions such as churches and service clubs still trying to adapt to the loss of farm people which has occurred especially over the past 20 years. Like all the other problem areas, there are many complexities; it is not a black-and-white situation of farm being good and country residential being bad.

As for the open countryside, so too an influx of 'newcomers' has invaded many existing settlements. Some of the smaller pre-existing places, of about 500 people, say, have been inundated and transformed into dormitory villages of several thousand people. Other places have grown from a few houses to over a thousand people. In developing land-use plans, a common thrust was first to encourage infilling of pre-existing settlements in preference to permitting open-country residential development. More recently, more emphasis has been placed on protecting the 'rural character' of some of these places themselves, an approach which involves specifying particular places to absorb population growth. While this approach is commendable, in some ways it raises the thorny issue of what is 'rural character' (Davidson and Wibberley 1977), and what places are to be chosen for growth.

Political management difficulties

If successful planning is to occur within the surroundings of our cities, not only must competition be handled in relation to the production, protection, place and play functions of land; it must also be handled between municipalities. There are many examples of a shopping centre or some other facility being located outside the incorporated city boundaries against the wishes of the city. We refer to this issue of competition between municipalities as a political management problem. Its roots lie in the fact that the functioning area of urban regions has generally not been under single planning areas coinciding with a single municipality for government and the administration of development. But urbanization processes operate at the scale of urban regions, not at the scale of individual municipalities whose boundaries were developed in different times when the technology of movement and communications was completely different to that of today's shrinking world. It is a political issue when elected governments are involved in planning; it is a management problem when elected governments through their employees and agencies are also responsible for administration of services needed by people. It seems clear that urban regions should be the building blocks of any efforts aimed at planning and administering the developments of the city's countryside, although this does not mean that regional government is the only form this can take. We shall return to the political management issues in much greater depth in Part III. Now, attention is turned to the various activities in the city's countryside and to a detailed consideration of the processes and problems which each activity both encounters and creates.

Further reading

Archer, R. W. (1973) Land speculation and scattered development: failures in the urban fringe land market, *Urban Studies*, 10, 367–72.

Bourne, L. S. (1977) Choose your villain: five ways to oversimplify the price of housing and urban land, *Urban Forum*, 3, 16–24.

Clawson, M. (1971) *Suburban Land Conversion in the United States: an Economic and Governments Process*, The Johns Hopkins Press, Baltimore.

Friedmann, J. (1973) *Retracking America: a Theory of Transactive Planning*, Anchor Press, Garden City, NY.

II The activities within the city's countryside

Introduction

In this part, detailed attention is given to the major types of land space and resource-use activities in the city's countryside. Underlying many of the changes in land uses are changes in land ownership which are dealt with in Chapter 4. This is followed by separate chapters on country residential development, agriculture, industry and commerce, recreation, and infrastructure and institutions.

The treatment moves from country residential development, the major expression of change in the cultural environment of the city's countryside (Ch. 5) to deal with economic production activities. Agriculture, the dominant land use around most cities, is discussed in Chapter 6, while aggregate production, manufacturing industry and commercial activities are discussed in Chapter 7.

The provision of recreational uses represents the first major discussion of public-sector involvement (Ch. 8), and this inevitably involves us in some public planning and management debate. The last activity chapter, Chapter 9, deals with infrastructure and institutional networks and nodes, again activities and uses which are often in the public or semi-public domain. These uses often generate intense conflicts. The new airport site, the pipeline, hydro line, highway route or large educational or medical institution are a few examples from a long list. Given the mix of people living in and using the city's countryside, somebody will usually protest a 'new' use. Most of these uses are place-function uses relying on a particular site having accessibility or having a resource advantage (e.g. water-supply reservoirs).Some of them, such as solid waste disposal sites or airports, are often considered incompatible with built-up urban uses. Others, just like some manufacturing uses discussed in Chapter 7, demand considerable space at lower land prices than are available in the built-up urban areas. All in all, these infrastructural and institutional uses add greatly to the variety of land uses (and conflicts) that occur in the city's countryside.

4 Land ownership and land conversion

Underlying many of the changes in economic and cultural activities in the city's countryside are changes in land ownership patterns. The processes involved in land ownership change and how they are linked to land conversion are complex, affecting all the activities in the city's countryside in one way or another; hence a discussion of land ownership and land conversion precedes the more detailed consideration of specific cultural and economic activities. In addition, changes in land ownership through the real-estate market sometimes reflect special types of activities – land dealing, speculation – which may have widespread effects on the other economic and cultural activities.

A useful way of thinking about land ownership change is to consider it as representing a latent 'landscape' with respect to land use. Changes in land ownership usually take place in advance of land-use change and the spread of the 'city'. Land ownership is itself a complex concept with economic, legal, political and cultural dimensions. Of perhaps most immediate interest is the motivation for land ownership, since this affects what value people place on their interests in land and how they might manage their property and eventually dispose of it. The motivations for land ownership are many – for speculation or as an investment, as a hedge against inflation, for the various play, place and production functions of land and, especially in relation to the public sector, the protection function of land. It is against this complexity of land ownership motivations that Found and Morley (1972, 1973) suggested that actual land use cannot provide a direct indicator of the likelihood of a property being sold and thus of what may happen to the property. It is because land ownership change is related to changing motivations for land ownership that we can talk of land ownership change as a latent force underlying the physical landscape.

Against this backdrop, the following themes are considered in this chapter: the actors involved in land ownership and land conversion; land values; impacts of such changes; and finally, geographic patterns of land ownership change. Much of the discussion draws upon the work of a recent synthesis and case study undertaken by one of the authors (Bryant 1982).

Actors in the market

Changes in land ownership occur within the market in land, a complex system with various submarkets that interact and overlap. It is useful to categorize the various actors involved according to their position in the land

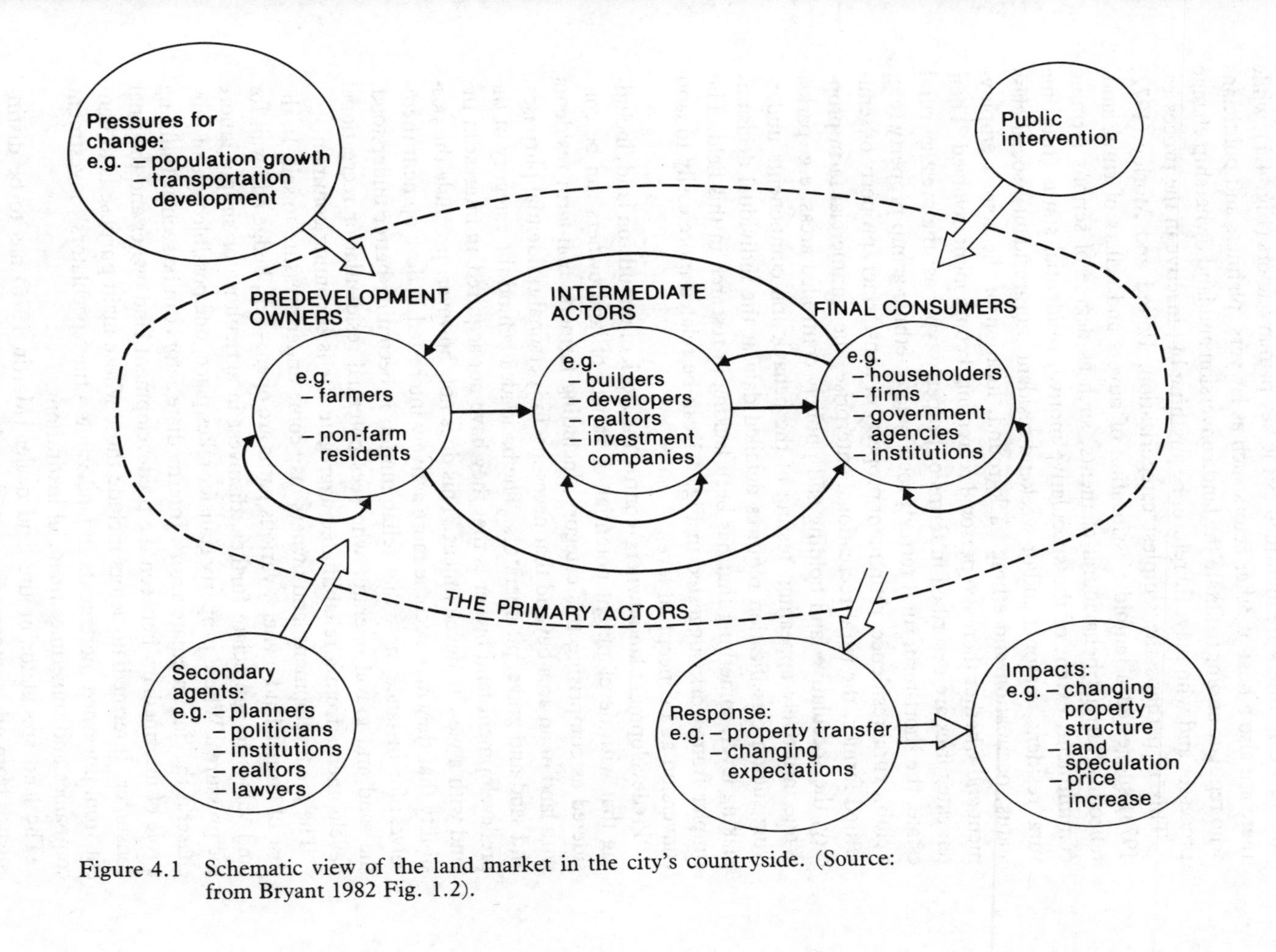

Figure 4.1 Schematic view of the land market in the city's countryside. (Source: from Bryant 1982 Fig. 1.2).

conversion process; thus, predevelopment land owners, intermediate actors and final consumers are identified as the key primary actors (Fig. 4.1), while there are also a host of other actors such as lawyers, planners and politicians who regulate and/or facilitate the land conversion and land ownership change processes and who may, therefore, be anything but inactive in the processes.

This is perhaps the simplest categorization. Found and Morley (1972, 1973) suggested a tenfold classification of buyers and sellers of rural land, reflecting various behavioural elements, such as degree of serious farming commitment, extent of the speculative motive, residential status (full-time rural resident, seasonal and/or weekend resident, non-resident), social class status, occupation and ethnic background, location of the actor's employment and whether there is a personal recreational component involved. Their ten categories are described in terms of property types as: the prestige rural estate, the short-term rural retreat, social and/or ethnic-group property (e.g. a club), rural residence, retirement property of non-farmer, property of semi-retired farmer, the rural recreational enterprise, the commercial farm property, the speculative land holding and publicly controlled areas, e.g. parks. While intuitively appealing, testing of the behavioural components underlying such a classification requires detailed data at the individual decision-making level, something that has been lacking in research in this field. The simpler framework suggested in Fig. 4.1 can be related more easily to land conversion at a conceptual level.

'Predevelopment land owners' control the stock of unbuilt-on land, including that with development potential. A variety of land owners can be considered as comprising this category, including farmers, non-farm residents with land of an area beyond that necessary for personal residential purposes, and sand and gravel pit operators. The basic idea behind the category of the predevelopment land owner is that they have not acquired an interest in the land with a view to development. This does not, however, preclude the possibility that they may become more actively interested in development themselves; for instance, now that rehabilitation is becoming better understood, the sand and gravel operator who sees potential residential or recreational developments from a rehabilitated aggregate site is becoming common.

The predevelopment land owners may come under pressure to sell. In the case of farmer land owners, various paths are open – sell, hedge and wait for land values to appreciate further, disinvest in agriculture or simply ignore the pressures. Where property transfer takes place, one possible type of purchaser is the 'intermediate actor'. Intermediate actors can be seen as fulfilling a role of intermediary between the predevelopment land owner and the final consumer. Intermediate actors include those whose main purpose is to benefit from unearned increments in land value – the 'speculators', investment companies and sometimes financial institutions.

The land speculator or the land dealer (Martin 1976) has to be distinguished from other intermediate actors such as land developers and builders in that his reward comes not from any 'improvement' he imparts to the land.

As we shall see below, this has given rise to substantial criticism of land speculators. But land speculators are not homogeneous, ranging from naïve land dealers and corporations with a poor understanding of speculative land markets, to 'clever' dealers (Martin 1976) who have a relatively sophisticated understanding of the processes involved. Other intermediate actors bring some 'improvement' to the land; some may assemble land, prepare it for development and public approval (land developers, and sometimes realtors) and even undertake the servicing and construction of dwellings, industrial parks, and so forth (developers, builders). It is certainly not easy to separate the various motives involved, even with behavioural studies. The same actor may hold several different motives, the relative importance of which may vary temporally. For example, the case of financial institutions in the UK has been noted as being particularly perplexing (Munton 1975); it was apparent that in the inflationary times in land values of the early 1970s in the UK, motives of financial institutions for acquiring land were mixed, some clearly representing efforts to safeguard the value of capital, some speculative and some involving a long-term commitment as an agricultural landlord.

Multiple transactions of the same property may occur between different types of intermediate actors before land ends up in the hands of the final consumer, although much simpler sequences exist with land going directly from farmer to developer, or to final consumer. The 'final consumer' also can include a variety of actors, including both private and public actors. In practice, overlap occurs with the other categories, e.g. the sand and gravel pit operator who becomes a speculator. Keeping in mind the problem of using this framework, an example grouping actors into these three broad types is shown in Table 4.1, based on information collected from title deeds in Land Registry Offices in the Waterloo area of southern Ontario (Bryant 1982).

Table 4.1 Grouping of actors in the land market

Predevelopment actors	*Intermediate actors*	*Final consumer*
Farmer	Developer Construction firm Realtor or investment firm	Industry Commerce Non-farm individuals Government and government agencies Institutions (churches) Social clubs

(Source: based on Bryant, 1981a: Table 2.5)

This framework presents a number of similarities to recent work on the Toronto fringe (Martin 1975b), in which actors in the land market are differentiated as either *primary* decision agents or *secondary* decision agents (compare Figs. 4.1 and 4.2). Primary decision agents include farmers, land dealers, developers, builders, households, and firms; secondary decision

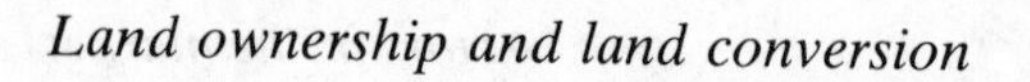

	Nonurban use	Nonurban use with pressures for change	Urban interest seen in land purchases; land use is transitional	Active purchase of raw land	Active development	Active purchase of developed land
Primary decision agents	Farmer	Farmer Land dealer	Farmer Land dealer Developer	Developer	Developer Builder	Builder Households Industries Firms
Secondary decision agents		Financier	Financier	Financier Lawyer Realtor Planner Politician	Financier Lawyer Planner Politician	Financier Lawyer Realtor

Figure 4.2 The land conversion process: stages of development. (Source: modified and developed from Martin 1975b).

agents, the regulators and facilitators, include financiers, lawyers, realtors and planners. The type of sequence of events illustrated in Fig. 4.2 is in reality only one possible chain, which may be considerably shortened or lengthened depending upon the circumstances. Furthermore, it is only really appropriate for dealing with potential urban development in the inner fringe, adjacent to nodes, or the case of clustered prestige estate development in the broader city's countryside. Thus, there is implicit here an assumption of large-scale development – subdivisions, estates – which are frequently going to create accretionary urban development. In other parts of the city's countryside, as already noted in Chapter 1 in our discussion of the *form* of the regional city, other types of use patterns are being created with sequences of property transactions very different to that presented in Fig. 4.2, e.g. scattered non-farm residential development.

Of course, some of the secondary agents may become involved directly as

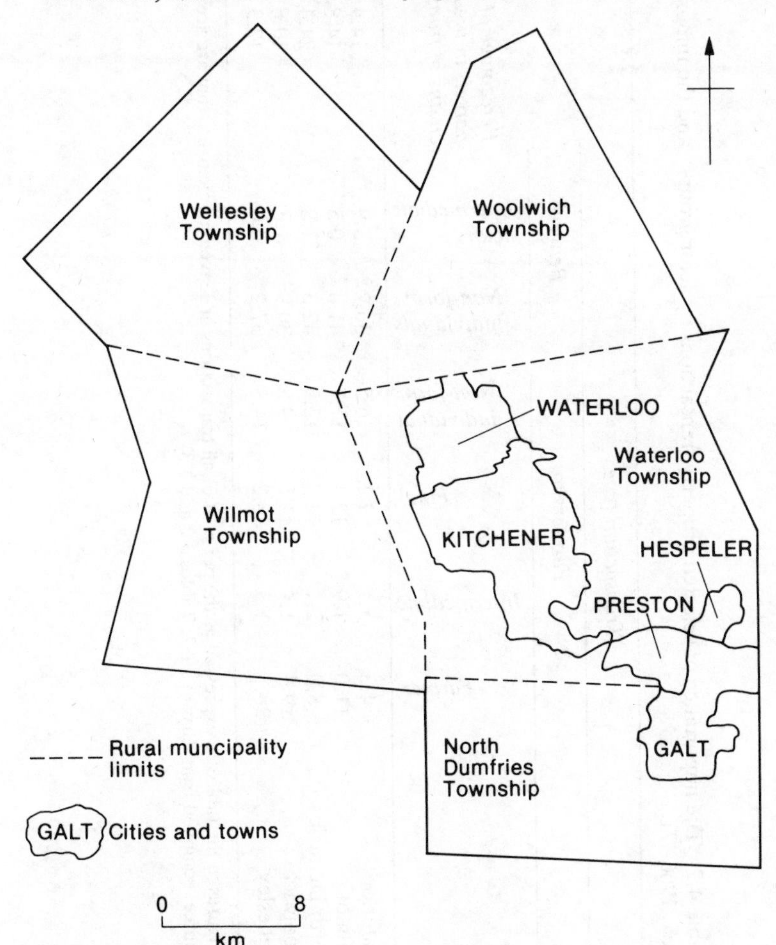

Figure 4.3 The Waterloo area.

Table 4.2 The importance of selected property transactions by actor groups* and the importance of multiple transactions: Waterloo area, 1966–71.

	Transaction type							
	Farmers to:				*Between:*			
	Farmer	*Intermediate*	*Final*	*Non-farm individual*	*Non-farm individuals*	*Intermediate actors*	*Percentage of separate parcels in the market in chains of transactions*	*Percentage of all chains of transactions involving an intermediate actor in at least one stage*
Waterloo	4.3	5.1	7.1	6.5	36.2	3.9	14.4	34.8
Wilmot	11.0	1.9	12.1	11.7	41.6	0.5	14.8	26.5
North Dumfries	8.0	2.1	14.7	12.9	42.3	1.8	24.4	17.9
Woolwich	19.4	1.4	11.5	9.8	30.9	1.3	10.8	25.0
Wellesley	28.3	1.3	15.2	14.3	37.2	0.0	12.3	10.0

* Figures in the table are expressed as the per cent of all transactions in a given municipality that are accounted for by the particular transaction type.
(Source: compiled from Bryant 1982: Tables 3.2 and 3.3)

primary actors; they can thus move from the role of facilitating and regulating the land market to the role of purchaser; hence realtors were included in Fig. 4.1 as intermediate actors when they were buying and selling land. Such secondary agents who change their roles may in effect be using extra knowledge of the land market gained through their role as secondary agent to help them determine where investments should be made.

By way of example and based on the framework of Fig. 4.1 and the classification of Table 4.1, the following observations are made on the relative importance of different actor combinations of property sales. The data were derived from Land Registry Offices for the Waterloo area in southern Ontario outside the urban area (Fig. 4.3) for the years 1966 to 1971 inclusive. Overall, the most important point is the major significance of non-farm individuals as actors (Table 4.2). Property sales between non-farm individuals were very important in all areas, often relating to the sale of property with a dwelling already present. The geographic variation in farmer-to-farmer transactions, farmer-to-intermediate actor and farmer-to-final consumer transactions as well as in transactions between intermediate actors is worth noting. A marked distinction appears between the township of Waterloo over the period 1966 to 1971, an area which can be assumed to include the inner fringe areas, and the remaining outer townships. This will be discussed again at the end of this chapter; before that, we now turn briefly to consider the nature of land values and some of the impacts of the land conversion process and the accompanying changes in land ownership.

Land values

The value of land at a particular point in time and space reflects pressures in the market place, the overall condition of the economy, the preferences of the various actors involved and their abilities and levels of knowledge, and generally, all of the factors – institutional, cultural and economic – that impinge upon the value of real estate. Thus, different factors affect the pattern of change in land values at different scales of analysis. An important perspective in investigating the determinants of land values can be obtained by considering the nature of supply and demand for land.

First, there are different dimensions to land supply. In the long term, it is possible to equate the supply of land with all the land that could possibly be placed on the market (Sévérac 1963). In a physical sense, the global supply of land in the long run is fixed; indeed, the long-term potential physical supply of raw land declines each year as new development, parks, communications infrastructure, and so forth, take their toll. Considering supply now as the quantity actually placed on the market for sale, Sévérac (1963) argued that because the sale of land is a rare act for most actors, excepting of course professional land dealers, and because price is not the only factor for consideration, then the short-term elasticity of supply with respect to price is weak. However, when we consider supply coming on to the market at a local or regional level, the elasticity of supply may be greater. It may still not be sufficiently responsive, though, to ensure an orderly and efficient process of urban development; hence some countries have seen the need to use compulsory purchase orders or similar schemes to try to obtain the right quantity of land at the right price in time and geographic space (Bryant and Martin 1976). Generally, the fact that land is fixed locationally also contributes to the inelasticity of supply. The overall fixity of land supply has thus contributed to the focus on demand as influencing land values in the literature (e.g. Brigham 1965).

Demand for raw land can also be regarded as being relatively price inelastic at a particular point in time and space; even at relatively high prices, some development will take place. However, demand is very complex, and there are many submarkets between which there is a certain amount of exchange. In any temporal analysis, it is impossible to ignore the interrelationships between supply and demand (Becker 1969). Under severe inflationary conditions, rises in price may simply encourage prospective buyers to buy more in anticipation of further price rises. Such speculative and hedging motivations are clearly partly to blame for the spectacular land price rises in the UK in 1973 (Munton 1976b) and the increase in land purchases by institutions over the same period (Munton 1975); once the 'bubble' breaks, that rare phenomenon of depressed and declining land prices may ensue (Munton 1976a). Such phenomena can exist on a more local scale too, with speculative spurts followed by depressed or stagnating values; for example, it has been suggested that the speculative activity associated with a major regional land assembly project may have been partly behind such price movements in the Waterloo region of southern Ontario in the late 1960s (Ferguson 1975; Bryant 1982).

Because of the complexity and heterogeneity of both supply and demand for land, it is probably illusory to talk of 'true' land values. Indeed, the term 'land value' itself is too simple in many respects, even though it is a commonly used lay term. It may be more appropriate to consider values *in* land; this depends on the view that land ownership can be decomposed into the ownership of a 'bundle of rights' in land, a concept that is particularly pertinent to English and Anglo-American jurisprudence (Denman and Prodano 1972). These rights are not fixed, and various institutional, cultural and economic constraints combine to circumscribe them and to influence the value attached to each right (e.g. the right of access, the right to develop) in a particular property. The idea of land ownership as a set of rights finds its most explicit expression in jurisdictions where certain rights may be bought, sold and exchanged independently of other rights in land, e.g. transfer of development rights and scenic easements.

It is also important to distinguish between 'market value' and 'use value'. Use value is simply the capital value of a piece of real estate under a particular use: it is possible, for instance, to talk of agricultural use value, a value which can be assigned to the land by calculating the capital value of future expected agricultural income from the land using an 'appropriate' time period and discount rate. This is the value that is commonly referred to in debates on the conservation of agricultural land as being exceeded by the market value of the land, thus jeopardizing the agricultural viability of a property. What, then, is 'market value'? This can be defined as the price that will be paid in a given property transaction between a willing seller and a willing buyer, where the seller and buyer have no family relationship to each other, i.e. an 'arm's length' sale. There will be many factors that can affect such a value, and it is to an enumeration and brief consideration of the most important factors that we now turn.

Factors that can affect the value in land in the market place can be identified broadly as factors *external* to the land owner and property, factors *specific to the property* and factors *specific to the land owner*. There is thus a hierarchy of scales implicit in these groupings,which are basically similar to Massie's (1969) three broad sets of factors that affect the land owner's 'reservation' price or minimum acceptable price, and the propensity of the land owner to sell or hold land.

Factors *external* to the land owner and property include both features of the overall economy and of the institutional structure. The importance of price inflation has already been noted in prompting hedging action by owners of capital, e.g. financial institutions (Munton 1975). The purchase of property in order to safeguard capital may not even be restricted to areas with some future development potential; as long as the investors' confidence is not shaken, rises in land prices will be simply taken as a renewed guarantee of the value of their capital (Sévérac 1963). The level of interest rates, and expectations of future changes in interest rates, may also be expected to influence overall levels of activity in the real-estate market.

Factors relating to the institutional structure that have been suggested as important include the costs of land transfer such as lawyers' and realtors' fees and the situation with respect to capital-gains taxation on unearned increments in land values. Martin (1976) suggests, for instance, that the 1974 Ontario Land Speculation Tax and the Land Transfer Tax perpetuated corporate apprehension toward the land market. In the UK, one source of inflation in agricultural land values prior to the end of 1973 came from land owners who had sold land for urban development, repurchasing farmland elsewhere (Munton 1973); this reinvestment in agricultural land partly reflected a wish to remain in agriculture (similar relocations for expropriated farmers have been noted in France in the Paris region – Bryant 1973a) but also partly reflected a 'roll-over' tax concession on capital gains from farmland sales accruing to land owners who reinvested those gains in a new farmland purchase within three years. The ending of this scheme in late 1973 thus reduced the incentive for the land owner to reinvest in farmland, so reducing one inflationary factor (Munton 1976a). Of course, more extreme forms of intervention in the market may see the substitution of some appraised use value (e.g. as under the 1976 Community Land Scheme in the UK) or of a carefully monitored and arbitrated value appraisal (e.g. as in the French *Zone d'Aménagement Différé* – Swan 1975; Bryant and Martin 1976) for market value.

Factors *specific to the property* that may affect land value include both broad locational characteristics and features particular to the individual property under consideration. The factors that have been studied can be seen essentially as having been identified because of their assumed pertinence as indicators of attractiveness to demand. Thus, a major locational factor that has been identified is that of *accessibility* to one or more nodes (e.g. Hepner, Lewis and Muraco 1976; Moran 1978; Hushak and Bovard 1975). This has found its most explicit expression in the rent-gradient models, from the agricultural location model (Hall 1966; Dunn 1954) to the urban and residential land-use models (Alonso 1964; Hoover 1971; Brigham 1965), which involve a relationship, generally non-linear, between accessibility to one or more nodes and land rent and thus, land value (Wilson 1979). Under such formulations, competition, between land uses leads to the allocation of land to the highest economic use. In tests of this relationship, measures of accessibility used range from metric road distance, to cost-distance and considerations of quality of road access to a property.

The general relationship between distance from the central business district (CBD) of cities and land values has weakened during the twentieth century (Moran 1978), resulting from the increasing dispersal of activities throughout metropolitan regions. Moran's own findings around Auckland, however, show that distance from the CBD provided increased explanatory power of 'unimproved' land values between 1955 and 1970; he suggested, though, that this situation may well have been due to some very localized changes influencing the results, rather than from some consistent pattern of geographic change. Other studies confirm the general negative relationship between value and distance from central locations, e.g. Hushak and Bovard (1975) concluded on the basis of a multiple linear regression analysis of land transactions for 1972 around Columbus, Ohio, that for each extra mile from Columbus, land values for residential or agriculturally zoned land were reduced by $509 per acre.

Another major locational characteristic, much more difficult to measure, concerns the *potential* of a property to move into a higher-valued use, e.g. agricultural land to residential development. In turn, this potential may be a function of broad locational factors such as accessibility, proximity to existing development and public utilities (sewage, water, gas lines), and of course, certain factors more particular to the individual property such as public planning designations (e.g. Hushak and Bovard 1975; Hepner, Lewis and Muraco 1976) and externalities such as adjacent land use. Such potential creates speculative or 'hope' value, and where the probability of a change in use to some type of nonagricultural use is high, as in the urban fringe, such speculative market values will exceed current use values. Where public planning is credible, restrictions on the rights of owners to use land as they wish, e.g. through agricultural land-use zoning, will reduce the value of land; on the other hand, the same planning process that restricts land use in one area, permits and even encourages development elsewhere, thus institutionalizing inequalities in landed 'wealth' and encouraging speculation in some areas. Munton (1976a), for instance, cites evidence that it has been common in south-east England for land with planning permission to reach prices in public auctions twenty or more times its agricultural use value while the overall effect of post-war policies of restraining urban growth in the UK has been to exaggerate price differentials between rural and urban land.

Other factors specific to the particular property include physical property characteristics, public planning designations, including property tax (Hushak and Bovard 1975), and adjacent land use, all of which have already been noted as important in affecting potential land-use change. Other property characteristics worthy of note include size, improvements, tenancies, amenity or aesthetic value, topographic characteristics and engineering or construction constraints. Again these are usually identified because of some presumed relationship to demand, e.g. amenity value may be important in attracting some types of country residential development.

Size of property affects market values per unit area; small parcels of agricultural land, hobby farms, and land for residential development characteristically fetch higher unit-area prices than larger lots even with the same physical characteristics (Bryant 1982; Munton 1975; Hepner, Lewis and Muraco 1976; Hushak and Bovard 1975). For example, existing farmers, interested in adding land to their current operation, would generally be prepared to pay a higher unit-area price for rounding out their operation than they would to buy a new farm; a premium might be paid then for this additional land, perhaps because it will reduce significantly the level of overcapitalization on the farm, or because of its location, it will contribute to a more efficient layout of the farm. Small farms also attract more attention from hobby farmers because of the smaller initial capital outlay required, resulting in higher unit-area prices.

'Improvements' to the land include structures, as well as (from an agricultural perspective) shape of property, and drainage improvements. Buildings, and their state of repair, and appropriateness for the new owner, for example, can either be a 'plus' or a negative factor. Often, it is difficult, if not impossible, to separate out site value from the contribution of 'improvements' (Hoover 1971), especially where in the case of agricultural land, the real value of the land resource has been realized through the application of capital and human toil for decades and even centuries. It is rare, indeed, to find data such as those produced by the Valuation Department, New Zealand, based on 'unimproved' values, which Moran claims as the 'best' available measure of the market value of the land less improvements (Moran 1978: 86).

Land ownership and land conversion

In jurisdictions where tenant–landlord relationships are regularized, significant differences may exist between land with vacant possession and that without vacant possession. Generally, one would expect land with vacant possession to command higher prices, because the owner is less circumscribed in what can be done with the property; analyses of agricultural land markets in the UK confirm this, although it has not always been the case that vacant possession creates a significant premium (Munton 1975, 1976a). In France, the *Statut du Fermage* creates similar attractions to land with vacant possession; leases are not broken, because of provision for compensation for improvements made by tenants, unless a substantial return can be anticipated from non-farm development.

Finally, *land owner characteristics* have been relatively neglected as an influence on land values and the process of land-use conversion, although some of the work relating to land speculation clearly ascribes a role to land speculators in pushing land prices upwards. However, in the work on residential development, land owner characteristics have frequently been relegated to an insignificant role. In the simplest residential development models (e.g. Donnelly, Chapin and Weiss 1964), land ownership characteristics are effectively viewed as one of the random disturbances in a probabilistic process. Thus, in the final analysis, this is like saying that 'everyone has his price' and that land ownership characteristics only introduce short-term rigidities into the land market. This narrow view of the importance of land owner characteristics is supported in a North Carolina study (Kaiser *et al.* 1968) where land owner characteristics became less and less important in predicting holding and selling behaviour as the built-up area was approached. Certainly, it is easy to see how land owner characteristics – their financial situation, expectations, attitudes to risk – can affect the spatial structure of the land market in the short term; each owner has his own 'reservation' price for his property (Clawson 1971) influenced by personal factors as well as his perceptions of what is happening in the surrounding environment and economy generally. On the other hand, land owner characteristics may have a longer-term effect as well on spatial patterns of land-use change in the city's countryside, thus contributing to evolving patterns of land values.

Impacts

The impacts of the land conversion process described above are several. Changes in land ownership patterns constitute one obvious impact; to the extent that they are reflected in a changing distribution of land uses, both economic and cultural, a major type of impact concerns the levels of future incompatibilities between changing activities. These impacts are treated in the following chapters of Part II. Other impacts, while still linked to changing land ownership, are more fundamental in the sense that they precede the land-use changes, paving the way for some of those future land-use conflicts, shaping and being shaped by the evolution of the regional city form. In particular, the phenomenon of land speculation and the level of monopolistic control over the supply of development land may not only affect land prices but may also help shape the evolving regional city form. It may also be regarded as creating problems for the orderly management and planning of the development process as well as adding to the more general problem of a maldistribution of wealth and income in society (Martin 1974).

It is possible to view many of these phenomena and impacts as arising because the real market place in land, as almost every other market place, is characterized by a number of imperfections, e.g. imperfect knowledge of market conditions of supply and demand by the key actors and an environment of uncertainty surrounding the future state of the market and of development patterns, when compared to the yardstick of 'perfect competition'.

Much concern has been expressed about land speculation and its relationship to land hoarding, price inflation and price spiralling. Land speculation has been regarded as wasteful, leading to inefficient patterns of urban development (Task Force 1969) and to the creation of idle land (Hushak and Bovard 1975). The land speculator is, however, not an easy actor to identify. To a large extent, it is the group of intermediate actors who have been singled out for attention – land dealers, land developers and builders. However, if we include any actor who holds raw land in order to sell it later without further improvements and reap an unearned increment, then we must include farmers and some 'final consumers' as speculators too. Land speculation is thus an activity open to anyone with sufficient capital and willingness to assume risk; indeed, far from being something aberrant, it has been regarded as simply the natural result of the economic and institutional structure of Western society (Clawson 1962). This being the case, it should be clear that it is no easy matter to control the phenomenon.

Land speculation is directly related then to actors' expectations. In a sense, land speculation is peculiarly optimistic, given the amount of land affected and the amount needed for development in the immediate future. It is this optimism which accounts partly for the phenomenon of the vertical and horizontal spread of high land prices. Each time a new sale of real estate takes place, other land owners' 'reservation prices' (Clawson 1971) are increased, reflecting rising expectations. Thus, a particular sale of land has a 'spillover' effect on to surrounding properties; some farmers, for instance, will begin to consider the rewards of land value appreciation and, in moving their 'reservation prices' upwards, they have certainly contributed in the past to the 'leap-frogging' of development and a greater dispersion of development than might otherwise have occurred (Archer 1973; Hushak and Bovard 1975). As well, some speculators have been criticized as being much more active in creating land price inflation, deliberately holding land off the market to force prices even higher. Other criticisms have included allegations of speculators making use of privileged information and of collusion and political favour-trading (e.g. Etherington and Anderson 1974).

On the other hand, it has been suggested that land dealers and developers, and speculators, play a positive role in the context of our economic and institutional structure. They interpret signals of changing supply and demand and transmit these back to the predevelopment land owner; they thus help ration land to its highest and best economic use; they assemble land and provide a stock of developable land; and they shoulder a large part of the risks involved in land-use conversion (Clawson 1971) – it is clear, for instance, that while some speculators make considerable profits, others lose very heavily (US National Academy of Sciences and National Academy of Engineering 1972).

But the evidence is not clear on many of these issues, although it is certain that land prices have increased by large amounts and exceed agricultural use values by astronomical amounts in many urbanizing regions (Schmid 1968; Clawson 1971; Munton 1976a) and even beyond such regions. On the other hand, the causes are more difficult to identify. Some have argued that strong monopolistic and oligopolistic tendencies in the land market have helped create land price inflation (see Dennis and Fish 1972, for a commentary on the Canadian situation; and Spurr 1976). Land price spirals, in which land is traded between actors relatively rapidly, may be partially interpreted as reflecting attempts to inflate the value of land prior to real development (Ferguson 1975; Bryant 1982). However, detailed data on the financial and decision-making linkages between the actors involved in such complex transaction chains is needed before such interpretations can be safely made.

Indeed, in one detailed investigation of corporate concentration in the land market on the north-east fringe of Toronto (Martin 1976) some doubt has been cast on the importance of such phenomena. For an area of 360 square miles, and for the period 1968 to 1974, Martin analysed corporate concentration among the 651 land dealer corporations that had been active. Of the 2,162 individuals who had served as directors of these corporations, 82 per cent had served as director of only a single corporation and another 12 per cent as directors of two corporations. From this perspective, and from a further analysis of family relationships between directors, Martin concluded that the amount of corporate concentration was small relative to the total number of actors involved. It was rather the case that a few corporations exhibited high degrees of cooperation and integration; if, of course, these actors can be thought of as leaders, their influence would be far more important than their absolute numbers would suggest.

Martin's work is important, for it emphasizes the complexity of the range of actors involved; not all land dealers can be tarred with the same brush. As he concludes (Martin 1976: 12): 'some land dealers are highly skilled at forecasting future land use and estimating the discounted value of that land...other dealers actually impede the functioning of the land market by fragmenting land ownership patterns, withholding land from prospective buyers, and inflating the asking price for land beyond realistic levels'.

A final complicating factor on this issue of monopolistic control in the land market should be noted; the existence of large holdings of land is not necessarily to be equated with attempts at controlling supply and thus prices. Indeed, it has been argued that such activities simply reflect a developer spreading the risks of getting or not getting development approval from the appropriate government agencies; and that the bureaucratic process for the granting of approval may sometimes hold up development, thus contributing to a restriction in supply and the inflation of prices (e.g. Kearns 1974).

Geographic structures

So far, some of the basic ingredients of the land conversion process have been discussed – the actors, land values, and, more briefly, impacts. But to what extent are the evolving land market structures differentiated geographically in terms of actors, their interrelationships and the resulting land values? To what extent are the spatial zones discussed in Chapter 1 – the urban fringe, the urban shadow, and so forth – spatially continuous or discontinuous? Answers to such questions must remain quite limited as yet, because of the lack of information on rural and agricultural land prices and changing ownership patterns at any fine geographic scale (Munton 1976a). There are some exceptions (e.g. Martin 1975b; Ferguson 1975; and Bryant 1982) but these have generally involved a laborious process of abstracting data from title deeds in land registration offices. While extensive records of both property assessment and real-estate transactions do exist, there have been few major attempts at exploiting these data in a *detailed disaggregated geographic sense*, except for studies dealing almost wholly with land values (e.g. Moran 1978). Furthermore, problems of access to such data still are encountered in some of the jurisdictions where they exist, thus limiting their exploitation. Our discussion thus is largely conceptual, while drawing upon direct personal research experiences.

Implicit in the simplified view of the land market in relation to land-use conversion (Fig. 4.1) is a notion of temporal sequencing in the land ownership structure as it moves towards some 'final destination'. This means that for any given period in which the land market is observed, different areas in a region are going through different stages in the land conversion process – the predevelopment stage, one involving perhaps intermediate actors, and finally one involving final consumers. Martin (1976) has even suggested a series of stages just for type of intermediate actor involvement; he suggested that corporate land dealer activities could be related to four phases in the development of a speculative market in land – the naïve sellers (e.g. farmers) selling to 'clever' dealers who have evaluated the land's potential; transactions between these sophisticated land dealers; the involvement of naïve land dealer corporations, often involving professionals such as lawyers and dentists investing capital, i.e. amateur speculators; and finally, a market dominated by naïve buyers and sellers.

In addition, any such sequencing is complicated by the fact that there is no unique final land-use structure to which land-use conversion must tend. Four broad categories can be distinguished:

1. urban development proper or accretionary urban development, the object of much of the discussion so far in this chapter, which would include residential, commercial and industrial uses;
2. development attracted to the smaller nodes in the regional city form – smaller cities, towns, villages;
3. scattered country residential development, including seasonal development in the form of cottages or second homes;
4. areas characterized by no urban development where the market in land remains an agricultural one.

Thus, the existence of different submarkets in land must be recognized. These different submarkets may overlap and interact both temporally and geographically. To a certain extent, land owners' expectations will be influenced by what is happening in the different markets; this is at the root of the phenomenon of land speculation. A farm land owner may therefore be influenced by the market for country residential lots or by the activity of speculators; the country residential lot market will be influenced by what land owners expect their land would fetch in a more development-oriented context. The interrelationship exists because of the substitutability of land between the different uses concerned; obviously, if this substitutability is reduced by, for example, strict land-use zoning, easements, inappropriate physical characteristics or poor accessibility, then the level of interlinkage between the different submarkets will be lessened.

A limited analysis (Bryant 1982) of temporal patterns of price per unit area for properties of different sizes around the cities of Kitchener and Waterloo of southern Ontario in the late 1960s, when these urban areas were growing rapidly, sheds some light on the level of interlinkage. Using property size classes of less than 5 acres, 5 to 15 acres, 15 to 50 acres, and over 50 acres, it was found that the temporal pattern of prices was closely interrelated for all property groups for Waterloo township (Fig. 4.3) but this was not the case for townships such as Wellesley and Woolwich. It was concluded tentatively that the various submarkets were much more closely interrelated in the immediate urban fringe than further out, and that this was partially so because of the greater involvement of intermediate actors there (Table 4.2). The importance of recognizing different submarkets in land which may be geographically differentiated is that the nature of evolving land-use patterns will be different, as will be the likely impacts and conflicts. Even where one ultimate land-use conversion path overtakes another, e.g. accretionary urban development moving into an area that was once characterized by country residential development, the form and the associated problems and conflicts will likely be different to the situation where accretionary urban development moves into an area of very limited, if any, previous country residential development.

The scene is set, therefore, for significant geographic variation, not only from zone to zone in the framework outlined in Chapter 1, but also in terms of lateral discontinuities. In the earlier discussion of values in land, various features were noted as possible explanations of land values. In different sub-markets, different features of land will be sought after, so that with geographic variation in these features, e.g. the natural environment discussed in Chapter 2, it is natural to expect evolving land ownership patterns to vary too. Furthermore, Hudson (1973) has argued that for nine metropolitan centres in the Middle West of the US, the process of settlement growth in the 'suburban fringe' was characterized by clustered growth rather than random growth, thus accentuating the phenomenon of discontinuity in the city's countryside.

What are some of the characteristics of land ownership change that have been found to discriminate between areas in the regional city form? Volume of real-estate transactions, the size structure of properties, the value of land per unit area, and the relative importance of transactions only involving farmers, farmers selling to intermediate actors, farmers selling to non-farm individuals, and of transactions between intermediate actors were all identified in Bryant's study (Bryant 1982) as key indicators. The general patterning of the importance of the transaction types by buyer and seller are informative (Table 4.2; Fig. 4.4). For example, farmer-to-farmer transactions are evidence of an agricultural market in land; they were much less important in the immediate environs of the cities of Kitchener and Waterloo and steadily increased with increasing distance from the urban boundaries (Fig. 4.4.). On the other hand, transactions involving farmers selling to intermediate actors decreased rapidly from the edge of the urban boundaries in this medium-sized city environment. Over the period studied, transactions between farmer and non-farm individuals increased with increasing distance and then fell off, reflecting both the fact that non-farm residential development had occurred significantly close to the urban boundary in some areas before the study period as well as the active involvement of intermediate actors in the inner fringe. Indeed, the presence of intermediate actors in chains of transactions was a major variable discriminating between inner fringe and outer fringe and urban shadow areas.

To test this situation further, factor analyses of a range of structural variables describing the land market were produced using various levels of aggregation of survey lots; similar sets of factors were produced at each level of aggregation. One dimension described the degree of development of an agricultural land market and conversely the degree of non-farm purchases of farmland; a second dimension dealt with the degree of involvement of intermediate actors in farmland purchases; a third one dealt with the level of farmer sales of real estate to 'final consumers'; and finally, a dimension of general land market activity was identified by overall volume of transac-

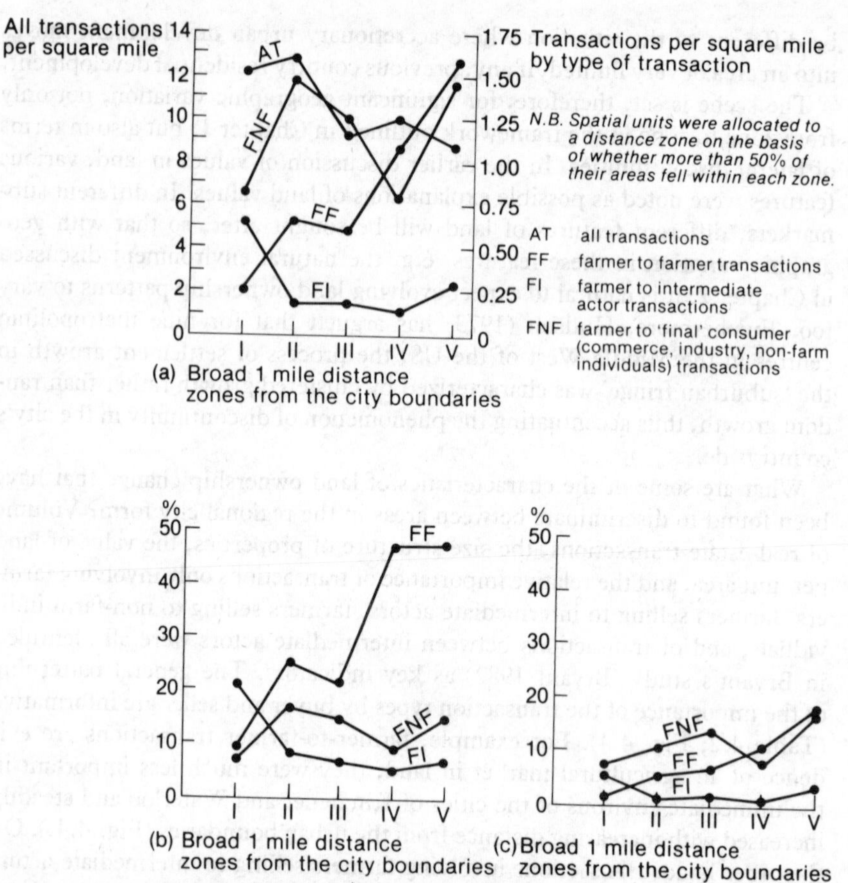

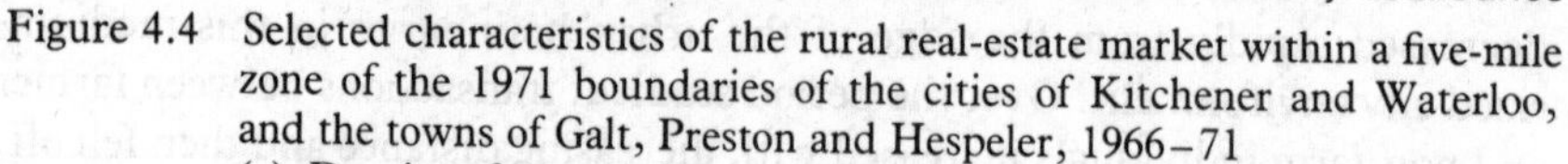

Figure 4.4 Selected characteristics of the rural real-estate market within a five-mile zone of the 1971 boundaries of the cities of Kitchener and Waterloo, and the towns of Galt, Preston and Hespeler, 1966–71
(a) Density of transactions
(b) Percentage of total area transacted accounted for by different types of farmland sales
(c) Percentage of all transactions accounted for by different types of farmland sales (Source: Bryant 1976a: Fig. 3, p. 76).

tions, values of land and the importance of small land parcels in the market.

The important point of this analysis was that the geographic patterns produced by combinations of factor scores only yielded a continuous 'urban fringe zone' at the highest level of aggregation of the data. Still more important, even when this zone was geographically contiguous and continuous around the cities, the zone was certainly not a homogeneous entity. Some parts of the zone were at different stages in the land-use conversion process, on their way to accretionary urban development; other parts of the zone were dominated by non-farm residential development of the single-family dwelling type; still other parts reflected the presence of the smaller urban nodes, with individual residential lots of small size, or the existence of special physical features, e.g. attractive hilly and wooded areas. Even though a common set of forces underlies the evolving regional city form which can be schematized in various ways, a very important consideration both for understanding the evolving structures and their associated problems is the great mix of people and environments involved. With this in mind, the discussion turns in Chapter 5 to country residential development, a major expression of the forces at work that are leading to changes in living patterns and the cultural environment of the city's countryside.

Further reading

Brigham, E. F. (1965) The determinants of residential land values, *Land Economics*, **45**, 325–34.

Bryant, C. R. (1982): *The Rural Real Estate Market: an Analysis of Geographic Patterns of Structure and Change within an Urban Fringe Environment*, Publication Series, Department of Geography, University of Waterloo, Waterloo, Ontario.

Clawson, M. (1971) *Suburban Land Conversion in the United States: an Economic and Governmental Process*, The Johns Hopkins Press, Baltimore.

Moran, W. (1978) Land value, distance and productivity on the Auckland urban periphery, *New Zealand Geographer*, **34** (2), 85–96.

Munton, R. J. C. (1976) An analysis of price trends in the agricultural land market of England and Wales, *Tijdschrift voor economische en sociale geografie*, **67**(4), 202–12.

5 Country residential development

Today, country residential locations provide an alternative living place and life-style to single-family suburbia or apartment living. This option has often been deemed a property right of individual owners even though some inevitable conflicts arise with agricultural and other resource-based production activities, and with the natural environment. This sentiment is stated well in a Halifax, Canada, planning study (Nova Scotia Community Planning Division 1976: 10.3): 'Lakes close to the metropolitan area and to the limited access highway interchanges are the high amenity areas under greatest pressure for year-round subdivision development. In general this pressure cannot and should not be resisted because people are entitled to freedom of choice as to where they want to live.'

First, it is necessary to define what we mean by 'country residential development'. Generally, the term includes relatively small properties or landholdings outside built-up nodes whose permanent occupiers depend on non-farm employment; countryside subdivisions can thus be included but second homes and cottage developments are not directly considered. Two questions immediately arise: what is 'small' and where do part-time and hobby farms fit in? It has been suggested in a Canadian study that 10 ha is a reasonable maximum (Russwurm 1976) but what size of holdings and what level of farming are included in different studies still varies almost as much as the name given to it, e.g. small-holdings, rural estates, rural retreats, ranchettes, country estates, exurban residential and rural non-farm development (McQuinn 1978). For instance, Troughton (1976) in a study of farm landholding types around London, Ontario, essentially excluded properties of less than 4 ha; an Auckland study interested in agricultural use defined 'small-holdings' as properties falling between 1 and 10 ha (Auckland Regional Authority, Moran, Neville and Rankin 1980); and a study with emphasis on hobby farms in Armidale region, Australia, defined rural retreats as being between 2 and 100 ha where the owner held an urban-oriented occupation (McQuinn 1978). This latter study suggested that nothing resembling commercial agriculture was possible on holdings under 2 ha. While it is probably inappropriate to draw a tight line, it seems reasonable to view country residential holdings (our preferred term) as less than 10 ha in size, the owner of which has an urban-oriented occupation, and which is located outside built-up nodes.

Urban demand for residences, expressed in various forms in the city's countryside such as scattered, ribbon and crossroad developments or as 'leap-frog' subdivisions, is widespread and is a key part of the emerging regional city form. This is particularly so where physical planning restrictions have been limited as in much of North America, which contrasts with the situation in the UK. According to Canadian empirical evidence to date (see below), scattered country residential population is about 5 to 15 per cent of the built-up concentrated core population, giving between 5,000 and 15,000 people living within 50 km of the built-up edge of a city of 100,000. Given current family sizes of about 3 people per family, this number of people would mean about 2,000 to 5,000 houses.

In discussing the country residential phenomenon, four basic questions are posed. What is the nature of the demand? What is the nature of the supply? What kinds of living patterns occur and what are the ramifications for the community? And what is the magnitude of the phenomenon itself?

Nature of the demand

Bauer and Roux (1976) see the expansion of population into the city's countryside as an 'explosion' of population at a subregional scale taking place within the broader 'implosion' or polarization that had developed until recently at a regional or macroscale. Though continuing increase of concentration of people into the larger cities is now in question in many countries, the dispersion of population into the city's countryside is still ongoing (Russwurm and Preston 1980; New Zealand Land Use Advisory Council 1980). A critical question is: what proportion of the urban population would live in the countryside given free choice? Though hard evidence is lacking, in the Canadian context it is suggested that the limit is somewhere around 10 per cent of the population living in the regional city. This model of a mature regional city thus postulates 75 per cent of the population in the concentrated built-up area, 15 per cent in the towns, villages and hamlets, and 10 per cent in scattered country residences.

Demand for country residences arises largely out of the social, economic and psychological desires of people living in the built-up city. Various studies have shown that most exurbanites originate from their nearby city though some uncertainty still exists on what proportion originally had a country background prior to living in the city (McQuinn 1978; Brunet and Lepine 1981). A largely unanswered question is: what kind of people are more apt to move to the countryside? Only limited information exists on this question and mostly concerns occupational categories and other demographic characteristics.

Factors underlying demand for country residences

Five general reasons given by people reflect 'pull' factors for living in the countryside: desires for greater privacy and personal space; values inherent in both the man-modified and the natural environment amenities of the countryside; freedom to carry on activities usually not permitted in the built-up area, e.g. keeping animals; attractions as a place to raise children; and the hope that economic advantages will result (Russwurm 1977a; Australian Department of Urban and Regional Development 1975; AREA 1973). Today sociocultural reasons rather than economic ones seem to be the dominating ones, and this is a phenomenon that has repeated itself in many different countries of the Western world.

Along with the pull factors, 'push' factors exist which represent essentially a negative image of the urban environment by exurbanites (AREA 1973). First, there is the reverse side of the coin of the five factors listed above, i.e. less privacy, amenity drawbacks in the urban environment, drawbacks for raising children, the impossibility of carrying out certain activities, and the costs of acquiring a house. Second, there are added problems of congestion, of air pollution and of the psychological 'rat race' syndrome of intense urban life, i.e. perceived disadvantages in the physical and psychological environment of the built-up city as a place to live. Put another way, the desire to live in the countryside may be a spiritual seeking for biophysical roots associated with man's evolutionary origins.

What does the evidence show about the nature of the demand for country living? In a study in Winnipeg, Canada, based on a mail questionnaire sent in 1973 to exurbanite households in five rural municipalities living on properties of less than 8 ha, respondents were instructed to select four choices from a list of fourteen asking why they moved to the country. The results were scored using a weighting of four points for a first choice to one point for a fourth choice (Manitoba Municipal Planning Branch and University of Manitoba 1974). The reason 'area less crowded' came out on top, while 'attractive landscape', 'more visual privacy around home' and 'lower taxes' tied for second, and 'wanted more land' came next.

In another mail questionnaire sent out to residents of the rural municipalities surrounding the city of Thunder Bay in Ontario, a random sample response of over 200 questionnaires was received. However, only five reasons were asked for concerning preferences for living in the countryside (Lakehead Planning Board 1974). By far the dominant reason given was 'to take advantage of the rural life style'. A definite second choice was 'less pollution and greater scenic beauty'. The other more economic reasons scoring relatively low were 'lower taxes', 'lower priced lots' and 'for investment purposes'. The investment motive, incidentally, is partially responsible for the phenomenon of vacant lots which can sometimes reach amazing proportions. For example, around Calgary, it has been noted the number of vacant lots approximately equalled developed ones (Calgary Regional Planning Commission 1977). Some of these are speculative lots, although most probably reflect the lag between purchase of a lot and actually building a home (Australian Department of Urban and Regional Development 1975).

Similar findings are reported from other countries. In a sample study of over 200 small-holders in New Zealand, the major reason given was a desire to live in a rural environment (77 per cent) accompanied by a desire to avoid living in the city (60 per cent) (Auckland Regional Authority, Moran, Neville, Rankin and Cochrane 1980). Other common reasons were to live off the land, to raise children in a rural environment, and for an investment. And a French study (AREA 1973) carried out in the Plaine de Versailles, south-west of Paris, noted a set of positive features of the rural environment (being close to agricultural activities which are indicative of rural life and the landscapes agriculture supports; having open space easily accessible for viewing and driving and walking; a slower pace of 'life'; 'the good air'; and being close to nature, especially being able to appreciate the seasons better) as well as a set of negative features of the urban environment (the 'threatening nature' of the urban environment and the lack of sense of personal freedom). Evident then from all these studies cited is the significance of more space and privacy and a perceived view of a more desirable living environment. But to put this into context, it should be stressed that the major advantage of living in the city's countryside is the ability to be close to nature, open space and all that they stand for *and* to be able to have access to the facilities of the city (Bauer and Roux 1976).

The people involved

If people of certain occupational classes, income levels, education levels, stage in the life-cycle, and so on, are more prone to move, then the demand for country residences may be predictable. One approach is to measure the proportion of country residents showing certain demographic characteristics in comparison to the proportion of the built-up city population showing the same characteristics.

Various studies have shown that most country residents move out from the adjacent city (e.g. Brunet and Lepine 1981; McQuinn 1978; AREA 1973). While the characteristics of families relocating in the countryside are varied, four attributes are pronounced. These families are more apt to be relatively early in the child-rearing stage of the life-cycle and to be from professional-managerial and craftsmen-production worker occupational groups. Somewhat higher incomes and a higher proportion of university-educated household members are the third and fourth attributes of country residents. The point about both professional-managerial and craftsmen-production workers being 'over-represented' in the city's countryside seems contradictory at first sight. Bauer and Roux (1976) confirm this and note in their analysis of 'rurbanization' in France that the city's countryside in comparison to suburban areas proper has a higher proportion both of the relatively well-off social categories (e.g. entrepreneurs, higher management executives and the liberal professionals) and also, although to a lesser extent, the least privileged social classes. The answer to this apparent contradiction is to be found partly at least in the fact that there are different types of country residential submarkets ranging from the exclusive and expensive large lot with expensive house or the rural estate to the smaller lot, often located closer to the city in a highway location, with a more modest house structure, where economic considerations of countryside living may be more important. One of the key implications of the different submarkets then is diversity, diversity of living environments and of life-styles available in the city's countryside.

As further evidence, in a Manitoba study (Manitoba Municipal Planning Branch and University of Manitoba 1974) residents of the city of Winnipeg were compared with a Winnipeg Region country residential sample. Country residential families were over-represented in:

1. technical occupational groups (26.0 compared to 18.9 per cent) and craftsmen and production workers (30.2 to 23.7 per cent);
2. university education (14.7 to 11.6 per cent);
3. household income over $10,000 (48.3 to 12.3 per cent):
4. average household size (4.0 to 3.6 persons).

While these four attributes do not show up consistently in comparisons of city and country resident populations from region to region, the larger average family size with more school-age children is a regular finding (e.g. McQuinn 1978; Russwurm 1977a). Interestingly enough, the youthfulness of households with children is a characteristic shared by many suburban areas proper and, consequently, gives more credence to views of country residential development as a further diffusion of the suburbs.

Nature of the supply

Having identified the nature of the demand in terms of why and who, the next step is to look at factors related to the supply of country residential lots. The nature of the supply concerns questions about the kind of sites, where they are located, and how new lots are created. Demand concerns motivations for purchase; supply concerns availability of the types of lots desired and motivations for selling the appropriate real estate.

First, a primary factor in the creation or availability of lots in many jurisdictions is planning and local government policy. Such policies tend either to eliminate, to regulate or to attract country residential development depending on the viewpoints held by planners and politicians. While upper-level government structures may provide some guidelines, most decisions on subdividing parcels of land from larger properties for country residences, an important part of the process of country residential development in North America, remain the responsibility of local municipalities. While strongly implemented policies at the municipal level have been rare, more and more regulations are being applied because of servicing, health or other environmental issues; thus, supply may be restricted to control undesirable consequences of too much development or of haphazard development. The issues of planning in relation to country residential development are taken up in Chapter 12.

Second, the supply of lots available can be viewed in various ways. One type of study has attempted to assess the site characteristics desired by prospective or actual country residents (e.g. Manitoba Municipal Planning Branch and University of Manitoba 1974; Australian Department of Urban and Regional Development 1975). This accent on demand preferences then would permit at least theoretically an assessment to be made of the total potential supply of lots in a region. Problems such as the effect of different densities of development on demand preferences, however, would make such an exercise extremely complicated. Furthermore, different regions possess different physical attributes so that the relative *value* placed on given sites by potential buyers and sellers alike will vary regionally.

In terms of the global supply of land for country residential development and based on evidence from several studies, Bauer and Roux (1976) point out that in the absence of significant planning controls, the supply of land for country residences normally appears to exceed demand over a wide area in the city's countryside. This is partly because land owners are overly optimistic about the chances of selling. This alone would thus permit a much greater scattering of country residences than would otherwise occur, even though constraints such as accessibility do exist. Furthermore, assuming a negative relationship between quantity demanded and total cost of a country residential lot (land price plus accessibility costs) and assuming a country residential lot of a given size and price, demand for such country lots will fall off with increasing distance as accessibility costs increase. If we further assume for the same-priced lot that willing suppliers are distributed in proportion to land area, then the supply of this same lot-type will increase with increasing distance from the built-up city edge. The net result would then be a tendency for supply to outstrip demand with increasing distance from the city edge, creating upward pressures on the lot prices near the city and depressing effects further from the city. The mechanisms underlying the land market for the country residential lots market is poorly understood so that the preceding remarks must be regarded as very tentative, and this is even more so for the supply side.

As noted in Chapter 4 as a general observation on analyses of the land market, supply has usually been regarded in terms of what property characteristics seem to be sought after by the buyers of land. The next section is therefore devoted to a consideration of accessibility and site preferences in relation to country residential lots.

Accessibility and site preferences

Most country residents are part of the daily urban system of their built-up

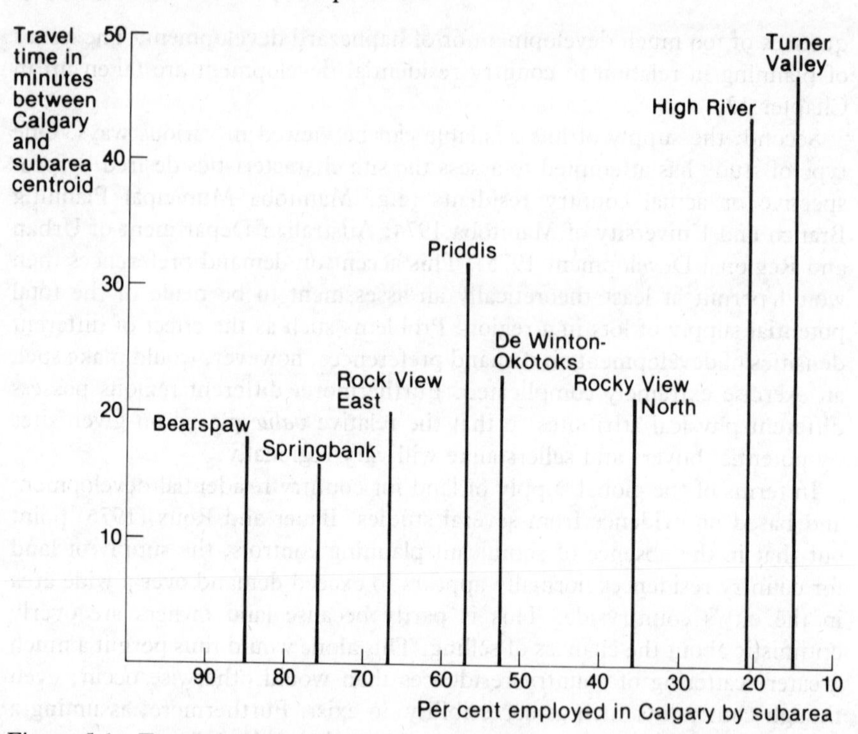

Figure 5.1 Travel-time distribution: Calgary. (Source: from data in Whitehead 1969: 17).

city, with one or more employed persons in a household working outside their immediate locale. While they may not recognize the full costs of living in the country (Phillips 1977), it seems that such commuters generally prefer to spend less than half an hour's travel each way. Figure 5.1 illustrates for Calgary a travel-time distribution similar in pattern to that occurring with some variations around other cities. In this Calgary study, almost half of the commuters spent only 20 to 29 minutes *en route* one way, while over 85 per cent of the daily commuters spent less than 40 minutes travelling to work. Similar findings were noted in two other recent studies (Ricour-Singh 1979; Taafe, Gauthier and Maraffa 1980). It is worth noting that travelling through the countryside is often easier and more pleasant than travelling through the built-up area. Nonetheless, when desirable sites are available, country residential location seems to reflect a distance-decay relationship, e.g. the correlation of distance with proportion of country residents employed in Calgary was –0.88, indicating an attempt to minimize commuting distance (Whitehead 1969)

With the time spent travelling to work affected by the principle of least effort, the location of country residents in relation to the road network and the type of roads will be important considerations. Road systems in the urban fields of cities have been consistently improved over the past 25 years, a phenomenon particuarly noticeable in areas where large sections of unpaved roads existed, e.g. North America. Again the principle of least effort (Zipf 1949) is invoked. Whitehead (1969: 22) concludes: 'few residences are found beyond two miles from a paved road, even though a gravelled road network makes much of the region accessible, and even though less costly and more scenic parcels lie beyond the two miles'. A similar conclusion was reached in a recent study west of Edmonton (Alberta Land Use Forum 1974). As the supply of sites becomes more limited, less accessible sites are increasingly used. Then, either the time spent on travelling to work increases or pressure is put on the local municipality to improve the road system.

Clearly, accessibility to the concentrated core of the regional city is important in determining what sites from the potential supply of land are more highly valued for country residences. But not all areas of land will be selected for a country home even if available, and only part of the journeys to work are to the concentrated core. People trade off accessibility, land costs and site preferences. Quite apart from planning controls, a mix of factors based on location and natural environmental characteristics, personal preferences and financial capability are thus commonly drawn upon to 'explain' the spatial distribution of country residences in the city's countryside.

Four aspects of the natural environment have been identified as being significant for urbanites in selecting a country residential site, viz. vegetative cover, proximity to water, scenery and topography, all of which relate to amenity considerations. In discussing the natural environment in Chapter 2, it was pointed out that what is important is what is available in the surroundings of a particular city rather than how such characteristics might be classified on a national scale. Where trees are scarce, areas of woodland are valued highly. For instance, around Winnipeg, treed areas are largely restricted to the valleys of the Red and Assiniboine rivers. In 1973, lots along the Red River within the municipality of St Andrews, north of Winnipeg, were selling at $8,000 to $10,000 per acre or approximately twice the average price for land away from the river (Manitoba Municipal Planning Branch 1974). Obviously, parcels of land possessing favourable amenity attributes and accessibility would be selected first. Later, as demand overtakes the most preferred locations, less preferred sites would be increasingly used. Thus, in southern Ontario, an early preferred site in the 1950s was a stream or lake location in a wooded area. Such sites if accessible were used up quickly; since then, many country residences have been located at the corner of a farm woodlot especially where such woodlots abut roads; these are an expression of a second-best choice.

Along with the vegetative cover and proximity to water preferences expressed in site selection by country residents, scenic views closely related to topography are important. In a private property market the most preferred sites fall to the wealthier segment of the population. Estate-type mansions are found at scenic sites such as rocky promontories of lakes, or rivers (e.g. Minneapolis–St Paul region), in glacial landscapes on large drumlins (e.g.

Guelph and Peterborough, Ontario) or hilltops of hummocky moraines (e.g. Calgary, Alberta). Lower-income groups usually end up with cheaper, flatter and less scenic sites.

All things being equal, as the supply of sites with superior natural environment qualities dwindles, other locations may be used increasingly. Then more and more country residential lots may be located on good agricultural land. However, this depends on the particular locational structure of agricultural land as well as on the existence of different types of submarkets for country residential lots. Thus, Greaves (1975) found residential severances densest on the good agricultural lands in Albion township; these lands happened to be closest to Toronto, so that accessibility considerations appeared paramount. The lot sizes there were also much smaller than in the more distant scenic areas, implying a difference perhaps between utilitarian commuter lots and country estate-type lots. Once the move onto cropland occurs for whatever reasons, then two critical issues may arise (Ch. 6). One is some loss of good farmland, the other is the greater potential conflict with farmers over dust, odours, trespass and other irritations.

Though generally most exurbanites might prefer sites reflecting natural-environment amenities when supply permits, some do choose lots close to active farm operations. It may be for family reasons, e.g. a lot severed by a son or daughter from the home farm; it may be from a preference for closeness to a pastoral scene; it may be the greater importance of accessibility to the city-edge industrial park and its jobs for a particular household; it may be the availability of an irregular parcel of land at a cheap price, e.g. a corner left over from a road-straightening project. In any event, country residential locations reflect supply–demand interactions, financial capability of the exurbanite and personal preferences, although these location factors are increasingly being modified by planning regulations.

Planning regulations

In the approach used so far in discussing country residential location, it has been assumed that no restrictions existed on the availability of sites except in those circumstances when demand exceeds supply. Thus, it was assumed that a family interested in locating in the countryside could locate wherever it wanted. All that was necessary was to find a property owner, normally a farmer, who would sell a piece of land. In North America particularly, just such a situation existed more or less until about 1960; and a similar situation existed in much of Western Europe, an exception perhaps being the UK, where the Town and Country Planning Act of 1947 had already tightened the situation considerably. Since then at various speeds between and within different countries, planning regulations have restricted the supply. With planning, the main concern has been to prevent undue costs for the municipality or more generally for society, as it was recognized how individual actions generated externalities (see Chs. 2 and 3), although concerns about maintaining 'rural character' have been increasingly common, too.

Planning approaches to controlling country residential development have included minimum lot sizes, minimum lot frontage, maximum densities of development, zoning for country residential development, encouraging residential development to cluster in existing hamlets and villages, or some combination of these. These are discussed at greater length in Chapter 12. Understanding and planning for country residential development in rural–urban fringe areas is a complex task involving people, land and institutional interactions as modified by overlapping natural, economic and cultural environments. Always it must be remembered that basically land is held as private property around cities. Even in areas like the states of Nevada and Arizona where only about one-fifth of the land is in private hands, most of this is found around the cities. Whenever regulations are applied they affect specific people in specific places. Underlying good planning regulations must be the intent to protect both people and resources. In some areas, supply may not meet demand because the land resource has to be protected; in other areas property rights of individuals may have to be protected from the activities of other property owners. Usually both aspects occur in most areas surrounding our cities.

Country residential living patterns

It was noted earlier that people have moved permanently outside the city to live in search of nature, more space, privacy, a better place for children, a place to raise animals, and fewer regulations generally. But once there, do people do things differently in their daily lives or do they simply transplant their urban behavioural patterns into the open space of the countryside? At present our knowledge about this question is still sparse but it is believed that urban patterns are initially transplanted and are then slowly modified over time (Walker 1975, 1976, 1977). Two broad overlapping categories of household activity, nondiscretionary and discretionary, are discussed and the paucity of research is noted.

Non-discretionary activities

These activities involve minimum choice on the part of the household. Most adults travel to work and household members have to travel to get the goods and services needed to maintain the household. In contrast, movement for discretionary (recreational and social) activities involves much greater freedom of choice (Bunting 1980). Travel to school is also an activity that involves little choice in most jurisdictions in a country residential location, and often involves considerable distance and time for children as well as parents, especially if their children are to participate in extracurricular school activities.

The journey to work is unavoidable for most adults. While some people can walk to work or use mass transit in cities, such possibilities are virtually nil for exurbanites. However, on average the inevitable commuting does not necessarily mean that people living in the city's countryside spend more time on the journey to work. Many journeys to work in the city's countryside are to employment nodes at the city edge like shopping centres, industrial parks and large educational complexes.

Detailed studies of commuting patterns of country residents are, however, still rare. Two fairly recent studies provide some interesting pointers though; one in the Hamilton–Toronto axis (Hoch 1974) and one from Kentucky (Phillips 1977). For well-separated single cities, especially smaller ones, it seems that the majority (usually 50 to 90 per cent) of country residents commute to the urban core of the regional city (Ironside and Williams 1980; Troughton 1981). But where regional cities overlap as in Nassagaweya Township north of the Hamilton (Ontario) Metropolitan Area, rather complex commuting patterns can arise (Hoch 1974).Nassagaweya Township is located from between 19 and 65 km (Central Toronto) of seven significant employment centres located outside the Township, which has only very limited nodes of employment itself. Accessibility is excellent via major highways including the limited-access Highway 401 and paved roads. Hoch sampled about one-fifth of the approximately 1,500 work force. Table 5.1 shows the complex spatial movements involved, with the average commuting distance one way being 34 km.

Considerable costs are involved in commuting patterns which may not be fully recognized (Phillips 1977). Based on his sample, Hoch estimated the daily journey to work for Nassagaweya residents to be about 96,000 km. As

Table 5.1 Commuting pattern, Nassagaweya Township, 1973

Attracting employment node	*Population 1971*	*Distance**	*Percentage of sample commuting†*
Metro Toronto	2,087,017	65	23.4
Hamilton	309,173	32	4.0
Mississauga	167,434	40	4.0
Oakville	58,440	40	8.0
Burlington	86,113	24	6.3
Guelph	62,659	21	4.0
Milton	14,257	19	26.3
Nassagaweya	3,445	–	11.7
Other	–		12.3

* Distance is from the centre of the township to downtown in kilometres
† Sample of 351 commuters
(Source: compiled from Hoch 1974; pp. 27–79

petrol costs continue to rise, such expense may become more of a limiting factor on further country residential development. At a commuting cost of about 20 cents per kilometre, the daily cost in this township would be close to $20,000. Yet the journey to work may have its advantages too; Bauer and Roux (1976) note that the car may be viewed as an extension of personal and private spaces in which the driver may cut himself or herself off from the hustle and bustle of work and family life.

In the Kentucky study, Phillips compared seven areas of country residential clusters within 80 km of Lexington with two sample areas within the city. This study area, containing a number of other employment nodes and

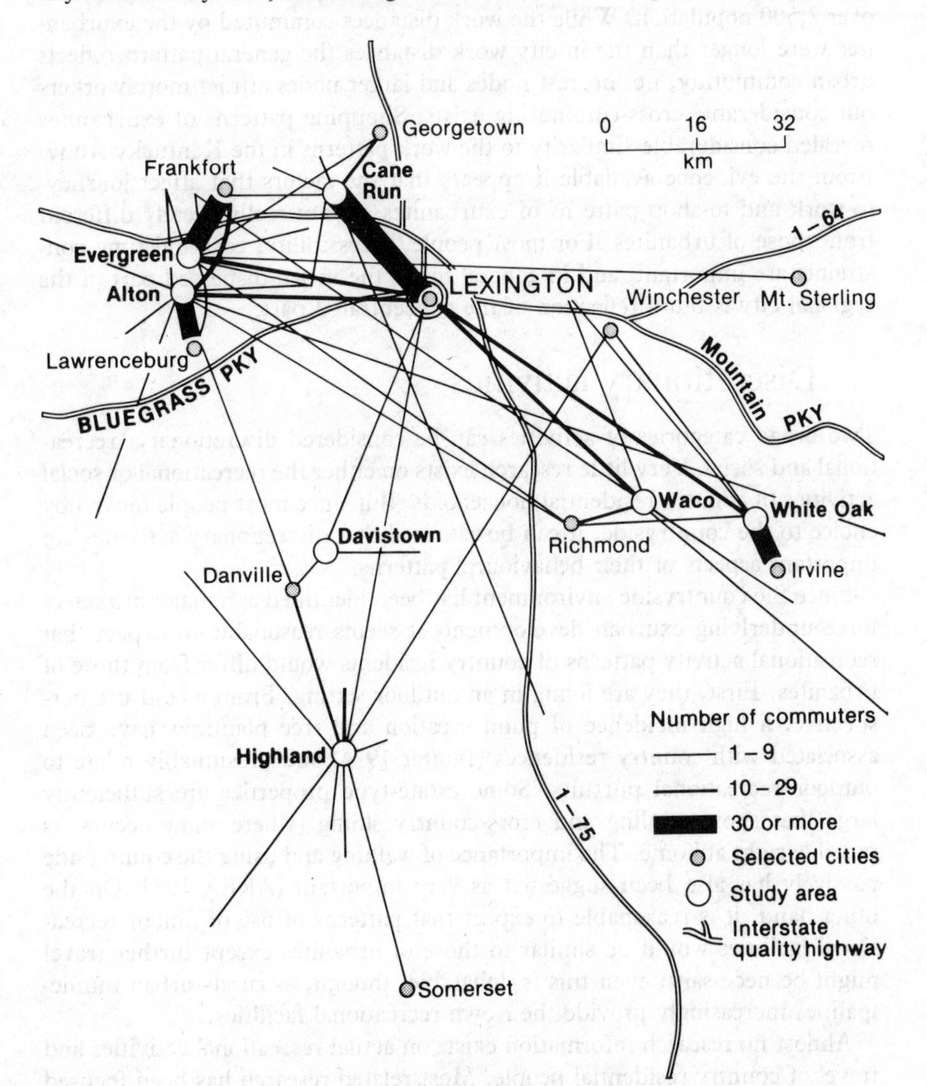

Figure 5.2 Commuting pattern: Lexington area. (Source: Phillips 1977: 31).

traversed by three interstate expressways, again had a complex commuting pattern and compares well with the study of Hamilton, Ontario (Fig. 5.2). Three characteristics are noticeable: most movement was to the nearest employment nodes; the pervasive influence of the largest city, Lexington, stands out; and considerable cross-commuting occurs, indicative of a complex system with multiple origins and destinations. Average commuting distance one way was 20 km and the exurbanites were five times more likely to commute to work in another county than were the Lexington sample respondents, whose average journey-to-work distance one way was 11 km. Urban places dominated the employment, with 87 per cent working in places over 2,500 population. While the work distances commuted by the exurbanites were longer than the in-city work distances the general pattern reflects urban commuting, i.e. nearest nodes and larger nodes attract more workers but considerable cross-commuting exists. Shopping patterns of exurbanites revealed considerable similarity to the work patterns in the Kentucky study. From the evidence available it appears that the factors that affect journey-to-work and to-shop patterns of exurbanites are not really greatly different from those of urbanites. For most people, accessibility, cost and time constraints are important, and in general terms the urban dispersed part of the regional city is but a reflection of the concentrated part.

Discretionary activities

Two broad categories of activities can be considered discretionary: recreational and social. Very little research exists on either the recreational or social activities of country residential households. But since most people moved by choice to the countryside, it can be assumed that discretionary activities are important aspects of their behavioural patterns.

Since the countryside environment has been identified as a major attractive force underlying exurban development, it seems reasonable to expect that recreational activity patterns of country residents would differ from those of urbanites. First, they are living in an outdoor setting. From a land-use perspective, a high incidence of pond creation and tree plantings have been associated with country residences (Punter 1974) and presumably relate to outdoor recreational pursuits. Some estate-type properties are sufficiently large that snowmobiling and cross-country skiing (where snow occurs) is possible right at home. The importance of walking and using the countryside passively has also been suggested as very important (AREA 1973).On the other hand, it is reasonable to expect that patterns of use of indoor recreational facilities would be similar to those of urbanites except further travel might be necessary; even this is debatable, though, as rural–urban municipalities increasingly provide their own recreational facilities.

Almost no research information exists on actual recreational activities and travel of country residential people. Most related research has been focused on the use of the city's countryside by urbanites (Greer and Wall 1979; Barker 1978). One specific study in part of the surroundings of Waterloo, Ontario, based on a sample of 50 households, living mostly on lots under 2 ha showed no real differences for a large number of outdoor recreational activities in activity patterns from those of urbanites (Fitzgerald 1977). Furthermore, use patterns of the surroundings showed no real influence of living in the countryside. Yet one concern regularly expressed is that country residential owners are 'locking-up' prime recreational lands for themselves (Australian Department of Urban and Regional Development 1975).

Aside from the commonly identified factors of leisure time, mobility and increased incomes, use of the urban surroundings for recreational purposes by all people in the regional city can be expected to increase because of rising energy costs. Increasing recreational use of private land is being proposed (e.g. New Zealand Land Use Advisory Council 1980) but can only lead to increasing conflict, especially with exurbanites who moved to the countryside for perceived environmental benefits and privacy. In relation to such pressures, it is interesting to note that recent legislation in Ontario has removed the possibility of a land owner being held liable except for irresponsible actions, and also encourages posting of land for specific types of recreational use (Ontario Ministry of the Attorney General 1979, 1980).

Social activities of country residential households are as little studied as recreational activities. It is generally held and supported by the few existing studies that exurbanites having come from the city will maintain most social ties with the city. In this field, the work of Walker (1975, 1976, 1977) stands out. In studies north of Toronto he has attempted to define the general form of social organization in the city's countryside by analysing visiting patterns, friendship choices and other social interactions among farm, country residential and village populations. Generally, he found that farm-household social networks were more distinctly patterned and that the exurbanites brought values, attitudes and behaviour with them which for the initial period in the countryside resulted in more circumscribed social interactions related to the city. He suggested, however, that with increased length of residence these networks would expand and incorporate farm and village families. One important factor is the young family stage in the life-cycle of many exurbanite households, resulting in many school and other related activities that can lead to social interactions.

An additional question stemming from the belief that exurbanites bring their learned urban values and behaviour with them concerns their responses to issues arising in the countryside. Evidence from three comparable studies around three different cities in southern Ontario shows that full-time, part-time and hobby farmers can be distinguished on a number of demographic and behavioural criteria (Troughton 1976; Seabrooke 1981; Hyslop and Russwurm 1981). Generally, hobby farmers (many of whom would fall under our definition of country residential) are more concerned about beautifying their property, about restricting further development in the countryside, and are more supportive of stronger planning controls.

Overall, then, the evidence available on both discretionary and nondiscretionary activities suggests that few differences exist between country residential households and city households with similar income, educational and stage in life-cycle characteristics. This is not surprising given the view of the urban-dispersed part of the regional city as an extension of the suburbanization process.

While push–pull factors are consistently listed high among reasons for locating in the countryside, many contradictions exist in the whole process of *citification* of the countryside, a point well made by Bunce (1981). One example of such contradictions is the overlapping use of the terms 'suburbanization' and 'exurbanization', a situation further exacerbated by the recently coined term 'counter-urbanization' (Berry 1976) although this latter term really refers to a more macroscale process. Another contradiction is that of people desiring a different life-style possible in the country, yet given all the urban-type services that are generally demanded, and the urban behaviour that is retained, it may be that the move to the countryside is really similar to the common city move from a first house to a more expensive second house.

Where planning controls and other restrictions on supply lead to rising costs for country residential properties, the countryside promises to become the enclave of the rich. Or perhaps the pattern of residential segregation noted as a key human consequence of urbanization in the US (Berry 1973) will follow in the city's countryside, a point already made in some studies (e.g. Punter 1974; Pahl 1965). Evidence points in this direction because different housing submarkets seem to exist. More often than not the higher status, higher-income groups (professional-managerial) and lower status, lower-income groups (craftsmen-production worker) occur disproportionately. If so, then it would follow that the suburbanization process in the countryside would be truncated somewhere short of the large numbers of middle status, middle-income groups becoming dominant. Obviously much remains unanswered on the social side.

The magnitude of country residential development

Some of the ramifications of country residential development, such as impact on agricultural resources, access to recreational lands, domination of local government councils and impact on 'rural character', depend in part at least upon the actual magnitude of country residential development. However, studies that deal with any broad geographic area are rare although some general indications can be derived from commuting statistics where they are collected in a national census (Bauer and Roux 1976). Commuting statistics do not usually permit the separation of nodal settlements within a rural municipality from the more open or dispersed part unless the settlement happens to be both a separate legal entity and of a large enough size. Therefore, it is appropriate to conclude this chapter by referring to two types of studies the authors have been involved in where this has been accomplished.

First, some interesting data on the various settlement components of the regional city form in the Canadian context have been developed in an ongoing study of agriculture in the urban field from 1941 to 1976 by Russwurm and Bryant. By manipulating Canadian census population data it was possible to obtain reasonably comparable data over time and space on the population

Table 5.2 Population components,* 1941–76, of Canadian regional cities with a concentrated urban population over 40,000 in 1976. ('000)

	Concentrated urban		*Dispersed urban*				
	Core	*Outlying*	*Nodal*	*Country residential (scattered)*	*Dispersed farm*	*Total farm and country residential*	*Total regional city population*
1941	5,113	357	664	261	1,073	1,335	7,470
1951	6,675	455	867	391	1,073	1,465	9,461
1956	8,106	524	1,023	501	1,045	1,544	11,197
1961	9,729	673	1,178	724	839	1,566	13,147
1966	11,040	775	1,302	764	790	1,554	14,671
1971	12,237	874	1,496	983	600	1,585	16,191
1976	12,925	984	1,657	1,403	425	1,829	17,395
Relative change							
1941–51	30.5	27.3	30.6	49.5	0.0	9.7	26.7
1951–56	21.4	15.1	18.1	28.1	– 2.8	5.4	12.7
1956–61	20.0	28.6	15.0	45.0	– 19.5	1.4	17.4
1961–66	13.5	15.0	10.5	5.0	– 5.8	– 0.8	11.6
1966–71	10.8	12.8	14.8	28.7	– 24.0	1.9	10.4
1971–76	5.6	12.7	10.8	42.7	– 29.2	15.4	7.4
1941–76	152.8	175.7	149.5	435.9	– 60.4	37.0	132.9
Percent of regional city population†							
1941	68.4	4.8	8.9	3.5	14.4		
1951	70.5	4.8	9.2	4.1	11.4		
1956	72.4	4.7	9.1	4.5	9.3		
1961	74.0	5.1	9.0	5.5	6.4		
1966	75.2	5.3	8.9	5.2	5.4		
1971	75.6	5.4	9.2	6.1	3.7		
1976	74.3	5.7	9.5	8.0	2.5		

* All data derived from Census of Canada: no census was taken in 1946. Concentrated urban outlying consists of free-standing urban nodes having 10,000 or more population, 1976; dispersed urban nodal consists of incorporated and unincorporated places between 50 and 10,000 population; dispersed farm consists of all population living on census farms which had similar definitions 1941, 1961, 1966 and 1971 but more stringent definitions 1951, 1956 and 1976.

† Regional city population consists of concentrated urban and dispersed urban and dispersed farm.

components of regional cities, viz. concentrated urban, dispersed urban nodal, dispersed urban scattered and farm population. The regional areas were defined as the areas with concentrated urban populations (urban built-up cores) of 40,000 or more in 1976 (52 in all, except for 1941 when St John's, Newfoundland, was excluded) extending outwards from the core for a radius of 50 km, thus comprising inner and outer fringe, and at least part of the urban shadow zone.

For these 52 urban fields, in aggregate, over the 35 years, farm population shrunk from 1.1 million to 0.4 million (Table 5.2) while scattered (i.e. country residential) population grew to 0.3 million from 1.4 million, almost a reversal of the numbers involved. It was approximately in 1966 that the country residential population equalled farm population with the gaps spreading widely from 1971 to 1976 (Fig. 5.3). About 20 per cent of this shift involves a more stringent definition of 'farm' adopted in 1976 (Parenteau 1981) but even so about a net quarter million people were added (420,000 country residential minus 175,000 farm) between 1971 and 1976 by the country residential category.

By 1976 this shift meant that over half a million people more were occu-

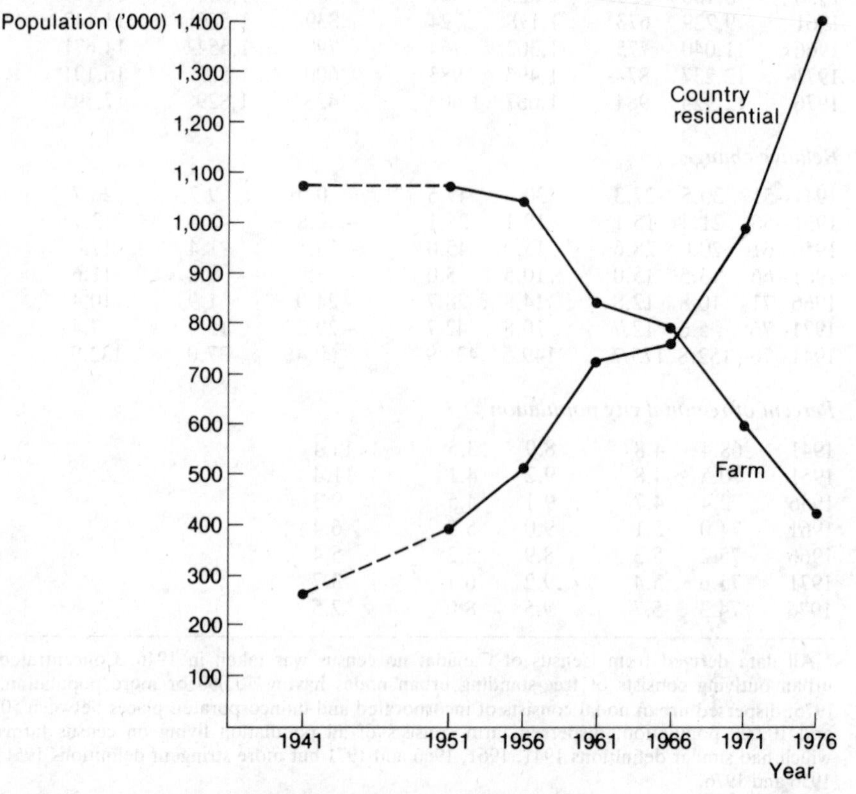

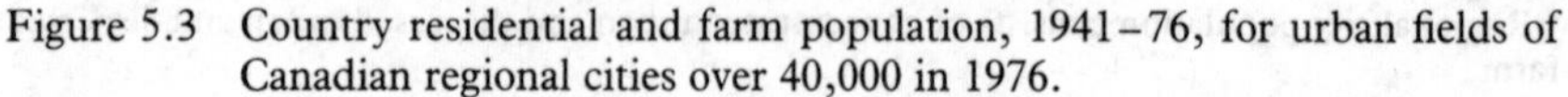

Figure 5.3 Country residential and farm population, 1941–76, for urban fields of Canadian regional cities over 40,000 in 1976.

pying the same undeveloped space as in 1941 and farm population was outnumbered three to one. Compared to the other population components, country residential generally grew relatively more quickly except between 1961 and 1966. Indeed, since 1961, all the population components of the city's countryside (except farm) have grown more rapidly than the built-up (concentrated) urban core. Thus, since 1961, the percentage of the regional city population living in scattered locations has risen from 5.5 to 8.0 while the concentrated urban core has retained its percentage at 74. Excluding farm population, these Canadian data suggest a relatively stable structure with 75 per cent of the regional city population in the concentrated core, about 15 per cent in outlying nodes and about 10 per cent scattered; however, given that the trend has been one of a gradually increasing share of the regional city population in the country residential category and there is some regional variation (Table 5.3) in the progression of country residential development, these figures will inevitably change over time.

For the second type of study, in methodology developed to classify geographic units on a rural-to-urban scale, Russwurm (1970) proposed the following categories:

1. 'rural', with at least 5 farm households for each non-farm household (country residential);
2. 'semi-rural', or between 5 farm households for each country residential household up to equal numbers of farm and country residential households;
3. 'semi-urban', or up to 5 times as many country residential households as farm households;
4. 'urbanizing', or more than 5 times as many country residential households as farm.

These categories were developed on the assumption that once non-farm or country residential households exceeded farm ones, then political control is more likely to be lost by the farming community; hence the categories 'semi-urban' and 'semi-rural'. Further, it could be argued that the greater the ratio of country residential households to farm households, the more likely farming will encounter difficulties in the long run. However, no test known to the authors has been made of any relationships existing between these different categories and the extent of political conflict or problems encountered by farmers.

To simplify analysis with these four categories, ratios are used of country residential to farm units; thus 'rural' is up to 0.2; 'semi-rural' 0.3 to 1.0; 'semi-urban' 1.1 to 5.0; and 'urbanizing' greater than 5.0. The approach can be used either with households or individuals as the unit. This method has been successfully applied in Canadian studies at the census subdivision (township) scale (Yeates 1975), at the one square mile scale (Krueger 1978) and at the quarter-section scale (Maguire 1979). Here it is applied at the urban field scale for Canadian Census Metropolitan Areas (CMAs) which by definition have more than 100,000 population (Table 5.3).

Table 5.3 Ratio of country residential to farm population, 1941–76, for urban fields of Canadian Census Metropolitan Areas, 1976

CMA	*1976 Concentrated urban population*	*1941* CR/F	*1951* CR/F	*1961* CR/F	*1971* CR/F	*1976* CR/F
1. Montreal	2,795,523	0.21	0.33	0.90	1.80	4.01
2. Toronto	2,704,040	0.44	0.73	2.04	3.24	6.60
3. Vancouver	1,013,290	1.02	1.60	5.07	7.40	19.01
4. Ottawa–Hull	615,032	0.11	0.24	0.75	1.13	2.77
5. Winnipeg	560,874	0.22	0.16	0.40	0.79	1.76
6. Edmonton	514,668	0.03	0.06	0.33	0.58	1.83
7. Quebec	507,626	0.11	0.22	0.48	1.04	2.40
8. Calgary	469,917	0.10	0.15	0.22	0.61	1.65
9. Hamilton	464,583	0.68	1.02	2.01	2.76	6.61
10. London	293,255	0.20	0.24	0.70	1.09	1.54
11. St Catharines–Niagara	275,054	0.46	0.47	1.20	1.94	3.19
12. Kitchener–Waterloo	250,876	0.23	0.24	0.50	0.90	1.11
13. Halifax	223,395	0.36	0.46	2.11	2.38	17.54
14. Windsor	219,974	0.40	0.49	1.28	2.41	3.82
15. Victoria	186,154	1.20	1.21	2.30	6.31	26.50
16. St John's	174,407	n/a	2.94	8.01	6.72	15.68
17. Regina	149,953	0.11	0.07	0.10	0.32	0.59
18. Oshawa	141,658	0.16	0.31	0.90	1.80	3.35
19. Saskatoon	133,750	0.11	0.08	0.25	0.24	0.62
20. Chicoutimi–Jonquière	131,835	0.30	0.44	1.09	2.77	5.96
21. Saint John	128,039	0.39	0.53	1.82	1.44	10.00
22. Thunder Bay	111,476	0.55	0.18	1.11	1.78	4.97
23. Sudbury	102,904	0.86	1.45	6.79	15.70	26.87

*CR/F : Country residential to farm population ratio

Application of these categories at the urban-field scale shows the steady urbanization trend from 20 CMAs in the rural categories in 1941 to 21 in the urban categories by 1976. Speeding up of the process by 1961 and then again between 1971 and 1976 is in evidence. The highest ratios are associated with regional cities having limited quantities of good farmland and much rocky terrain, e.g. Sudbury, Victoria and Halifax. Also affecting the ratios are the historical settlement patterns of coastal spread and a lack of nodal settlements in some urban fields, e.g. Vancouver and St John's. Throughout, the prairie cities of Winnipeg, Edmonton, Calgary, Regina and Saskatoon have more rural ratios, reflecting the widespread farm base of the economy and the free-standing nature of prairie cities.

The significance of the country residential population in the regional city is clearly demonstrated by the above data. Nevertheless, it should be noted that within all urban fields there will be areas that are still rural. In applying the rural–urban ratios at the aggregate scale, irregularities are smoothed out and the general distinctions between inner fringe, outer fringe and urban shadow zones are obscured. These points are picked up again in Chapter 11. Meanwhile, one of the major concerns about the magnitude of country residential development in the city's countryside is its relationship with the resource base, especially agricultural land, the land-use activity discussed in the following chapter.

Further reading

Ironside, R. G. and Williams, A. G. (1980) The spread effects of a spontaneous growth centre: commuter expenditure patterns in the Edmonton Metropolitan Region, Canada, *Regional Studies*, **14**, 313–32.

Pahl, R. E. (1965) *Urbs in Rure: the Metropolitan Fringe in Hertfordshire*, Geography Paper 2, London School of Economics, University of London, London.

Phillips, P. D. (1977) *Exurban Commuters in the Kentucky Bluegrass Region*, Monograph 5, Centre for Real Estate and Land Use Analysis, University of Kentucky, Lexington, Kentucky.

Walker, G. (1977) Social networks and territory in a commuter village, Bond Head, Ontario, *The Canadian Geographer*, **21** (4), 329–50.

6 Agriculture

Agriculture represents perhaps the most basic activity carried on within the countryside in terms of the human life-support system. The very existence of city life can be viewed as being dependent upon agriculture. The development of agriculture to a point where it was no longer a subsistence activity provided a surplus to support urban populations and at the same time released a large proportion of the human race from having to engage in food production and made them available for non-agricultural employment. Agricultural development has therefore been viewed as being an essential ingredient for the 'urban revolution' that occurred in early Mesopotamia (Childe 1942), and for the Industrial Revolution that occurred in Western Europe largely during the late eighteenth and nineteenth centuries (Mumford 1961).

Furthermore, areally, agriculture represents the major land-use activity in most metropolitan regions in North America and Western Europe. The landscape around our cities, therefore, owes much of its structure and appearance to agriculture. Particular types of agriculture present different visual characteristics; in many areas of Western Europe, the impact of past agricultural technologies on the landscape has left a heritage that remains treasured, and has spurred attempts at conserving such landscapes (e.g. Préfecture de la Région d'Ile-de-France 1976a,b). Equally, changes in farm practices and technology may lead to significant changes in the landscape, e.g. field consolidation and hedgerow removal. For all of these reasons, then, it is imperative to appreciate the characteristics of agricultural activities and the pressures that affect agriculture and thus, the landscape. The need for understanding these characteristics and changes is especially critical with the build-up of the pressures in the period after the Second World War. Our discussion in this chapter focuses on the interrelationships between urbanization and agriculture, highlighting both positive and negative interactions, while the existence of other forces and their effects is also noted.

Urbanization and agriculture: a general framework

Research related to agriculture in metropolitan regions has been dominated by an urban perspective for over 30 years (Bryant 1976b). This has given rise to a particular image of urban fringe agriculture whereby:

1. agriculture is characteristically seen as responding to pressures induced by urbanization;

2. such responses are viewed dominantly as negative for agriculture;
3 this image does not make any allowances for regional or environmental variation (Bryant and Greaves 1978).

Munton (1974), in support of the first point, suggested that much research on urban-fringe agriculture has considerably underestimated the extent to which urban-fringe farming has, and still is, responding to important technological and managerial innovations, quite unrelated to metropolitan influence.

Undoubtedly, urbanization is one of the most important processes that has accompanied general economic development, with far-reaching effects upon agriculture. However, other forces also cause pressures on agriculture, and in Fig. 6.1 three urbanization or metropolitan factors are identified as well as four non-metropolitan forces. *Urbanization* can be seen as producing three sets of 'demands' that may elicit some response from the agricultural sector (Bryant 1970, viz. those related respectively to increasing employment opportunities in urban areas, increasing market opportunities and increasing demands for land for urban development.

First, urbanization has been associated with *growing employment opportunities* in urban areas. The attractions of urban employment have produced rural depopulation, farm amalgamation opportunities, and have encouraged capital substitution for labour in agriculture. While stresses are clearly created in the agricultural sector by such stimuli, the attractions of urban employment together with technological change have produced what most people would label as a 'normal' and 'desirable' process of change in agriculture. Although non-farm employment opportunities can result in such high opportunity costs that land abandonment ensues, this is more likely to occur in the harsher agricultural environments for which an appropriate agricultural technology has not been available to the same degree for substitution for labour. Part-time farming represents another form of adjustment by some farmers to alternative employment opportunities, although the ranks of part-time farmers have also been inflated by hobby farmers and exurbanites.

Second, some urban regions constitute very significant *market concentrations* which cannot fail to exert some influence in the surrounding agricultural areas (Thompson 1978). While interregional competition from low-cost producing areas has intervened, market proximity still conveys certain advantages to local producers (e.g. Chassagne 1977; Davidson and Wibberley 1977). The theme of market influences on agricultural production can be traced from Von Thünen's classic work (Hall 1966) through various studies of specialized agriculture such as dairying (e.g. Fielding 1962) and market gardening (e.g. Pédelaborde 1961; Smith 1966), and through studies treating intensive agricultural production generally (e.g. Russwurm 1967; Golledge 1960; SEGESA 1973).

Finally, urbanization produces *a demand for land* for urban development of various kinds. It is this theme that has probably received the greatest

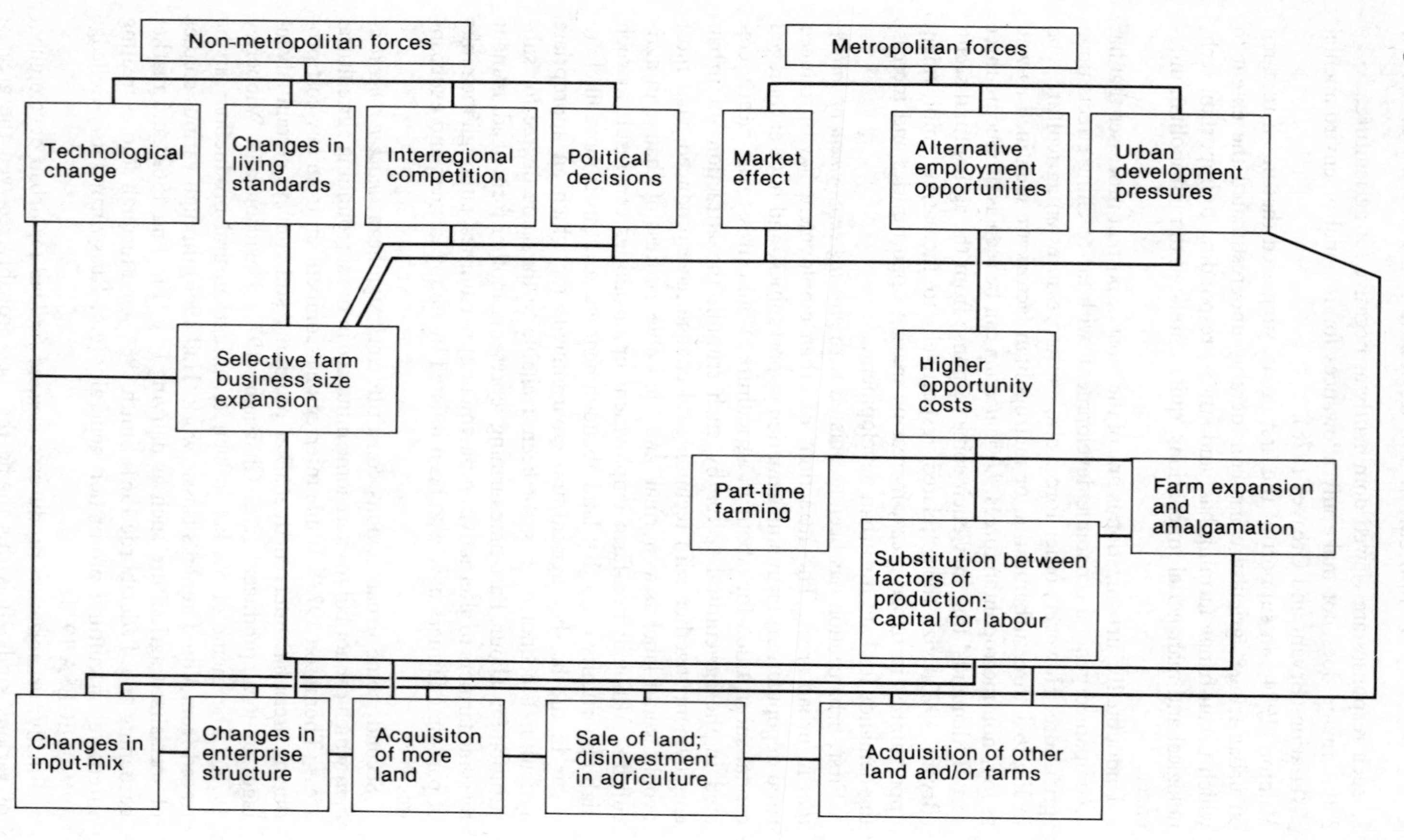
Non-metropolitan forces
Metropolitan forces
Technological change
Changes in living standards
Interregional competition
Political decisions
Market effect
Alternative employment opportunities
Urban development pressures
Selective farm business size expansion
Higher opportunity costs
Part-time farming
Farm expansion and amalgamation
Substitution between factors of production: capital for labour
Changes in input-mix
Changes in enterprise structure
Acquisiton of more land
Sale of land; disinvestment in agriculture
Acquisition of other land and/or farms

amount of attention in terms of research into agriculture in the city's countryside. The dimensions that have been dealt with are numerous, including the loss of agricultural land, especially the higher-quality land (e.g. Wibberley 1959; Gierman 1977; Sermonti 1968; Krueger 1959, 1978) and some of the more indirect effects on agriculture such as the uncertainties for agricultural investment (e.g. Sinclair 1967; Bryant 1973b).

These urbanization forces have operated simultaneously with other forces, which are largely independent of metropolitan and urban development. *Technological change* has undoubtedly been one of the basic forces behind agricultural change in the nineteenth and twentieth centuries (Pautard 1965). Furthermore, *general changes in living standards* have exerted pressures on farmers, forcing some to abandon agriculture, others to enter the ranks of part-time farmers and still others to increase the size of the farm business. *Increasing interregional competition*, both national and international, as transportation costs have been progressively reduced relatively, has created difficulties for many specialized agricultural sectors that developed close to major urban areas in a time when the contemporary transportation technology created a virtual monopoly for local producers (e.g. Tricart 1948). Finally, *political decisions* constitute another non-metropolitan force; while such decisions can be made in relation to urbanization pressures, other decisions relating to such fields as import duties, supply management through quotas and even interest rates are of tremendous significance for agricultural production, in the city's countryside as elsewhere.

Clearly, urbanization pressures can produce both positive and negative responses from agriculture; more importantly, however, is the way in which these forces interact with the non-metropolitan forces. This interaction can be either *complementary* or *conflicting* (Bryant 1976b). *Complementarity* can be seen in the 'normal' pattern of agricultural change described earlier, in which technological changes and the pull of non-farm employment opportunities have combined to produce a reduction in the agricultural population, farm size expansion and increased mechanization in many regions; or again such complementarity can be seen in the possibilities for farm business expansion through rental of relatively cheap land from the increasing numbers of non-farm land owners in many metropolitan regions (e.g. Fielding 1979). *Conflict* exists where urbanization pressures reach a threshold beyond which agricultural 'progress' is thwarted, e.g. excessive farm fragmentation and very uncertain investment planning environments. Finally, the nature of these interactions is subject to regional variation, partly because of regional specialization in agriculture and the fact that some of the forces of change affect some enterprises more than others.

Figure 6.1 External forces of change affecting agriculture in the city's countryside. (Source: adapted from Bryant 1970: Fig. 2.5, p. 43).

Urban development and agriculture

The effects of urban development on agriculture have been categorized as *direct* or *indirect* (Bryant and Russwurm 1979). By *direct impact*, we refer to the actual removal of land from its agricultural production function – an essentially negative impact – while by *indirect impact*, we refer to interactions between urban development and the continuing agricultural structure which may result in modifications to the agricultural system, in terms of either input, product-mix or flexibility of the agricultural system. These indirect impacts may be either positive or negative for agriculture.

First, the locational structure of urban areas in relation to the agricultural land resource is important because much concern for the impact of urban development on agriculture can be related to this. Although the actual correlation between urban populations and high-quality agricultural land resources depends upon the specific configuration of land resources and city distributions for any given country, the relationship is a positive one in many countries (Vining, Plaut and Bieri 1977; Manning and McCuaig 1977). This was pointed out long ago for the UK (e.g. Wibberley 1954), while the expansion of Paris, France, has been making inroads into some of the most fertile agricultural lands of Western Europe for some time. For Canada, where climate places severe restrictions on the potential of the agricultural land resource (McKeague 1975; Manning and McCuaig 1977), a recent study compared the cumulative distribution of urban population and of census farmland rated agroclimatically and found that the 'best' 5 per cent of the farmland is coincident with 50 per cent of the urban population (Williams, Pocock and Russwurm 1978).

The fact that the agricultural land around our cities tends to be of higher quality should not be of great surprise since many cities developed in the richest agricultural areas. The industrial revolution is barely two centuries old, while the history of agriculture and urban growth is considerably longer! Furthermore, towns and cities have always presented market potential which has often encouraged the increased application of human labour and capital in areas close to cities to improve land productivity (Pautard 1965; Schultz 1953). On the other hand, while there is this general relationship, some cities have developed in very poor agricultural environments, e.g. the Atlantic provinces in Canada, northern England (Best 1974, 1977a) and parts of southern and south-western France.

Nevertheless, the prime quality of much of the land lost to urban development has been a key issue in many debates. The food-shortage issue loomed very large in the early debates in England – not surprisingly given the difficulties of the war years (Best and Ward 1956; Wibberley 1954); in Canada, the food issue has become important, not only for our own populations, but also for serving the needs of less well-endowed nations (e.g. Rawson 1976); and the US has provided ample scope for similar debate (e.g.

Lessinger 1958; Hart 1976). However, concern over loss of food production capacity has been tempered by serious overproduction in many Western countries, e.g. as witnessed in the Canadian cereal economy in the 1950s and 1960s (Craddock 1970), in the payments by the US government to farmers in some areas not to produce certain crops, and in overproduction of dairy produce in the European Common Market in the 1960s and 1970s. This situation is partly due to the tremendous advances in agricultural productivity in the post-war period, related to technological and structural change in agriculture. In the UK, Best (1977b) estimated that agricultural production has increased by about 20 per cent per decade while agricultural land lost to urban development amounted to only 1 per cent of the agricultural land inventory per decade. Such processes lie behind the estimates cited by Davidson and Wibberley (1977) that the UK would be 70 to 75 per cent self-sufficient in temperate foodstuffs by the year 2000. Such figures suggest that concern for the loss of agricultural food production capacity has to be based on food production *potential* rather than current marketable food supplies; thus quality of the resource removed from agriculture is of at least equal importance to the absolute quantity being removed.

Agricultural land is a *renewable resource*, i.e. with appropriate management, the productivity of the resource can be maintained in the long term. However, when land is *built over*, to all intents and purposes we have to regard such conversion as an 'irreversible' change in terms of normal planning horizons. Our attitude therefore should be influenced by the quality of the land that is being converted. First, there is a direct relationship between land quality and agricultural productivity (Centre for Resources Development 1972). Second, and more important, prime-quality land has *a wider range of production possibilities* than poorer land, so that loss of prime agricultural land reduces society's *range of choice* more than if poorer land were taken. So even though the overall loss of agricultural land is a small proportion of the total agricultural land inventory of most nations (e.g. Williams, Pocock and Russwurm 1978; Shields and Ferguson 1975; Hart 1976), two facts combine to fuel the farmland conservationists' case:

1. the limited extent of *prime* agricultural land;
2. the positive correlation of this land with urban population.

But there is more to the agricultural land resource than simply 'land'. Agricultural land does not become a productive resource until successfully incorporated into the socioeconomic system of production and, therefore, into the farm unit. People and land together constitute a self-maintaining agricultural production system. Consequently, in the following sections, we make a distinction between, on the one hand, the impact of development in terms of the *physical conversion of land* from agricultural to urban-oriented land-use activities (direct impact) and the *functional removal* of land from agriculture generally, and, on the other hand, the impact of development on the continuing agricultural structure (indirect impact).

The functional removal of land from agriculture

The loss of agricultural land

The *conversion* of land from one use to another is the final stage of a potentially long process; prior to this stage land may have been left *idle* for a period of time. Such land, although not converted to another use, is nonetheless removed from its former function, although the intent (on the part of the land owner) is still oriented towards development. Other land may also be idle, but without such intent, and may therefore be termed *abandoned*, i.e. there is no intent of moving such land into another economically or socially functioning land-use activity.

Attempts to calculate the amount of land converted to urban uses with primary data have been rare. It has been more common to utilize secondary sources, e.g. agricultural census data, as the basis for inferences. For instance, the Canadian province of Ontario, highly urbanized in its southern parts, lost 1.85 million ha of census farmland between 1941 and 1966 (Patterson 1968), a reduction of 20.4 per cent. However, these census data only indicate that the land *managed within* census farms has declined. While some of this loss certainly reflects conversion of land to non-agricultural uses, other land has simply been reallocated to afforestation or has been abandoned.

Because land removal from agriculture can be attributed to so many processes, care must be exercised in interpretation of this type of data. Studies in which the area of land 'used', say, per 1,000 increase in population has been calculated, have frequently fallen prey to such interpretation problems. Although both Bogue (1956) in his classic study of farmland loss in the US and Crerar (1963) in his study of Canadian metropolitan regions, acknowledged the existence of other factors, they assumed that little abandonment of land would take place because of the superior market position of farmland in metropolitan regions.

However, this assumption neglects the important regional variation in agricultural resources in many countries which influences the regional viability of the agricultural system. As an example, evidence from a recent Canadian study of agricultural change in metropolitan regions (Bryant 1976b; Bryant and Greaves 1978) shows that the relative rate of removal of agricultural land was greatest (1961 to 1971) where urban population growth was small, i.e. around the Maritimes' cities and the northern Ontario and northern Quebec cities (Table 6.1). A substantial portion of the land loss in the Maritimes is land that is uncompetitive agriculturally. Similarly, a US study (Ziemetz *et al.* 1976) using the more direct approach of air-photo analysis, identified considerable regional variations in the relationship between urbanization and agricultural land supply, with some urbanizing counties, e.g. Florida, experiencing a net increase in cropland while others, e.g. the Piedmont region, experienced cropland removal involving conversion to forests or abandonment. The study concluded that much of the cropland decline

Table 6.1 Population change and farm area change around Canadian Census Metropolitan Areas, 1961–71.

	Percent change 1961 to 1971 in:		
*CMA-based region**	*total census farm area*	*improved census farm area*	*CMA population*
Toronto	– 19.0	– 19.5	36.9
Montreal	– 17.3	– 14.7	23.8
Windsor	– 7.0	– 4.2	19.1
Hamilton	– 8.4	– 5.7	24.3
Regina	– 0.2	5.6	23.7
Winnipeg	– 2.5	0.7	13.4
London	– 3.9	0.4	26.2
Quebec	– 32.8	– 25.4	26.7
Edmonton	– 5.8	14.3	37.8
Calgary	– 6.2	2.2	44.5
Saskatoon	0.3	4.1	32.2
Kitchener	– 10.1	– 9.6	46.4
Ottawa-Hull	– 21.2	– 18.9	31.8
Thunder Bay	– 34.3	– 18.9	9.8
Sudbury	– 40.0	– 37.9	22.0
Chicoutimi	– 27.3	– 23.7	4.8
Victoria	– 24.0	– 22.7	25.7
Halifax	– 34.0	– 14.7	15.1
St John's	77.4	– 14.4	23.5
Saint John	– 32.5	– 28.3	8.8
St Catharines	– 13.4	– 12.3	17.7
Vancouver	– 9.7	– 4.6	30.9
Canada	– 1.7	4.6	

* Each region is defined to include Census Divisions falling mostly within 40 km of the CMA, except where the CMA had a population of over 1 million in 1971, when 56 km was used.
(Source: compiled from Bryant 1976b: Tables 3.2 and 3.10)

could be attributed to the impact of changing agricultural technology and increased productivity in other regions.

Some studies have tried to estimate or measure land conversion directly. Gierman (1977) calculated that for Canadian cities over 25,000, some 70 ha of rural land were converted to urban uses for each 1,000 increase in the urban population between 1966 and 1971 and that 76 per cent of this land was formerly in farming. Densities of development have generally fallen over time, contributing to land loss beyond sheer growth of population. Best (1977a) quotes figures of 16,000 ha per year of agricultural land transferred to urban uses in England and Wales, while Petersen and Yampolsky (1975) cite US Department of Agriculture figures of about 121,000 ha per year of cropland conversion. While these figures are interesting, a more important question is the significance of this land conversion, a question that requires consideration of economic aspects such as the immediate value of the agricultural output involved, economic linkages with other economic sectors and foreign currency earnings from exports, as well as less tangible aspects such as the morality of saving land for future generations and other less fortunate countries.

The preference of urban development for good farmland

We have already suggested that the quality of agricultural land can affect the rate of land removal from agriculture; naturally, another question arises: are different types of non-farm development associated with different types of farmland? First, it is a reasonable hypothesis that better-quality land might be more resistant to development. Similarly, land associated with more intensive or valuable agricultural production might be expected to offer greater resistance. Differences in agricultural structure and intensity, then, may well account for short-term rigidities in the supply of land for non-farm development, a point which Munton (1974) has made quite strongly, although empirical evidence is lacking.

Second, however, non-farm development may prefer certain types of agricultural land quality. As already noted above, our principal urban regions often coincide with high-quality agricultural areas, so it is no surprise that urban development takes over much good farmland. Various studies have shown that urban development takes place in areas with a good agricultural land resource (Howard 1972; Gierman 1977). However, these studies do not demonstrate that prime-quality land is 'preferred', only that development occurs in regions with good agricultural land resources. To answer the preference question accurately requires an analysis of the importance of prime land used for non-farm development in relation to its importance in the total land base available. It is interesting that, in the US study cited earlier (Zeimetz *et al.* 1976), of the sources of land converted to urban uses, cropland accounted for 35 per cent of the conversion, only a slightly higher proportion than its proportion in the total land base – somewhat surprising considering the usually greater ease (cf. Wibberley 1959; Sermonti 1968; Bogue 1956) of construction on such land. Furthermore, one might expect the proportion of prime land in land converted to be even higher, given that much 'poor'-quality agricultural land has been protected for other planning reasons, e.g. flood-plains and scenic areas (e.g. part of the Niagara Escarpment area, southern Ontario). We also have to recognize the existence of different types of non-farm development. The question that must be posed is whether, *all other things being equal*, prime-quality land is preferred to poorer-quality land.

Greaves's (1975) study of severances in Albion township near Toronto showed that the incidence of severances (and therefore presumably potential removal of land from agriculture) was highest on prime agricultural land. But on the other hand, the area of prime land in this township was also closest to the principal urban areas. An analysis of maps of the distribution of prime agricultural land and non-farm residential development in the Winnipeg region (Manitoba Municipal Planning Branch 1974) leads to the same conclusion.

Indeed, a survey of the case-study literature suggests strongly that the major factor affecting the geographic distribution of farmland sales for non-farm residential development is that of accessibility to the urban areas. However, certain types of non-farm residential development, e.g. the large lot, high-value country estate (Found and Michie 1976), seem to prefer poorer-quality farmland, partly because such land is frequently, though not always, associated with rolling topography, presence of woodlots, and other features of scenic value. Harker (1976), for instance, found that in Grey County, Ontario, an area well towards the outer part of the urban shadow of Toronto, farmland and farm buildings purchased by non-residents tended to occur on the rougher agricultural land, often with streams and woodlots adjacent to, or on, the property. This phenomenon may reflect both the scenic and recreational attractiveness of such properties and the fact that they may tend to be less viable for agriculture.

One very important point needs to be made, that much of the land taken over by non-farm owners is *not* functionally removed from agriculture because, particularly where large tracts of farmland are purchased, much of the land is rented back to farmers. Depending upon the circumstances of this arrangement, this may be either a very beneficial process or a potentially negative process for agriculture.

We are already anticipating the next section, for we have recognized that the introduction of urban elements into the landscape may lead to much more than the mere removal of certain lands from agricultural production.

Impact of development on the continuing agricultural structure

The process of urbanization can effect both positive and negative impacts on farm structure. On the one hand, urbanization has created a market of non-farm job opportunities which has attracted agricultural labour, including many farm operators, to move from farm employment into urban employment. This has often released land and made it available for remaining farmers to expand their land base, a process known as 'farm consolidation' in North America and 'farm amalgamation' in Western Europe. Simultaneously, the subsequent labour shortage has encouraged, even necessitated, the move towards a more capital-intensive type of farm structure. It is no coincidence that many of the most capital-intensive agricultural regions and the most rationalized farm structures are often found within our major metropolitan regions. Large markets for agricultural produce further encourage intensification. Overall then, we can envisage potential beneficial or complementary interaction between urbanization forces and agricultural development forces.

On the other hand, it is incontestable that urban forces may also thwart those of continued agricultural development. We only need think of land speculation, increasing property taxes, farm fragmentation and incidents of trespass and vandalism to obtain an idea of the range of these more indirect negative impacts. We would expect this type of conflicting interaction to be most typical of the rural–urban fringe, especially the inner fringe. To the extent that some actual loss of agricultural land is inevitable given the regional pattern of population change and non-agricultural investment, then these indirect impacts may be of more significance than the more direct impact of actual land loss (Rodd 1976; Bryant and Russwurm 1979).

Public concern over the indirect impacts on agriculture has been quite extensive in some countries, e.g. Canada, the US and the UK, with most advocates of farmland conservation arguing that these indirect impacts can lead to premature removal of land from agriculture. Concern for the agricultural land resource base has not been enunciated as clearly in some of the West European countries, e.g. France, but rather the concern has been more related to considerations of landscape amenity and the structuring of the urban form. However, even from this perspective, such indirect impacts may be of considerable consequence, because they can effect changes in farm structure, the main support of the landscape in the city's countryside. One classic attempt at estimating the magnitude of such indirect impacts (Krueger 1959) suggested that twice as much land was ruined for agricultural production by them than was actually converted for non-agricultural purposes. As we shall see, however, the empirical basis for such statements on the magnitude of many of these indirect impacts is quite limited.

The anticipation of urban development

One aspect of *indirect impacts* that has spawned an important research literature is concerned with the impact of *potential* urban development on farm structure. The basic idea is quite straightforward, viz. in areas where farmers consider urban development is likely there will be a disincentive to maintain investment in agriculture. Sinclair (1967: 78) summarizes the argument well: 'As the urbanized area is approached from a distance, the degree of anticipation of urbanization increases. As this happens, the ratio of urban to rural land values increases. Hence, although the absolute value of the land increases, the relative value for agricultural utilization decreases.'

We can follow the development of the various ideas by referring to Fig. 6.2. The classic Thünian model (Fig. 6.2(a), curve *a*) describes the situation where no potential for rural to urban land use is considered; relying upon the concept of economic rent and how this is affected by increasing transportation costs from a central market place, the initial Thünian model yields the well-known sequence of concentric zones of different agricultural land uses. Muth (1961) utilized the same basic framework for investigating the conversion of rural land to urban uses. However, Sinclair (1967) argued that, because transportation costs to a central market were no longer signif-

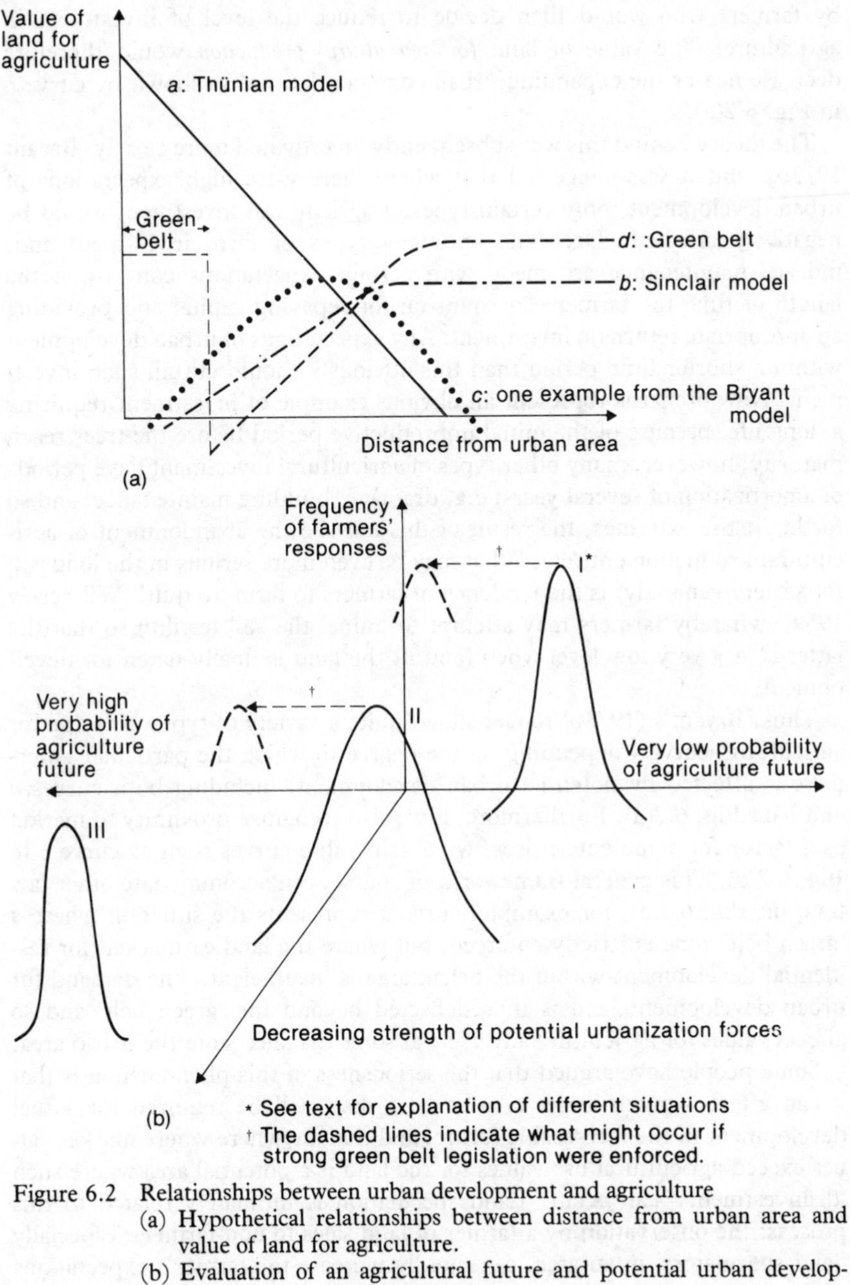

Figure 6.2 Relationships between urban development and agriculture
(a) Hypothetical relationships between distance from urban area and value of land for agriculture.
(b) Evaluation of an agricultural future and potential urban development. (Source: Bryant 1981: Fig. 1, p. 29).

icant in the Western world, continued and rapid urban development in some regions constituted a new factor in agricultural land-use location. The smaller gap between agricultural and urban land values near the expanding urban area would be taken as indicative of a high potential for urban development by farmers who would then decide to reduce the level of investment in agriculture. The value of land *for agricultural production* would therefore decrease nearer the expanding urban edge, a relationship shown by curve *b* in Fig. 6.2(a).

The theory behind this was subsequently investigated more closely (Bryant 1973b), and it was suggested that where there were high expectations of urban development, only certain types of agricultural investment would be negatively affected. Decisions on many types of farm investment and, indeed, maintenance are made with certain expectations concerning the length of time the farmer can count on for repaying capital and providing an appropriate return on investment. Any expectations of urban development within a shorter time period than this obviously should curtail such investment. New orchards represent an obvious example of investment requiring a 'long life' because of the initial unproductive period before the trees reach maturity; however, many other types of agricultural investment have periods of amortization of several years, e.g. drainage, building maintenance, and so forth. At the extremes, the result of this may be the abandonment of agricultural production entirely. What may be even more serious in the long run for society generally, is the tendency of farmers to farm 'to quit' (Wibberley 1959), whereby farmers may attempt to 'mine' the soil fertility so that the latter is at a very low level when (and if) the land is finally taken for development.

Thus, Bryant's (1973b) model allows quite a variety of types of 'value for agriculture' curves, depending on the degree to which the particular enterprise is affected by potential urban development, including both curves *a* and *b* on Fig. 6.2(a). Furthermore, if we also recognize proximity to market as a factor for some enterprises, we obtain value curves such as curve *c* in Fig. 6.2(a). This general framework, of course, can accommodate other factors; on Fig. 6.2(a), for example, curve *d* represents the situation where a 'green belt' zone is strictly enforced, but where the land earmarked for residential development within the urban area is insufficient. The demand for urban development land is thus deflected beyond the 'green belt' and so affects values for agriculture adversely at some distance from the urban area.

Some people have argued that the seriousness of this phenomenon is that it can affect a much larger area of land than will be required for actual development in the foreseeable future; and that anywhere where market values exceed agricultural use values for the land is a potential area where such 'disinvestments' can occur. Land speculation is intimately related to this process: the observation by a farmer of land sales to non-farmers, especially 'land speculators' in an area, can rapidly increase the farmer's expectations of the value of his own property, and act as a 'signal' to the farmer of the potential value of his own property. It is in this manner that a large area of land can be affected, particularly if 'leap-frogging' of development also occurs. The inefficiency of such a process arises from the over-optimism of the people involved and the 'falseness' of many of their expectations (Conklin and Dymsa 1972).

At the same time, however, these models create a false impression of homogeneity of response on the part of the farming community. More recently, then, an attempt has been made to investigate the extent of homogeneity of farmer responses to the threat of potential urban development (Bryant 1981). Focusing first on the farmers' evaluations of the likelihood of urban development, a framework was developed (Fig. 6.2(b)) in which it was suggested that, while the 'average' evaluation of a non-agricultural future was directly related to measures indicating a high potential for urban development, e.g. proximity to existing development and incorporation within designated urban zones, the range of variation in farmer's evaluations would vary systematically with the strength of these potential urban development indicators. In areas either where the indicators were very strong or very weak (respectively, situations I – e.g. in the inner fringe – and III – e.g. in the outer parts of the urban shadow – on Fig. 6.2(b)), the size of variation in expectations would be small, while in areas intermediate in terms of potential development indicators (situation II), the variation would be large. In the empirical case study, it was found that:

1. farmers' evaluations of a non-agricultural future did indeed conform to such a model; but that
2. no systematic relationship existed between either the indicators of potential urban development or the evaluations and farm investment behaviour.

In explaining this, it was suggested that this lack of correlation reflected two facts:

1. although farmers in areas showing strong development potential tended to recognize the development pressures, they often were able to recognize and take advantage of the benefits of a near-urban location, such as direct sale of farm produce to the consumer on an important scale;
2. although the farmers would invariably recognize the many problems in such environments, e.g. trespass and vandalism, it appears that such problems were more like irritants than major financial problems. Some research in the UK (UK Ministry of Fisheries, Agriculture and Food 1977) supports this idea.

Other impacts related to increasing land values and non-farm land ownership

Increase in land values, both actual and anticipated, can have significant impacts in other ways on farm structure. For instance, it is increasingly difficult for farmers to *purchase* additional farmland in order to increase their productive land bases. The figures on farm size increases in metropolitan regions partially reflects this, e.g. in Canada, in the Toronto region (Bryant 1976b), the average farm area increased from 1961 to 1971 by only 3.9 per cent, for Vancouver 0.0 per cent, for St Catharines 3.7 per cent and for the Montreal region by only 14.3 per cent, compared to an increase of 29.2 per cent for Canada as a whole.

Expansion of the land base of the individual farm has been an important dimension of structural change in agriculture in the Western world; it has permitted the adoption of capital-intensive techniques of production necessitated by the continued movement of labour into nonagricultural employment, and has represented an attempt by many farmers to maintain, and even increase, their net incomes from farming in the face of the 'cost-price squeeze'. As long as most farmers desire *to own* the land they cultivate, areas of high land values inevitably become zones where farmers find it difficult to expand their productive land base. In the Niagara Fruit Belt, Canada, for instance, Reeds (1969) pointed out that in 1969 fruit farmers could afford a maximum of $5,655 per ha; given that many properties were selling for up to $15,000 per ha, this underlines the difficulties farmers have in remaining competitive, and how increasing land values contribute to an agricultural area becoming non-viable both economically and socially over time. However, we should in fairness note that some part of the increasing land values, especially near the edges of metropolitan regions, is due to farmers competing for land for farm expansion and to the effects of farmers relocating away from the inner fringe areas (e.g. Bryant 1973a; SEGESA 1973).

Other factors related to the process of non-farm development contribute to the weakening position of agriculture as well. One factor that has received attention in the North American context is the effect of non-farm development on property taxes. Classic studies such as those by Barker (1949), the Lower Mainland Regional Planning Board, BC (1956), Walrath (1957) and Krueger (1957) have demonstrated that, characteristically, small residential lots, although having a high unit area assessment value, contribute less to municipal revenue than they generate in terms of local taxation, while the reverse is the case for farm properties – the implication being that farmers are subsidizing some non-farm elements in the countryside.

Subsidization of one sector of the community by another is, of course, nothing new in countries with social welfare programmes; however, it may be of concern if the farmers are less able to bear such costs than those they are subsidizing. Basically, where property taxation constitutes an important source of municipal revenue, farmers in the rural–urban fringe may pay higher taxes than 'normal' for two reasons. First, their properties may be assessed at higher values nearer the urban area – even with the system of assessment of value 'in use', non-farm influences in the property market can influence assessed values. Obviously, programmes of equalization of assessment, e.g. the standardization of assessment on a regional basis in Ontario, are aimed at eliminating the most obvious effects of this. Second, in these communities in the rural–urban fringe, municipal costs are frequently greater because of the additional demand for services made by non-farm components. This, of course, simply means that the farmers there will pay more per dollar of assessed value than if there were no non-farm elements. Programmes involving preferential assessment, roll-back taxes, and (as in Ontario) tax rebates all attempt to ease the costs involved to the farmer (although not all are aimed specifically at rural–urban fringe problems), because such increased costs may worsen an already precarious cost-price squeeze situation for many farmers (Hady and Stinson 1967; Whyte 1968).

Farm fragmentation

The fragmentation of the rural farm landscape and of farms by non-agricultural land-use development can also create additional costs to the farmer, although it may be difficult to evaluate these objectively. New highways, or the upgrading of existing ones, can create additional problems of access to fields for the farmer, both in terms of cost and time. Some of the worst examples of this are found in the most heavily urbanized areas of metropolitan regions, e.g. the Vancouver region, parts of the London Green Belt and the suburbanized agricultural communities surrounding Paris. Utility corridors may also present their own access problems – hydro corridors, for instance, if in sufficient density, may restrict aerial crop dusting, as well as creating additional obstacles for field operations. 'Strip' or 'ribbon' development also helps fragment the farm landscape. Additional vehicular traffic generated subsequent to new housing developments also has potentially disruptive effects on the movement of farm machinery; moreover, extensive ribbon development may create enclaves of agricultural land with very limited access.

Social impacts

Finally, a number of social and/or cultural impacts are felt which in some areas have added to a sense of insecurity. On the one hand, many farm areas are subject to detrimental pressures from non-farm people – trespass; damage to hedgerows and fences; stealing crops from fields (Hall 1976); and complaints about 'normal' agricultural operations. This sort of infraction, which around some cities is very serious, helps create an atmosphere of mistrust between farmers and non-farm people, even if the total damage involved may be quite small. Furthermore, many communities within metropolitan regions have witnessed a transfer of municipal power from the rural and often farm group to non-farm populations; while this in itself is not surprising, taken together with the other factors mentioned earlier it can help confirm a feeling of future change in the orientation and function of an area.

Such essentially detrimental impacts or interaction between urban and agricultural development forces are likely to be more intense in the rural–urban fringe than in those areas which could be described as urban shadow. It has been suggested elsewhere that in regions characterized by high levels of urban development, a strong differentiation occurs between those areas experiencing degeneration in farm stucture and those experiencing continued agricultural investment (Bryant 1976b), which could be linked to differences between zones in terms of urban development pressures. However, we must recognize that there are circumstances in which the introduction of non-farm elements into the countryside may interact with agricultural development forces to produce a beneficial environment for agriculture, as mentioned earlier.

Some beneficial relationships between urban pressures and agriculture

While most of the existing literature tends to paint a picture of impending gloom for agriculture within metropolitan regions, the evidence suggests that, for medium-sized city regions at least, the area of the city's countryside in which agriculture is unequivocably undergoing disinvestment is relatively limited in extent. Even in some of the larger city regions, it is remarkable how often one encounters very viable and dynamic farm structures even adjacent to developing urban areas; research by one of the authors in a growth area near Paris, France, confirms this view (Bryant 1981). Frequently, one is led to the conclusion that agriculture is maintained despite the difficulties partly because of the very strong attachment of farmers to the land, but also because there are forces at work leading to a beneficial interaction between urban and farm areas.

One of the most interesting ways in which a beneficial interaction can occur is through the rental back to farmers of farmland which has been purchased by non-farm interests. Obviously, from a purely economic perspective, it may be more attractive to a farmer to rent land in order to ensure its use as a factor of production rather than to purchase the land and encumber the business with a heavy mortgage. It also has the advantage of releasing more of the farmer's capital for improvements rather than tying it up in land ownership. How attractive leasing of land is depends largely upon the conditions surrounding the lease. Some non-farm owners of farmland may not actually desire to farm their land – land ownership may be a goal in itself, or while the primary objective may have been to secure a base in the countryside, planning regulations may have necessitated the purchase of a whole farm (e.g. restrictions on minimum parcel sizes). In these circumstances the land owners may be more than willing to rent back the land to local farmers, often quite cheaply. Sometimes, special conditions are set (e.g. the owner requiring that the farmer maintain fences and ditches) which may constrain a farmer's choices, but essentially this provides a source of cheap land.

Providing leases are not viewed as precarious, the result can be a long-term improvement in farm structure and the maintenance of the agricultural landscape. Close to North American cities, non-farm ownership of land is often high and rental of land back to farmers is fairly common (Bryant and

Fielding 1980; Conklin and Dymsa 1972). However, the speculative motive for owning such land is undoubtedly high and the leases might be viewed as potentially precarious – if so, while farm expansion is permitted, this may only be 'temporary' and farmers may begin to 'mine' such land. In North America, land renting tends to be more precarious than in many West European countries because leases in North America tend to be very short, often on an annual basis, and the legal structure for compensation for tenant investment on the land is practically non-existent, in contrast to countries such as France.

But how 'temporary' is 'temporary'? Around some cities considerable areas of farmland are in the hands of non-farm owners, who presumably have some future alternative use in mind. But frequently the area so owned is so large it is unlikely that development will occur within even a 10 or 15 year time-span – or ever. The medium-sized cities which have been growing rapidly may provide the best examples of this, e.g., Kitchener–Waterloo, Ontario, where despite high growth rates, absolute levels of development are still low compared to Vancouver, Montréal and Toronto. Quite unlike the intense fringes of the latter urban areas, much of that of Kitchener–Waterloo is characterized by substantial farm size increase through additional farmland rental (Fielding 1979). On the basis of the evidence available (e.g., Bryant 1976b), we must tentatively conclude that areas of high levels of development, even with relatively low rates of growth, often exhibit degeneration of agricultural structure, while areas of low levels of development but high rates of growth may well possess conditions suitable for continued agricultural progress.

Yet another potentially positive factor already alluded to several times is that of the urban market. The proximity to huge urban markets presents an opportunity for the farm entrepreneur to engage in direct sale to the customer; the result can be seen in a variety of ways, ranging from the small roadside fruit-stand or the 'pick-your-own' enterprise to the large-scale garden centre with supporting nursery production. The sod farm found around many North American cities is a classic indicator of the potential and actual influence of the urban-market factor.

Part-time farming

Most of the foregoing discussion has stressed the impact that urbanization may have on investment, on land, and on farm production through the processes of land conversion and land development, and the market factor. But urbanization also affects people. We have already noted that the movement of farm labour to non-farm employment in urban areas can lead to farm amalgamation and substitution of capital for labour in the farm input mix. But there are other forms of adjustment possible, and that of part-time farming is one of the most interesting. Part-time farmers have been, and continue to be, the subject of much debate (see for instance, Fuller and Mage 1976; Troughton 1976; Gasson 1966, 1977). Are part-time farmers 'good' farmers?

Do they have a different management perspective from full-time farmers? Do they encourage efficient utilization of our agricultural land resources? Are they but ephemeral creatures, representing just one stage in the transition from rural to urban employment? How do we recognize part-time farmers?

Attempts at definition of part-time farmers basically use one, or both, of two dimensions: amount and/or proportion of time devoted to, and amount and/or proportion of income derived from, an off-farm job. The 1966 Census of Canada, for example, defined a part-time farm operator as one who reported income received from agricultural and non-agricultural work off the operator's farm of $750.00 or more *or* who had worked 75 days or more off the farm during the previous 12 months. The fact that some off-farm work does not entitle a farmer to be called a part-time farmer partly reflects the fact that in many respects, some form of multiple job holding associated with agriculture might be expected as 'normal' in a temperate climate where a distinct seasonal round of activities is found on the farm with workloads varying tremendously from season to season. Whatever the exact definition of part-time farming, one thing is clear – that some form of multiple job holding is a prevalent feature of today's agriculture (de Farcy 1976; Harrison 1975).

Part of the problem in providing answers to many of the questions raised previously regarding part-time farming is the existence of many different types of part-time farmer (Mage 1974). Broadly, we can distinguish between the part-time farmer and the hobby farmer; the distinguishing feature is basically that the hobby farmer is less dependent upon agriculture for a source of income compared to the part-time farmer (Troughton 1976). It has been found that hobby farmers tend to originate in urban areas, often have little background in farming, and their move to the countryside has been influenced as much by a desire to 'get back to nature' as to engage in farming (McKay 1976).

One interesting but tentative conclusion that seems to be supported by empirical evidence from several regions is that the less dependent the operator is on agriculture for income and the more important the social motivation for having a combination of farm and off-farm jobs, the more stable the land use appears to be. Such operators seem more concerned about the appearance of their holdings and appear less willing to contemplate sale of land for potential non-agricultural development. Furthermore, when we compare operations of *similar* scale and enterprise-mix, there is a lack of evidence suggesting that part-time farmers are any more or less efficient than their full-time counterparts (Gasson 1966; Auckland Regional Authority, Moran, Neville and Rankin 1980; McQuinn 1978). All in all, we must conclude that part-time farming is a prevalent feature of the countryside around our cities; it includes significant amounts of the total agricultural resource; and it is certainly more than a transitional feature. Indeed, it seems more appropriate now to view part-time farming, in its many forms, as representing a range of viable and alternative life-styles.

Finally, we must reiterate that the changes discussed above are taking place within the context of overall development, both in agricultural and non-agricultural sectors. Even in the most highly urbanized regions, there are areas undergoing what we commonly regard as a 'normal' process of change in agriculture. Naturally, all this has its own impress on the landscape and we will return to consider this in Part III. The continued existence and even development of intensive enterprises in highly urbanized regions partly reflects the concentration of demand in urban areas, and partly the increasing purchasing power that is so frequently associated with economic development. Again, the impact on the landscape is marked, e.g. sod farms, nurseries, greenhouses. On the other hand, change in agricultural structure and land use cannot always be explained by urbanization forces alone – the market structure, price structure and international trade environment can all act to create, or add to the uncertainty of the farmer's environment (Munton 1974). It is important to recognize the existence of these other forces of change, for it means that land-use controls directed at eliminating urban-based forces of agricultural instability in the city's countryside cannot alone be a guarantee of conditions of agricultural viability.

Further reading

Bryant, C. R. (1973) The anticipation of urban expansion: some implications for agricultural land use practices and land use zoning, *Geographia Polonica*, **28**, 93–115.

Bryant, C. R. and Russwurm, L. H. (1979) The impact of nonagricultural development on agriculture: a synthesis, *Plan Canada*, **19**(2), 122–39.

Munton, R. J. C. (1974) Farming on the urban fringe, Ch. 10, pp. 201–23 in Johnson, J. H. (ed.), *Suburban Growth*, John Wiley and Sons, London.

Sinclair, R. J. (1967) Von Thünen and urban sprawl, *Annals of the Association of American Geographers*, **57**, 72–87.

Vining, D. R. Jr., Plaut, T. and Bieri, K. (1977) Urban encroachment on prime agricultural land in the United States, *International Regional Science Review*, **2**, 143–56.

Wibberley, G. P. (1959) *Agriculture and Urban Growth*, Michael Joseph, London.

7 Industry and commerce

While agriculture is the most important land user of the economic activities in the city's countryside, there are other economic activities present of major significance to the people living there: industry and commerce. Some of these activities have developed as a result of forces peculiar to the city's countryside. On the one hand, some of these other economic activities are, like some intensive agricultural production, both dependent upon natural resources found in the natural environment and attracted by locational considerations, e.g. the aggregate industry and some commercial recreational enterprises (the latter are left for consideration until Chapter 8 because of the complex interrelationships between the private and public sectors in the supply of recreational opportunities).

On the other hand, there are secondary industries and commercial activities that have developed in the city's countryside because of accessibility and locational considerations (the 'place' function of land) as well as a host of other factors. All such developments are of significance to the evolving regional city form in that the greater dispersion of economic activities implied can create additional pressures for residential expansion in the countryside as well as creating other impacts. Yet even in a recent book on planning and the rural environment (Davidson and Wibberley 1977) little mention is made of these activities, except for a very brief note on the sand and gravel industry. Our discussion focuses first on the aggregate industry, then on manufacturing and finally on commercial activities. The processes and factors underlying the development of each activity in the city's countryside are considered, as are some of the impacts with which they can be identified.

The aggregate industry

The aggregate industry produces commodities that are key raw materials in the process of urban development and all its associated infrastructure. In addition, the industry can contribute substantially to overall economic activity; in the US in 1965, crushed stone and sand and gravel were the two leading mineral commodities both in terms of tonnage produced and value (US Department of the Interior 1967). Crushed stone and sand and gravel are the basic materials of concrete for residential development, industries and airports, and provide the raw material from which highways are built. For the US it was once estimated that between 13 and 18 tonnes of aggregate materials were 'consumed' *per capita* yearly (US Department of the Interior 1967).

The demand faced by this industry is strongly urban-oriented. Yet the industry is also dependent upon the occurrence of natural raw materials, which may be unconsolidated materials (e.g. glacial drift deposits, alluvial deposits and beach materials) or rock. Thus, at least in the *siting* of the activity, access to the raw material is a must. The aggregate industry falls then into the natural environment-economic environment intersection of Fig. 2.1, and the presence of the raw material in the natural environment is, of course, a prerequisite for the activity's existence. Furthermore, depending upon the type of raw materials present (e.g. glacial drift, alluvial gravels, appropriate rock formations), the type of aggregate industry present will vary in terms of technical operation (contrast dry-surface gravel pits with drag-line operations in river beds, and again with the rock-blasting that accompanies quarrying), in terms of the relationships with, or impacts on, other land uses in the cultural and economic environment, and in terms of the rehabilitation difficulties and potential of each type of site. The discussion here is focused upon the sand-and-gravel portion of the industry.

Given the presence of appropriate raw materials, there are several reasons why this economic activity is of concern to the student of the city's countryside. First, it is a surface mining activity that leads, inevitably, to major landscape disturbance during its operation. At the same time, since the deposits worked are generally quite shallow, being rarely more than 20 m in depth, the land area required to satisfy its present and immediately future needs can be very large. A recent study (McLellan, Yundt and Dorfman 1979) of the Waterloo area in southern Ontario identified approximately 2,400 ha of land occupied by some 60 active sand-and-gravel operations and an additional 127 abandoned pit sites occupying 307 ha of land, making the industry the second largest user of land beyond the built-up urban area after agriculture in this county. In the much larger area of the London Green Belt, UK, it was estimated in the mid-1970s that some 3,320 ha of land were in active mineral workings with another 3,040 ha approved for future workings (Standing Conference 1976). Although the area worked or to be worked amounted to less than 2 per cent of the total Green Belt area, the importance of mineral workings was considered to be underestimated because they tended to be localized in areas with significant land-use pressures.

Second, while the site of this extractive industry is tied to materials, raw material sources close to the urban markets earn an economic rent over sources further away because of the high transport costs on the bulky commodities of low value per unit weight produced by the industry. For instance, even before the rapid rise in energy costs in the mid-1970s, transport costs accounted very often for close to 60 per cent of the delivered price of aggregate materials in Ontario (Yundt 1973). Thus, the industry is attracted to locations within the city's countryside in which it must compete, as we have seen, in a very competitive land market. Depletion of existing near-urban raw materials and the implications of higher transport costs of utilizing more distant reserves have led some public jurisdictions, e.g. Ontario (Proctor and Redfern 1974; Bryant and McLellan 1974) to undertake detailed inventories of raw material deposits in an effort to ensure that all available sources are utilized as far as possible. Other jurisdictions have been prompted to undertake technical studies in an attempt to produce acceptable products from local materials other than those traditionally used, e.g. the study of fine sands and their utilization in the Paris region (France Ministry of Industry 1979).

Third, because of the negative externalities that accompany the industry, it has entered into serious conflict with the various functions and users with which it competes for the land resource. The bulky materials are transported most often by highly visible truck traffic, causing concern from rural residents over safety for children and, of course, increasing road maintenance; noisy machinery, especially with stone crushing, generate other complaints. And the landscape disturbance destroys amenity value. As Davidson and Wibberley (1977: 98) put it: 'Mining, particularly open cast mining, raises the important disparity between private costs and social costs in a capitalistic economy'. A particularly good illustration of the detrimental impact that sand-and-gravel operations have had is seen in the extensive number of derelict sites around urban areas (e.g. McLellan, Yundt and Dorfman 1979). In an investigation of landscape deterioration in London's Green Belt, mineral workings were found to be very frequently associated with 'damaged landscapes' and were often the prime source of the damage (Standing Conference 1976). The challenge of such derelict landscapes is considerable and only recently have concerted, though localized, efforts been aimed at them (e.g. McLellan, Yundt and Dorfman 1979). Despite progress in terms of rehabilitation and restoration (e.g. Bauer 1970; Earney 1975) and the progress in some jurisdictions in terms of regulating the industry (e.g. Ontario 1971), the industry retains an image of being involved in a 'robber economy' (Davidson and Wibberley 1977) and of somehow being 'a sneaky business'.

Critical to any consideration of the problems created, and faced, by the aggregate industry is understanding that conflicts arise from two sources:

1. the resource underlies other resources that are valued economically and culturally by other 'users' of the city's countryside;
2. the industry generates significant negative externalities that place it firmly in the public eye, which became increasingly critical as awareness of the environment developed over the late 1960s and 1970s.

In terms of other economic activities, agriculture – another extensive space user – is frequently displaced by aggregate mining activities, even though in the long term it is possible to restore some level of agricultural production capability. Other functions of the city's countryside that may be negatively affected by sand-and-gravel extraction are groundwater supplies and the amenity function, including the maintenance of natural habitats. It is pertinent to note that the development of a technology to utilize hitherto little-used resources as substitute materials will often lead to other conflicts, sometimes of even greater magnitude; a particularly good example of such conflict is the potential utilization of the fine sands of Fontainebleau in the Paris region and the inevitable conflicts that this would pose in terms of historic landscape maintenance. Impacts on the amenity resources thus constitute a major negative externality of the aggregate industry.

The aggregate industry, wherever it is located, faces a dilemma, which is all the more acute in the city's countryside because of its visibility. The products of the aggregate industry serve a necessary and useful function – without them urban development as we know it could not exist. Yet nobody wants a gravel pit or a quarry in their backyards, a dilemma they share with some noxious industries and sanitary landfill sites. The challenge to land-use planning is to be able to reserve significant resources in the city's countryside, where they exist, for the aggregate industry, while providing a regulatory environment plus control over other land-use developments that permit a harmonious operation of the industry (Bryant and McLellan 1975a).

In the long term, the essential interim or 'temporary' nature of this land use provides a partial solution to the dilemma, for the land can often eventually be restored to a useful function. For instance, in an analysis of past and present sand-and-gravel operations within the city boundaries of Toronto (Yundt and Augaitis 1979), 68 of the 78 past operations identified had been rehabilitated to support recreation or conservation areas, housing, schools, industrial uses, sanitary landfill sites and shopping centres (in that order), most of which had taken place without a coordinated regional planning intervention. The potential is thus great, although careful planning is required where several operations are concentrated in the same area – there is a limit, for instance, to how many recreational areas can be justified in a given area (Standing Conference 1976; Bryant and McLellan 1974).

Furthermore, while through a combination of multiple use and progressive rehabilitation (McLellan 1979) it is often possible to restore workings to acceptable and valuable after-uses, the aggregate industry faces severe public-image problems – after all, it is one thing as a disinterested observer to note that the gravel pit is temporary because its life-expectancy is only 30 years; it is quite another story when that pit happens to be the observer's neighbour! And in terms of public planning, the industry also has a long way to go to become acceptable; in a 1976 report on Green Belts in Scotland, for instance, extractive industry was still labelled an 'inappropriate' use (Countryside Commission for Scotland 1976). Finding ways to deal with the mistakes of the past may well prove to be a significant step in rehabilitating the industry (McLellan, Yundt and Dorfman 1979).

Manufacturing industry

Research oriented explicitly to the study of the role of industrial development in the evolving regional city form is rare. Wood (1974), in his discussion of manufacturing in the urban fringe, comments on several pertinent general statistical analyses, some of which have been very general while others have been quite detailed. But little effort has been expended in undertaking more microanalyses at the firm level in the context of the regional city. There are, however, three areas of literature corresponding roughly to three different scale levels of analysis which contribute to our understanding of the processes influencing industrial development in the regional city form.

First, work relating to overall patterns of regional economic development provide the broad context within which regional cities have been developing. Within this field, interesting insights into industrial development in the city's countryside come from the now classical models of regional economic development (e.g. Myrdal 1963; Hirschmann 1958; Friedmann 1966) as well as more recent work on trends in 'rural' or 'nonmetropolitan industrialization' (e.g. Haren 1974; Summers and Selvik 1979; Lonsdale and Seyler 1979).

Second, some interesting work has been undertaken on redistribution of industry within the urban area, sometimes including urban fringe areas. This work has been largely statistical (e.g. Reeder 1954, 1955), and has generally confirmed the trend towards 'suburbanization' or 'decentralization' of industry (Struyk and James 1975; Hoover and Vernon 1962), though the term 'decentralization' has been quarrelled with (Wood 1974) for reasons that are examined below. The term 'suburbanization', especially when used in North American research, seems frequently to include the settlement nodes within the urban fringe as well as suburban areas proper. This type of research is the easiest to identify with the concern of the evolving regional city form and the city's countryside. It merges, inevitably, into the third body of literature which is characterized by the collection and analysis of data at the microscale, undertaken as part of industrial location and development studies (e.g. Fulton 1974; Shively 1974) in which firms are asked to respond in terms of advantages and disadvantages of current and past sites and, sometimes, to rationalize their locational evolution. These three areas thus provide the basis for the following synthesis.

At the macroscale, against the background of the regional-income divergence models of Myrdal (1963) and Hirschmann (1958), the history of regional economic development trends has been dominated until quite recently by polarization and increasing regional disparities. Growth of job opportunities was not only concentrating into urban areas (Bryant 1980) as secondary and tertiary activities became dominant, but the concentration benefited primarily a limited number of metropolitan regions. This polarization process has thus created one of the main stimulii, i.e. population increase, underlying the development of the regional city form and the juxtaposition of nonagricultural and agricultural activities in the city's countryside. With population increase and job creation differentiated regionally, it can be argued that the level of development of the regional city form would vary regionally too, and, as a corollary, that the locational distribution of any industrial growth would be affected by the overall size and rate of expansion of the regional economy.

Hoover (1971) argues convincingly that sheer urban size affects the spatial structure of economic activities and land use in the urban area. Hypothetically, as population increases in an urban area with a single focal point of economic activity – the central business district – distances between place of work and place of residence increase. At some point, compensatory adjustments are made to reduce the costs of overcoming distance: 'Subcenters for various single activities or for groups of activities play a growing role in a larger urban area, because the total market in the area, . . ., becomes big enough to support two or more separate production or service centres at an efficient scale rather than just one' (Hoover 1971: 324). By extension we can apply the same logic to the *regional city form* both in terms of commercial activities (see later) and in terms of manufacturing activity. Thus, in the mature regional city form, we can envisage not only clusters of suburban industrial development but also the strengthening and development of industrial activity at various settlement nodes in the city's countryside – smaller cities, towns and villages. And in terms of industrial development there are factors other than market size that help accentuate this dispersal of industrial development among the nodes of the city's countryside.

At the broad regional scale, then, polarization forces can be seen as attracting industrial growth (*in situ* expansion of existing plants, relocation and expansion of existing plants, or new plants) to particular regional cities, with growth in the nodes of the city's countryside being perhaps more sharply developed around the larger metropolitan areas. At another scale, industrial growth in the city's countryside can also be seen as the result of limited spread effects, as outlying nodes benefit from expansion and development of the core area. Some of these spread effects can also be seen in terms of the trend towards 'rural industrialization' noted in recent work (e.g. Bryant 1980; Lonsdale and Seyler 1979). In the US, Haren (1974) used State Employment Security figures to show that non-metropolitan areas increased their share of US manufacturing employment from 22 to 25 per cent between 1960 and 1970; however, there was a significant concentration of new manufacturing jobs in the non-metropolitan counties in and adjacent to the Great Lakes Industrial Belt, reflecting both infilling and some decentralization of activity from places such as Cleveland, Detroit and Chicago, as well as much infilling both in and around the Southern Industrial Crescent and the Carolina Coastal Plain. Thus, while some of the patterns of change in the distribution of manufacturing reflect the increasing importance of centrifugal forces relative to centripetal forces (e.g. Keeble 1976) which has sometimes acted in favour of peripheral areas of the economy, including some previously non-industrialized rural areas, it is clear that much of this 'rural' growth is related to the extension of broad urban-industrial regions, the ultimate expression of which is perhaps the megalopolis (Gottman 1961).

The regional city is thus seen as a stopping point on the road towards megalopolis, although megalopolis is not the inevitable destination. It is when we consider the complex settlement, economic activity and transportation structure of the mature regional city (e.g. the New York Metropolitan Region described by Hoover and Vernon, 1962) that we can appreciate Wood's criticism (1974) of the term 'decentralization' of industrial development; the core no longer becomes the appropriate vantage point from which to observe industrial development (or, for that matter, commercial and residential development), e.g. in the overlapping regional cities around London, UK, or those of the 'Golden Horseshoe' at the western end of Lake Ontario in Canada.

Part of the changing industrial structure (*in situ* expansion, differential growth, relocation and new development) in the broad urban-industrial region can thus be regarded as *redistributional*, as opposed to *developmental*, the latter occurring when the changing industrial structure affects the relative position of one broad region *vis-à-vis* another (Sant 1975). It is therefore important, given our concern with the city's countryside, to understand the factors operating in favour of the dispersed part of the regional city in terms of industrial development.

First, industrial development is of various types – *in situ* expansion, relocation, and 'new' activity – which may be affected by different processes. As yet, research has not been directed towards these different types of growth in terms of differential location within the metropolitan area (Wood 1974) and thus in the regional city. In terms of the overall distribution of industry within regional city forms, it is important to recognize the dominance of urban areas, and the influence of inertia on industrial change. Clearly, manufacturing is urban-dominated; in the US, the 'central cities' of metropolitan areas accounted for 35 per cent of manufacturing employment in 1960 while 'other urban' areas within metropolitan areas had 27.8 per cent in 1960 (Bryant 1980). While important changes took place over the 1960s, with the share of central cities dropping to 29.9 per cent and the share of other metropolitan urban areas increasing to 31.5 per cent by 1970, the importance of the core urban areas is still considerable.

Now, if we argue that expansion of plant capacity from an investment-management perspective will be more likely to occur *in situ*, providing site conditions allow (Wood 1974), a major component to industrial change within a metropolitan area will be affected by the existing distribution of industry. Given that conditions for expansion are frequently not ideal in core urban areas (see below), we might expect the net result of this incremental process to benefit other urban areas in the city's countryside. These nodes have often had a long history of manufacturing activities in any case. Of course, this is a type of process that feeds upon itself.

This suggested redistribution of capacity by differential *in situ* expansion is therefore accentuated by actual relocation or 'decentralization' movements. Given that actual physical movements of industry are often short-distance moves (Sant 1975), relocation will similarly tend to emphasize locations on the periphery of the built-up area as well as locations close to other industrial areas within the city's countryside such as existing nodes and in certain transportation corridors. Both *in situ* expansion and relocation can be expected to contribute to the development of manufacturing in the city's countryside, with existing industrial areas acting almost as seedbeds in a diffusion process, in which concentric, axial and multiple nucleii components can be present. Thus, various parts of the city's countryside benefit from these processes of change largely due to proximity to existing industrial areas.

Secondly, there are some factors which discriminate against central-city types of location for industry and those that draw industry into the city's countryside, not only in terms of decentralizing industries but also new firms and plants and differential *in situ* expansion. Technology has been important in both *forcing* some plants outside the central urban areas and in *permitting* the subsequently greater dispersal. Hoover and Vernon (1962) note how the development of continuous material-flow systems in many branches of manufacturing has necessitated more substantial horizontal plant layouts; expansion *in situ* in the urban area has often been hampered by the existence of obsolescent buildings and inadequate space for horizontal expansion and parking facilities (Hoover 1971), not to mention the costs of land in urban areas both in terms of land values and taxes.

At the same time, transportation technology especially truck and highway technology, has permitted many industries to take advantage of more dispersed locations on the urban periphery, or beyond, where they can benefit from *greater space availability*, at lower unit costs, and where industrial parks can be more easily developed with the supporting infrastructure. The use of truck transportation, provided adequate highway facilities exist, has greatly facilitated the dispersal of manufacturing through the regional city. Also, the highway transportation facilities of many urban areas were not conceived of in terms of large truck transportation, thus adding to the problems of urban-core industrial expansion. The 'central' location is not necessarily the most accessible location; this is even more important where the industrial activity (firm, plant) being considered serves more than a local or even regional market. For activities whose markets are extra-regional, access to any single central location is likely irrelevant; it is more important to have access to a transportation system that links the plant with several regional markets (Johnson 1974).

One result of locations peripheral to the urban area being no longer the least accessible locations, but rather being among the most accessible locations, is that *external economies* (e.g. having the opportunity to make use of specialized repair services, financial services or being able to farm out parts of a manufacturing process to subcontractors) are no longer as localized as they once were for many industries. Frequent contact between an industrial unit in the city's countryside and a core area (or areas) may not be essential – it is not a daily commuting constraint on dispersal that is important. However, given the increased mobility afforded by highway communication over the past four decades, the need for regular, but infrequent, contact may permit the industrial units concerned to locate at distances involving travel times of two hours or more from the core area(s). Development of industry in these broad urban-industrial regions, the next step beyond the regional city, represents the extension of urban fields within which access to markets (regional and extra-regional), transportation availability and external scale economies are maintained, permitting key linkage and contact patterns to be retained (in the case of relocating industry) and developed (for 'new' industries) (Norcliffe 1975). In certain industries, where industrial processes have been considerably subdivided (e.g. electronics), there are examples of 'concentrated dispersal' (e.g. Parry 1963) in which the various units of the industry are spread over a wide area to tap a dispersed labour pool but where they are sufficiently close to maintain adequate contact between units.

The same change in transportation technology has also eased a considerable constraint on some industries, that of *access to an adequate labour pool*. With the increased personal mobility afforded by the automobile and the dispersal of residential development, even a 'greenfield' site in the city's countryside may be able to draw on a large enough labour pool in its catchment area. The spread of residential development in the inner fringe and beyond, and the increasing dispersal of industrial employment opportunities constitute mutually reinforcing processes which have benefited pre-existing nodes in the city's countryside as well as in suburban locations.

There are other factors that have pushed or kept manufacturing away from core urban areas and attracted them to suburban areas and the city's countryside. Within urban areas, industrial units have not only had a hard time finding space for expansion and battling traffic congestion, but they have frequently been hampered by being 'unwanted'. Public planning, especially through zoning by-laws, has made survival in the urban area extremely difficult for some industries. This has been the case particularly for industrial zones that have become surrounded by residential development, and is most noticeable in the case of noxious industries and 'nuisance' industries (Hoover and Vernon 1962), or those that create negative externalities in terms of danger, noise, dust (e.g. cement pipe works), smell and even aesthetics. These would include the low-value unwanted activities (e.g. auto-wrecking yards) that Firey (1946) talked of when noting the degenerative character of many 'rurban' fringes. Inevitably, they have found themselves forced into the areas beyond the contemporary urban area where they may still produce their negative externalities – the only difference is that there are fewer people to complain. These industries may not be very large in total number, but their localized effects can be considerable.

On the other hand, the city's countryside offers specific attractions to some industries; of particular interest because of its intimate relationship with the evolving settlement structure of the regional city form is the attractiveness to labour of living in rural areas. This amenity and life-style factor has been noted by several researchers (e.g. Haren 1974; Fulton 1974; Keeble 1976) based either upon general patterns of association between certain types of development and attractive living environments, or surveys at the level of the individual firm. This may be more important for some types of industry than others, e.g. high-technology industry and research-oriented activities such as laboratories which rely heavily upon a professional labour force (Hoover 1971; Norcliffe 1975). The small town within the orbit of a major metropolitan area may provide the attractiveness of 'small-town living' with the advantages of having access to the commercial and cultural facilities of a metropolitan area.

Finally, one last point of considerable importance at the intra-regional scale is that the regional city form and the even broader incipient megalopolitan structures are composed of many local municipal units – small cities, towns, counties and villages (Hepner, Lewis and Muraco 1976). This political fragmentation at the local scale has inevitably involved competition between political units to attract industrial development in order to improve local tax bases, improve or maintain services and provide support to local commerce. Town councils have been quick to take advantage of all the factors discussed above that have encouraged some industries to consider the city's countryside for their relocation or start-up. While it is difficult, if not impossible, to separate out the real impact of this factor, it nonetheless adds a twist to the evolution of industry in the city's countryside that cannot be ignored.

Commercial activities

There are certain similarities between the factors that have led to the increasing dispersal of manufacturing within the regional city form and those affecting the spread of commercial activities. But at least one factor is quite specific to commercial activities in the city's countryside. Retail activities constitute the most easily identified type of commercial activity. Being highly consumer-oriented, any change that affects market distribution thus will exert some influence on the changing distribution of retail activities (Brush and Gauthier 1968).

Hoover's (1971) previously noted argument concerning the effect of sheer size of the urban area upon urban land-use activities is particularly appropriate for retail activities. Increased size of urban area associated with the increased dispersal of both day-time (place of work) and night-time (place of residence) populations leads to greater travel times and costs if one starts with the hypothetical single focal point, the central business district. Eventually, as market threshold sizes are reached, the dispersing market demand becomes served by a larger number of centres. For some activities, the point at which this occurs is reached very rapidly, e.g. the convenience stores or neighbourhood stores that seem to follow the construction of practically every new housing subdivision around North American cities.

The expansion of the urban area also has had effects on overall patterns of accessibility. With the increased personal mobility afforded by the automobile, downtown or central locations have been placed at a disadvantage, both because of increased distances between consumers and central locations and lack of parking facilities. Dawson (1974) notes that in 1970, more than 80 per cent of US families owned a car while in the UK over 50 per cent of families owned a car. He notes that this underestimates the situation considerably in the suburbs (and, of course, the city's countryside) because of the generally higher income structure of families there. Against the backdrop of parking becoming an increasingly important consideration for accessibility, peripheral urban locations becoming more accessible with the development of ring roads and freeway developments, and the greater dispersal of consumer-demand, the peripheral development of shopping malls can be appreciated. The planned, large-scale developments that have characterized so much of the changing pattern of retail activities in North American cities possess considerable economies of scale, e.g. in terms of parking, and the individual shops benefit from external economies of scale such as shared parking facilities and shared physical infrastructure in terms of heating and lighting; the closed-in shopping malls furthermore capitalize on and encourage the multipurpose shopping trip. Such developments inevitably involve conflict with downtown shopping areas; almost every planned peripheral shopping development sees protests from downtown merchants' associations, and it would seem that, in the UK, the potential competition between the two types of development led the planning system to opt against any wholesale decentralization of retailing, at least up until the mid-1960s (Dawson 1974).

The large, planned shopping development is not always a strictly suburban development: sometimes, it is linked with a major secondary node in the city's countryside; sometimes it is an integral part of a planned residential community separate from the built-up urban core (e.g. Parly II to the south-west of Paris, France); and sometimes it may be practically in a 'greenfield' location, though in this case it is almost inevitably linked to a major highway transportation corridor (e.g. the extensive commercial developments located along the RN10 south of Paris).

Other retailing activities are on a smaller scale than these large developments, but they have also been affected by similar forces. Of interest are the fortunes of retailing in many of the smaller nodes within the city's countryside. Research that has dealt with this explicitly in terms of the forces underlying the evolving regional city form is rare, although some localized studies do exist (e.g. Amos 1979). One body of research that is of significance, however, is that which has focused on the changing fortunes of rural service centres in agricultural areas. This is interesting because it provides a contrast with what has been happening in the city's countryside. Generally, the decline and thinning out of rural service centres (e.g. Hodge 1965) in many agricultural areas has been attributed to changes in agricultural technology and the subsequent migration of population following decreases in agricultural labour requirements, as well as to changes in consumer mobility and scale of retailing operations. Clearly, these same forces are present in the city's countryside as well, but at the same time, the dispersal of non-agricultural consumer-demand provides a counterbalancing force to the agriculturally based forces. An influx of country residential residents and development attached to settlement nodes can have a beneficial impact on the viability of retail activities, creating not only an environment in which existing levels of service provision can be maintained but in which expansion may also occur (e.g. Harrison 1976; Amos 1979).

Still another component to the retail structure of the city's countryside involves a combination of entrepreneurs capitalizing on many urban residents' desire to drive into the country – the shopping trip and journey to shop as a recreational type of pursuit. Hence, the development of antique shops, and even clusters of craft-oriented shops, can be seen as catering to a 'back to nature or countryside' feeling on the part of urban customers. The revitalization of many country pubs can be seen in a similar vein. In a sense, where there are clusters of such stores, they can be viewed as 'tourist-oriented' developments with the tourists coming from the nearby urban area, although they may, of course, develop a much broader clientele too.

Sometimes, this outward move of retail activities is also linked to a need for substantial space, which is relatively more abundant in the city's countryside; hence, the development of furniture stores in various nodes in the city's countryside around, e.g., many southern Ontario cities (Russwurm 1977a). This need for space and for being accessible to urban markets puts some of the retailing activity in the same situation as certain manufacturing industries and wholesaling activities. Large space-using warehousing and wholesaling operations are therefore found both in peripheral urban locations, e.g. along major highway axes into the urban area, as well as in other settlement nodes. Sometimes, such developments may be part of a major planned infrastructural development involving substantial public investment, e.g. the development of the fruit-and-vegetable wholesaling centre at Rungis, south of Paris, which replaced the crowded and congested Les Halles wholesaling area in central Paris (Fédération Française des Marchés d'Intérêt National 1969).

Finally, we should at least mention the area of commercial office employment. Obviously, substantial numbers of strictly office jobs may go hand in hand with any dispersal of retailing, wholesaling and manufacturing. In addition, while office employment is still of tremendous significance in downtown areas, certain types of office employment may find advantages in suburban locations and beyond. Again, offices represent a people-oriented activity and considerations of accessibility and parking space are similarly important in understanding the development of office complexes (often the administrative function of an industry unit), for example, along the main Highway 401 artery south-west of Toronto. Amenity considerations may also be of significance here too.

All in all, the changing pattern of industrial and commercial activities within the regional city form, particularly the dispersed part of the city's countryside, are part of a complex set of processes, both generating and responding to new interactional patterns. Some forces have discriminated against urban-core locations, such as lack of space and congestion, while others have favoured peripheral urban locations and beyond. Underlying all of this has been the complex change in transportation technology, based on the personal automobile, the commercial truck, substantial public investment in highway networks and cheap energy. In some regions, the resulting form is no longer a regional city with a single dominant urban core, but a complex system of interacting settlement and economic activity nodes in which it is no longer pertinent to view the processes from a central-city perspective. Any speculation as to what the future of such settlement and economic activity forms holds as the result of increasing energy costs must consider the fact that the development of these systems has reached different levels in different regions, implying different degrees of inertia in the system; we shall return to consider these issues in our concluding chapter.

Further reading

Hoover, E. M. (1971) *An Introduction to Regional Economics* (1st ed), A. A. Knopf, New York.

Hoover, E. M. and Vernon, R. (1962) *Anatomy of a Metropolis*, Anchor Books, Doubleday and Co., Garden City, New York.

McLellan, A. G. (1979) Aggregate mining and rehabilitation, *Minerals and the Environment*, **1**(1), 31–5, J. W. Larman, Cambridge.

Wood, P. A. (1974) Urban manufaturing: a view from the fringe, Ch. 7 **pp. 129–54** in Johnson, J. H. (ed.), *Suburban Growth*, John Wiley and Sons, London.

8 Recreational activities

While leisure is an age-old phenomenon, it has only become widely available to the general population following the social and industrial reforms in the wake of the Industrial Revolution. Mass production, an increasing division of labour, unionization and shorter working weeks have provided increasing amounts of discretionary time for the average family to devote to the pursuit of leisure and, therefore, various recreational activities. The right of access to recreational opportunity has become increasingly entrenched during the twentieth century, with both citizens and governments concerned with the provision of recreational facilities and opportunities. On the one hand, this has led to an increase in the acquisition of private recreational properties, e.g. cottages and second homes (e.g. Bielkus, Rogers and Wibberley 1972) and, on the other hand, public bodies have become increasingly involved in acquiring or protecting scenic areas, historic sites and other 'valued' areas. Furthermore, both public and private sectors have become heavily involved in providing more intensively used recreational facilities.

Thus, a wide range of potential opportunities exist for recreation: funfare or carnival, museums, exhibitions, parades, observation or participation in a wide variety of sports activities, soccer, baseball, tennis, golf, horseback riding, active water sports, sailing, swimming, surfing, camping, hiking, fishing or simply dozing on the beach – the list seems endless and difficult to rationalize.

However, there are several useful criteria which we can use to classify recreational activities:

1. Where are the activities carried out, e.g. in urban areas, in the city's countryside, or in more distant locations such as mountain zones, 'wilderness' parks or the tropics? This is, of course, a perspective that fits well into the geographic focus of this book.
2. Does the activity require the provision of special facilities? A useful distinction can be made between activities that are very extensive in their use of space, requiring relatively few facilities, e.g. hiking, driving for pleasure and cross-country skiing, and those that are more intensive in their use of space, requiring the provision of specialized facilities, e.g. swimming and sports activities generally, camping and picnicking.
3. Is the activity accommodated dominantly on public lands, on lands and facilities provided by the private commercial sector, or does it involve the informal use of private lands, made available with or without the land owner's permission?

The locational matrix of recreational activities

It is possible to view recreational activities and opportunities as being differentiated on the basis of a minimum time spent on an activity and distance travelled to engage in that activity. If we integrate the sort of spatio-temporal pattern of recreational activities portrayed by Wall and Sinott (1980) with our view of the regional city form, four broad types of zones can be identified (Fig. 8.1) when viewed from the perspective of the concentrated urban core. First, a zone of daily leisure extends into the urban fringe. On the one hand, for many leisure-time activities, our own homes provide all the necessary facilities: witness the many hours spent reading, relaxing and

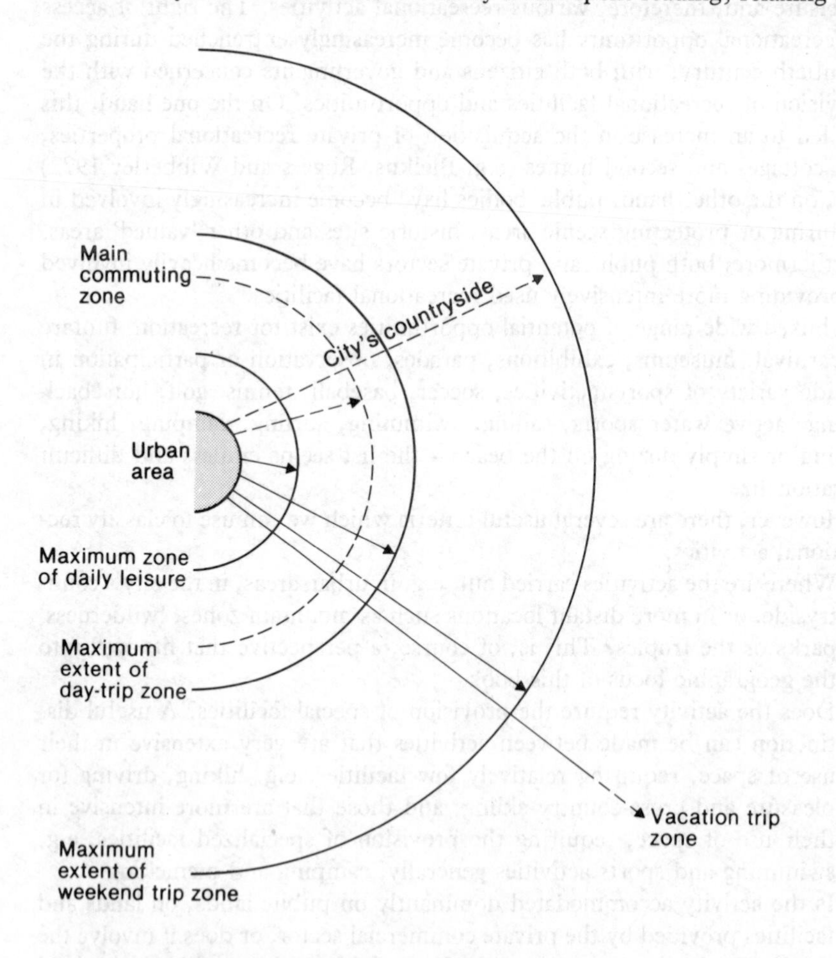

Figure 8.1 Recreation zones around an urban area

watching television (Davidson and Wibberley 1977). On the other hand, some people spend additional leisure time outside the home on organized recreational activities, e.g. ice hockey, baseball, soccer and tennis, or using private commercial facilities, e.g. cinema, theatre and musical entertainment, or frequenting nearby parks.

A second spatial context for recreational activity covers most of the city's countryside as we have defined it, where urban residents 'escape' from their urban environment to the most accessible rural areas. Driving for pleasure, hiking or walking, visits to farms with pick-your-own facilities, cross-country skiing or simply countryside viewing – all demand access to this extra-urban spaciousness without a large time commitment. This zone can be viewed as incorporating the day-trip zone, as well as the zone of daily leisure activities.

The outer limit of the third zone of recreational activity demands considerably more effort and travel time and would not be normally accessible for day use. This is the zone accessible to people willing to make a weekend trip, and would include the regular weekend seasonal recreational space represented by many cottage or second-home areas, e.g. the Muskokas north of Toronto or Normandy to the west of Paris. Finally, the fourth zone of recreational activities extends to include the longer visits to remoter 'wilderness' parks and the annual family vacation including those abroad. Access to both of these last two zones would normally be much more demanding in terms of time and financial commitment than the two other location types.

It is worth noting that this geographic zoning is, of course, at a much broader scale than that which we used to describe land-use changes occurring within the regional-city context. We would expect this as recreational travel will not be affected by the costs of distance as much as commuting, although

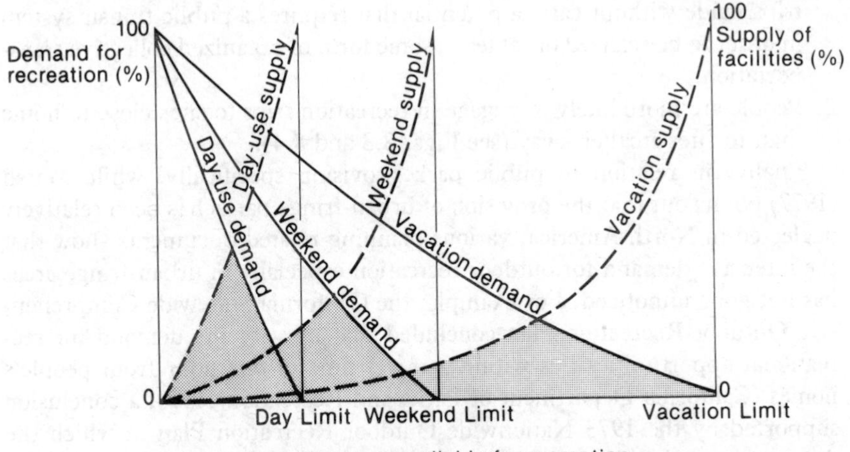

Figure 8.2 Intensity of demand and supply of recreational opportunities and distance from source of demand. (Source: Greer and Wall 1979: Fig. 30, p. 229).

the demand for day trips, weekend trips and vacation trips are affected by distance to different degrees as the framework of Greer and Wall (1979) shows (Fig. 8.2). Furthermore, there is considerable overlap between the different zones. Depending upon particular amenity attractions, it is possible, for instance, to find cottage or second-home areas in urban fringe, urban shadow or much remoter locations. The criterion of minimum time spent may thus be respected but the distance or travel-time involved may vary widely for the specific recreational activity and use. The key difference between the zones, then, is to be found in differences in the intensity of demand for recreational experiences, a differentiation that is heightened by general differences in potential supply of recreational opportunities (Fig. 8.2).

The importance of accessibility for urban fringe locations is implied in Burton's (1967a) study of visitors to Windsor Great Park in the UK, where 36 per cent of the visitors were found to have come from *within* 16 km, rising to 68 per cent in some parts of the park, demonstrating the intensity with which near-urban recreational opportunities can be used. Other research by Burton and Wibberley (1965) provides further evidence of the relatively short recreational distances travelled by a large proportion of car-trippers. For some types of recreational trips, e.g. to sports facilities, distances travelled seem to be characteristically even shorter, so that such facilities tend to be fairly widespread in relation to demand (Bowen 1974), even though some areas are not as well provided for as others.

Furthermore, Travis and Veal (1976) note two conclusions based on the research in which the effect of accessibility on the incidence of car-use for travel to parks has been evaluated:

1. Urban-fringe sites have the potential to attract considerable numbers of trips made without cars, a potential that requires a public transit system in order to be realized or, at least, some form of organized collective transportation.
2. People are more likely to engage in recreation trips to sites close to home than to sites further away (see Figs. 8.3 and 8.4).

Finally, in relation to public park provision specifically, while Marsh (1977) points out that the provision of urban-fringe parks has been relatively neglected in North America, various planning-related documents show that the intensive demand for outdoor recreation especially in urban-fringe areas has not gone unnoticed. For example, the California Statewide Comprehensive Outdoor Recreation Plan concluded that most of the demand for recreational opportunities lies within a travel time of one hour from people's homes (California Department of Parks and Recreation 1972), a conclusion supported by the 1973 Nationwide Outdoor Recreation Plan in which the day-use recreation zone, including approximately one hour of travel time, was identified as critical for publicly provided recreation opportunities (Bureau of Outdoor Recreation 1973). Furthermore, it was estimated in the mid-1960s that by the year 2000, while the American population would dou-

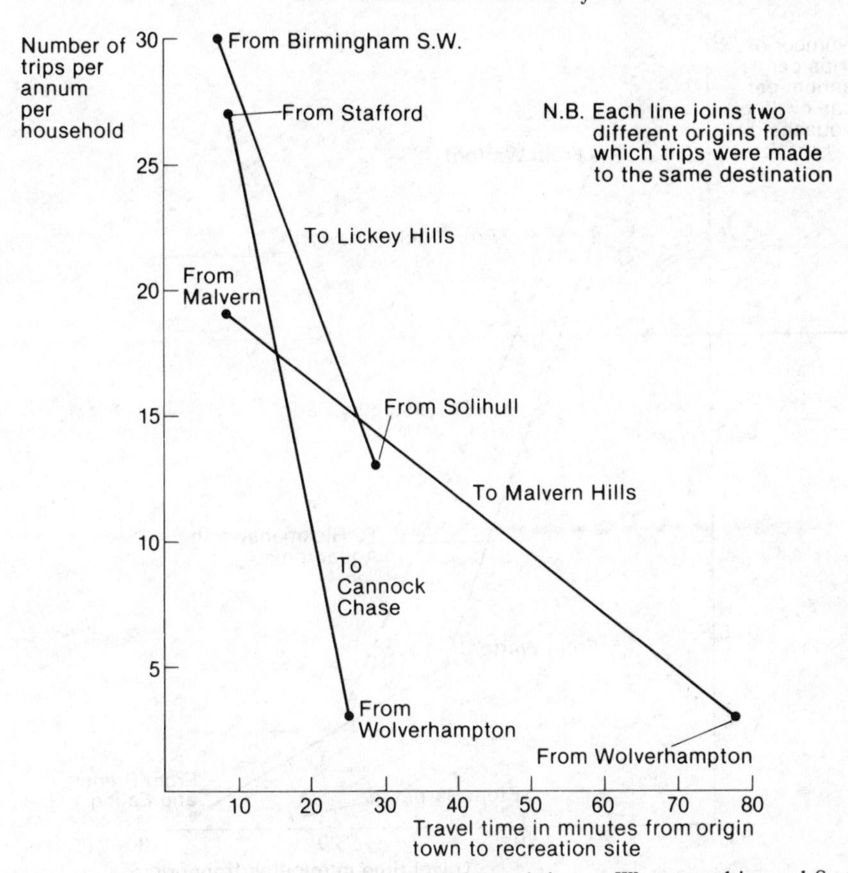

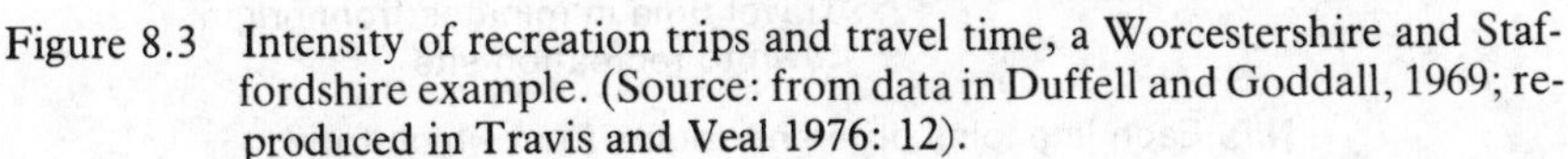
Figure 8.3 Intensity of recreation trips and travel time, a Worcestershire and Staffordshire example. (Source: from data in Duffell and Goddall, 1969; reproduced in Travis and Veal 1976: 12).

ble and the general outdoor recreation demand would triple, the demand for recreation opportunities within 'a half-hour from home' would increase tenfold (US Department of Housing and Development 1965).

Of particular interest to us then, is that part of the zonal structure covering the daily leisure space and the day-trip zone which would account for the greater part of the dispersed component of the regional city, the city's countryside. Recreational activities undertaken in the city's countryside have been given relatively little attention by researchers until recently (Davidson 1976), despite the fact that increased car ownership and city expansion have greatly increased accessibility to the city's countryside for a large number of people since 1945. This is not for want of recognizing the potential in the city's countryside: witness the frequent concerns expressed for the provision of recreational opportunity in green-belt areas (see Ch. 12). And in the last five years in Europe and somewhat more recently in North America, a new economic reality has developed that may lead to increasing interest in recrea-

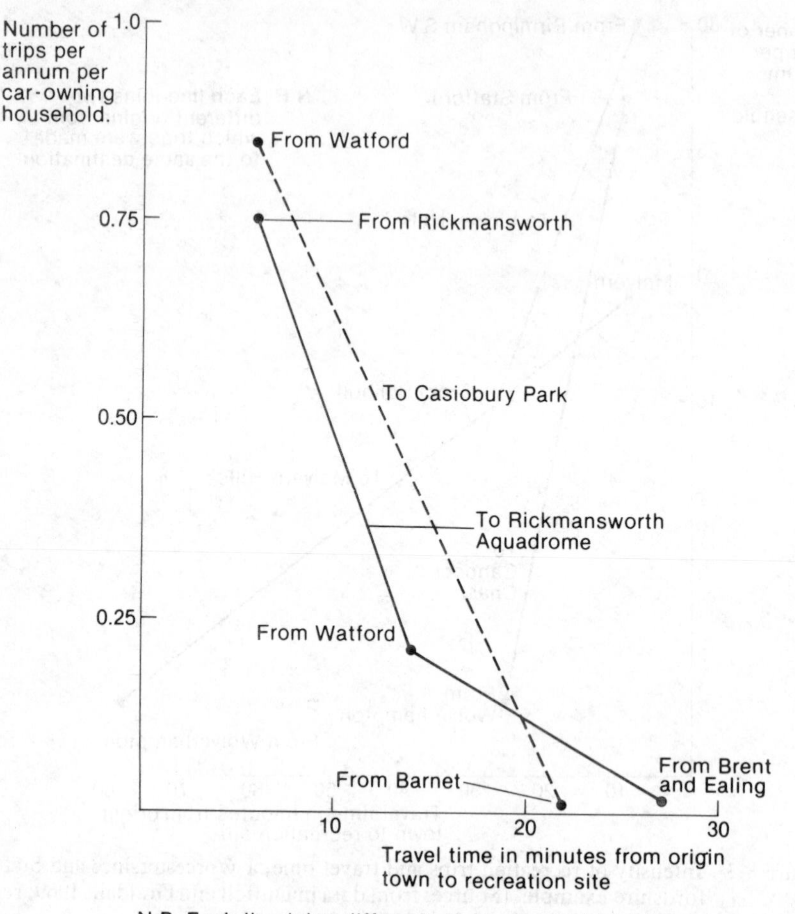

Figure 8.4 Intensity of recreation trips and travel time, a Hertfordshire example. (Source: from data in Duffell and Peters 1971, reproduced in Travis and Veal 1976: 13).

tional opportunities in the city's countryside – rising petrol prices. If the price elasticity of demand for access to recreational opportunities is sufficiently high, it may well be that people will begin to substitute shorter-distance recreational travel for longer-distance travel, thus increasing recreational demands on the city's countryside. The evidence so far is sketchy, though, and does not allow us to draw any firm conclusions (Travis and Veal 1976).

If there is a process of substitution underway between outdoor recreational opportunities in distant and near-urban locations, the relative roles of informal private versus commercial or publicly provided recreational opportunities are raised more clearly than in the past. Most of the land surrounding our cities is owned by neither commercial nor public interests but rather by farmers. Accessing this land for recreational activity without removing it from agriculture is perhaps one of the greatest challenges of the city's countryside. We are faced by a set of problems involving the degree of compatibility of different uses of the same land, different attitudes towards land, the often inadequate state of trespass laws, and the fascinating questions of compensation and who pays. It is to the task of providing some insight into the characteristics and associated problems of recreational activities in the city's countryside that we now turn.

Recreation in the city's countryside: why, who and what?

Why?

Underlying the increased participation in outdoor recreational activities which may be expected to influence the city's countryside to a significant degree because of accessibility considerations, are both positive attractions of rural countryside and negative features of urban areas. The upswing in outdoor recreation can be seen at a general level in the context (Davidson and Wibberley 1977) of increased levels of personal mobility, increased leisure time and greater spending power. In addition, outdoor recreational experiences, be they in near-urban locations or the remoter 'wilderness' experience, can serve a useful function by providing people with a sense of psychological release from the stressful environments characteristic of many large urban areas (Kehm 1977).

Thus, the upswing in urban-fringe recreation has been viewed (Travis 1976) as resulting partially from a failure to meet changing demands for recreation within cities. In redevelopment schemes in the urban core, for instance, recreational opportunities have not generally been developed and it has fallen to the lot of urban fringe zones to provide the opportunities required. This is less true of newer schemes, particularly waterfront urban locations where former urban and industrial sites have sometimes been rehabilitated for recreational use in a most satisfactory way, e.g. the walkways along the rehabilitated River Kelvin in Glasgow.

The people: actual and potential involvement

But who uses the city's countryside for recreation? In terms of potential involvement, an interesting fact which emerged from an early study (Wager 1967) was that 'accessible' park areas provided a useful recreational opportunity for particular social groups – the poor, those without cars, older people and children. For many of these people, National Parks and the like are remote, expensive and inaccessible. Because of such accessibility considerations, even amenity resources that are of mediocre value when compared with some national or international standards, e.g. the Swiss Alps, may become of real significance in the city's countryside.

However, the need of some social groups for access to outdoor recreational opportunity may be more latent than real, actual behaviour patterns being constrained by the economics of access and availability of opportunity (Fitton 1976). Because access to many existing facilities and amenities requires the use of a car, it is no surprise really that many surveys of the characteristics of day and half-day trippers show that car-owning young and middle-aged families from suburbia tend to be disproportionately represented (e.g. the studies summarized by Davidson and Wibberley 1977).

Again, the latent demand for outdoor recreational opportunity has been underlined even in the North American context. For, despite the 'general mobility' of North Americans, a recent study suggests that nearly half of those living in the inner-city areas of America have neither automobiles, nor the funds for public transportation to recreation areas even if it was available (University of Missouri 1972). Kehm (1977) draws similar conclusions for inner areas of many of the larger Canadian cities. Such statements demonstrate the latent demand for public recreation that could affect the city's countryside.

The activities

Recreational activities can be differentiated on the basis of intensity of use of the land resource per recreationalist. *Intensive-use activities* require relatively little land but may require substantial capital investment in terms of facilities, e.g. swimming pools, playgrounds, golf courses, sports fields and campgrounds. Of course, the level of facilities required varies quite considerably; contrast for instance a no-frills campsite with a trailer/caravan campsite with electrical hook-ups and a whole range of associated infrastructure. Such activities would often be user-oriented and specific resource endowments would generally not be significant, except for activities like sailing and boating. Most of these activities involve an *active* use of space, but intensive-use activities also include visits to certain historic monuments and sites, a more *passive* use of space (Bowen 1974).

Extensive-use activities involve relatively large areas of the land space resource per recreationalist. On the one hand this includes activities such as driving for pleasure, hiking and countryside viewing, relatively passive uses of space. Interestingly enough. several of these activities follow a linear spatial form. The general landscape amenity resource is clearly of prime importance here. On the other hand, there are extensive activities that are more active in their use of space, e.g. cross-country skiing, hunting and fishing, in which both amenity values, specific resource endowments and access to the land are important.

Often, one of the extensive space-use activities is combined with an intensive space-use activity, e.g. driving for pleasure or countryside viewing and camping or use of sports facilities or picnicking. And, of course, what we have argued above is that the *overall demand* for all of these activities is likely to be more intense in the city's countryside than beyond, e.g. even though cross-country skiing may be an extensive space use from the perspective of the individual recreationalist, we would expect cross-country skiing facilities to be more intensively used by the general public closer to urban areas than beyond. This greater intensity of use has significant implications for the level of management required in meeting the demands, both from private informal sources, commercial sources and public sources.

Recreational resources in the city's countryside

In the Western European context particularly, considerable potential for meeting some of these activity demands already exists and has been partially realized. For instance, substantial properties with recreational potential, e.g. attractive landscapes and historic buildings within large estates, royal or state forests and parkland, are all part of the heritage of the city's countryside around many Western European cities. Longleat with its lion park, the Duke of Bedford's estate, Windsor Great Park and Blenheim Palace are only some of the more outstanding examples in the UK, while in France, private estates that have been opened to the public are also quite common, e.g. the safari park of the Château de Thoiry and the estate of the Château de Brétuil, respectively west and south of Paris. Publicly owned land is particularly significant in this respect in some countries, e.g. in Britain the National Trust holds 160,000 ha of moorland, coastland, woodland, bridges, canals, castles and even whole villages and prehistoric and Roman sites (Clay 1978), some of which are found within the city's countryside. Furthermore, Ferguson and Munton (1979) show that if we count sites in which a public or semi-public body has either an interest in management or ownership, then close to 500 informal recreation sites can be identified in London's Green Belt, covering 31,000 ha or 5.7 per cent of the Green Belt area.

Thus, there are clearly many types of recreational opportunities and potential in the city's countryside, ranging from intensive recreation areas either privately or publicly operated, to buildings and sites of particular historic or scientific interest, and to the countryside generally which provides amenity value in the landscape and sometimes opportunities for multiple use of private land for walking, skiing, and so forth.

Recreational activities

In the remainder of this chapter, and by way of example, we focus on three types of recreational opportunities that involve substantial land areas. First we consider the role, characteristics and potential of near-urban parks. These may both serve some of the latent demand for outdoor recreation not currently catered to and relieve pressures on surrounding countryside by providing a specific focus for some users of the countryside. This involves both intensive and extensive space-use activities. The discussion draws substantially upon two recent conferences (Travis and Veal 1976; National and Provincial Parks Association of Canada 1977). Second, the role of privately owned land, particularly farmland, in providing recreational opportunity is discussed, drawing upon recent comparative work at the University of Waterloo (Cullington 1979, 1980); the focus here is on relatively extensive space-use activities. Third, some brief comments are made on commercial recreational enterprises.

Near-urban parks

The arguments for major parks in the urban fringe (Cripps 1976) include the following:

1. Many existing parks have constraints on use including those relating to access and particular management policies.
2. Many people without private transport do not have effective access to the countryside, but park development could focus demand so that public transportation might be viable. Thus there is an opportunity to cater to a broader segment of the population (Davidson 1974; Fitton 1976), with the understanding that this includes the less privileged classes of urban areas.
3. Provision of parks can lead to environmental improvement in the city's countryside, e.g. conversion and use of derelict sand-and-gravel workings (McLellan, Yundt and Dorfman 1979).
4. Open space in the city's countryside provides relief from the 'concrete jungle' and helps maintain a 'green lung' for cities. Large blocks of land or parks may provide an important strategic component for ecosystem protection, representing both biological and visual buffers to adjacent heavily built-up areas.

Various types of public recreational facilities have been developed that are located in the city's countryside. They range from areas of land which support recreational activities even though their prime purpose is not recreational, e.g. many of the Conservation Areas in Ontario, to parks designed specifically for recreational opportunity, e.g. the English Country Parks and the near-urban park. There has, indeed, been an increase in interest in providing park facilities in an urban context even on the part of agencies traditionally associated with 'wilderness' and remoter park facilities. Thus, the large-scale urban recreation proposals for the New York and San Francisco areas that developed out of the 1960s involving the National Park Service (Smith 1972) reflect this redirection in thinking about where major new developments in park provision should be located. Similar trends are noticeable in other countries too, e.g. in Canada (Marsh 1977) and the more general concerns of the UK Countryside Commission in urban-fringe areas. Let us focus now on the concept of near-urban parks or 'urban-fringe parks' as they have been referred to in the UK (Standing Conference 1976). Their definition remains somewhat elusive. However, Marsh (1977) identifies two basic dimensions to the concept, both essentially spatial, 'urban'and 'nearness'.

The 'urban' component can be resolved largely by reference to some population threshold of an urban-centred region, a criterion reflecting the notion of concentration of demand and need. The term 'near' involves proximity to these urban areas, both with respect to time and distance. Given the nature of the demand, it seems reasonable to suggest that 'near' means within the half-day use hinterland of an urban area. Moreover, such parks must also be accessible in an economic sense, and given the concern for the lower-income and non-car-owning families, near-urban parks must be accessible by public transport (Marsh 1977). Even so, people dependent on public transportation face a much reduced range of choice in destination, owing to the almost inevitable increase in travel time implied, a problem that is exacerbated in the larger urban areas (Fitton 1976).

Given this locational context of near-urban parks and the variety of possible outdoor recreational experiences, it is not surprising to find that their advocates suggest multiple functions. Among such functions we find the provision of a diversity of recreational opportunities, the preservation of natural landscape elements, the integration of historically and educationally important sites into a park setting, and their integration with broader open-space policies within the dispersed part of the regional city.

With so many functions possible, it is inevitable that dilemmas are posed in terms of the compatibility of, e.g., preserving natural environment elements and catering to very intensive use of such a park. However, given areas of sufficient size, e.g. the 800 ha site of Bronte Creek Provincial Park near Hamilton, Ontario, it seems possible to design an overall facility that contains elements both of the intensively used facilities characteristic of many urban parks, e.g. playgrounds, swimming pools and other sports facilities, and the characteristics of the more remote 'wilderness' type of parks, as well as providing for those activities that simply need lots of space, e.g. cross-country skiing, cycling, and so forth. This obviously involves intensive land management within the park perimeter, especially keeping more sensitive zones away from intensively used and travelled areas. Thus, near-urban parks almost invariably would contain elements that are not 'rural' and they are much more intensive than the Country Parks which have been promoted under the Countryside Commission in England and Wales since 1968; in this sense, they do not fit well the conventional image of green belts and unadulterated countryside (Standing Conference 1976).

Near-urban parks obviously have great potential – especially at a time when increased desires for outdoor recreational opportunities and more leisure time may be tempered by rapidly rising petrol and transport costs. However, these near-urban parks represent only one type of recreational opportunity which complements other opportunities, e.g. the linear recreational opportunities offered by rehabilitated canal networks such as the Chesapeake and Ohio networks in the eastern US, and the possibilities of utilizing smaller sites, e.g. abandoned sand-and-gravel pits or small roadside woodlots, as wayside picnic spots (McLellan, Yundt and Dorfman 1979). Furthermore, while near-urban parks may serve as a 'honeypot' in focusing demand, thus relieving some of the pressures that are otherwise created on the open countryside (Fitton 1976), these parks cannot provide a substitute outdoor recreational experience for everyone, and demands of one kind or another will continue to be placed on privately owned land.

Farmland and recreation in the city's countryside

The land in the city's countryside, although mainly farmland, has an important role to play in providing for recreational opportunities. This land is often scenically attractive and it has been suggested that the 'domesticated' character of agricultural landscapes may be more appealing to many people who may feel 'threatened' by a wilderness landscape (Ironside 1971); even land that is not absolutely of tremendous scenic value may nonetheless acquire substantial value as an amenity resource because of the heightened values conferred by accessibility considerations. Furthermore, from the recreational perspective, the combination of open spaces and scrubland, floodplain zones and woodlots which are not vital to farming activities, have the potential of being incorporated into a general recreational plan, particularly when some trail or footpath network though the countryside is involved. And from the agricultural perspective, some activities may generate additional income for the farmer, although we must not exaggerate the magnitude of such benefits.

Even though it was not directed towards farmland in the city's countryside, this latter perspective encouraged people involved in rural and agricultural development to think of recreational enterprises as heralding a solution for low-income farmers. Several manuals were published on how to develop rural areas for recreation (e.g. Smith, Partain and Champlain 1966). Farm vacations, leasing permits for hunting and fishing, horseback-riding facilities and snowmobiling were among the many enterprises seen as capable of supplementing farm income while maintaining the integrity of the farming enterprise. However, the employment and income potential of many of these recreational enterprises has subsequently been questioned (e.g. Burton 1967b), although the ingredients for success of certain activities are more likely to be encountered in the city's countryside. Overall, though, it is more realistic to think of farmland as having a more important role to play in the supply of opportunities that generally do not entail payment for access to the land.

However, the potential role for farmland in this respect has not been fully realized, because of the existence of difficult questions, relating to trespass, liabilities and compensation (Cullington 1979), most of which relate to attitudes held towards accessing privately owned land for recreational activities. These attitudes differ widely internationally, depending upon the particular historical and legal situation. Cullington (1980) identifies Sweden and Norway as classic examples of countries where the use of private land for recreation is accepted. In both these countries, access to private land is accepted, provided no damage occurs and the land owner's 'personal space' is not infringed upon. On the farmer's side, the farmer must not erect fences or obstruct this movement unless there is a recognized and justifiable purpose for such fences (Lambden 1975). The emphasis is thus on people's common sense not to cause damage or enter areas where they would be unwelcome. In the UK, Scottish attitudes owe much to Viking and Nordic traditions and although Cullington (1980) argues that Scottish attitudes are slightly more restrictive than in Scandinavia, the public use of private land for recreational purposes, excepting for such activities as hunting and fishing, is well entrenched in recreational behaviour.

In England and Wales, while there are slightly more constraints, public access to private land is still a major part of the recreational scene. The tradition of access to private land dates from pre-Norman times, and one of the most remarkable assets is the network of footpaths that evolved before the eleventh century, a network that was formalized under the 1949 National Parks and Access to the Countryside Act. As a result of this legislation, maps were developed that now show uncontested routes, which land owners must not obstruct.

The same Act set up the National Parks of England and Wales, which contain large areas of private land; while these parks were not conceived initially in terms of recreational opportunities in the city's countryside, some of them serve this function by virtue of their location, e.g. the Peak District Park adjacent to Sheffield (Strachan 1974). The *de facto* as opposed to *de jure* access enjoyed by the public to these areas shows the importance attached to public access and use of private land in England and Wales, even though the problems of multiple use of such land in an urban-fringe context are much greater than elsewhere. It is against this legacy of attitudes and action with respect to access to private land in the UK that the work of the Countryside Commission, set up by the 1968 Countryside Act, in urban-fringe areas must be viewed (see Ch. 12). In the North American context, such attitudes are not part of the cultural heritage generally, and trespass laws relating to liability have sometimes been regarded as a major deterrent to land owners in permitting access to their lands, e.g. in Ontario until 1980 (Cullington 1980). Such problems underlie the difficulties associated with establishing *de facto* access to privately owned land in the city's countryside, where the potential for conflicts is so much greater owing to the intensity of demand, e.g. the difficulties encountered in maintaining the voluntary Bruce Trail along the Niagara Escarpment in southern Ontario, which passes through several cities' countrysides.

Of course, if public access to private land is deemed a significant issue then questions of compensation arise. Clearly, however well intentioned the average user, some damage seems inevitable; furthermore, permitting access more freely may entail costs in any case, e.g. special fences or gates, as might maintenance of particular landscape features. We are not able to tackle these thorny compensation issues in this book, but it is worth while noting that potentially compensation can take several forms, e.g. awards for claims against damages incurred, financial incentives for landscape maintenance including negative rents that could be paid farmers and manipulation of the taxation system (Davidson and Wibberley 1977).

The entrepreneurial approach

We have not as yet examined the role of commercial recreational enterprises. Most contemporary statements agree first with the assumption that the 'dark horse' of the past – urban-fringe recreation – will demand greater attention in the future. But the second issue is what role the private commercial sector has to play.

Even a casual look at the past reveals that some entrepreneurs have been responding to changing demands and initiating recreation opportunities. There is a great variety in the scale and type of commercial recreational enterprises, from the golf course and horse-riding enterprise, to the restaurant with a few added amusement attractions, to the safari parks and their often associated amusement area, to the large-scale Disney-type attraction. At the lower end of the scale, we might find some of the enterprises run by farmers that were mentioned at the beginning of the last section, or the fish-farm run with relatively little capital and small areas of land. At the upper end of the scale, large areas of land with a high degree of accessibility are required, not to mention large capital requirements. Urban locations can no longer provide suitable venues because of space needs and land costs for such large-scale endeavours, but the conflict-prone urban fringe seems an ideal location. Marinelands, safari zoos and, more recently in North America particularly, 'theme' parks are all typical examples. The theme parks range from a water base, e.g. Sea World in Florida, to country music, e.g. Opryland, Tennessee.

In terms of the large-scale enterprise, perhaps the Disney Corporation has been the most successful – and the most extreme. The wonderland atmosphere, the integration of cinema imagination and the opportunity for real-life adventures have seen Disneyland develop on the edge of Los Angeles and then in 'urban-fringe Florida'; these have probably become two of the most popular recreation sites in the world. New large-scale assemblies of land for medieval theme parks, Star Wars theme parks or multiple theme parks are being developed in urban-fringe locations ranging from Maple, 20 km north of Toronto, to Warwick Castle in the urban midlands of England. New technology is constantly improving and diversifying the themes of these parks. Audio animatronics, lasers, highly sophisticated robots and machines, medieval worlds and Star Wars – the attractions in near-urban theme parks that distract the visitor from today's problems are only at an embryonic stage.

In the context of the Western world, government involvement in such activities is probably more appropriately kept to the area of the monitoring of health and safety standards and ensuring the integration of such developments in the broader regional setting. The recreation opportunities provided by the Disney Corporation seem to show that large corporate structures are capable of providing for public enjoyment with a minimum of stimulation or overseeing from government. And if Fitton's tentative conclusions (1976) about the needs of the less privileged classes of society are correct, there may be more benefits from these intensive urban-type parks and their publicly provided cousins, the near-urban park, than any amount of attention to broader landscape amenity considerations and the wide-open, out-of-doors experience. Or is this an elitist comment? Yet Davidson and Wibberley's comment (1977) that recreation policies have for long been dominated by resource protection concerns and the preservation of fine landscapes to the detriment of urban-fringe recreation where the need for variety may be greater, lends some credence to such a perspective.

It should be clear that recreational activities in the city's countryside are tremendously varied, both in terms of the demands they place on the environment and in terms of the appropriate means of supplying the opportunities. Unlike the production activities, e.g. agriculture, industry and commerce, which are dominated by private-sector involvement, and the residential activity phenomenon which is also dominated by the private sector both in demand and supply, our discussion of recreational activities shows a mix of formal and informal private-sector and formal public-sector involvement on the supply side. This mixture is partly because the activities differ enormously in terms of their land-space needs and the degree of management needed of that space, and partly because the provision of some recreational needs would not be fulfilled through a market system, e.g. landscape amenity and preservation of natural environment elements.

Further reading

Fitton, M. (1976) The urban fringe and the less privileged, *Countryside Recreation Review*, **1**, 25–34.

9 Infrastructure and institutions

The land-use activities discussed so far have been largely private-sector activities, with the exception of some recreational facilities, discussed in the previous chapter. There are also several other land uses or activities that exhibit a strong involvement by the public sector, e.g. communication infrastructure, utility networks, and hospitals and educational facilities. In some countries, the public sector has become dominant in all areas, including telephone communications, e.g. the UK and France, while in other places, a mixture of private and public involvement is common, e.g. in Canada, where the telephone system is dominated by the large Bell Corporation whose operations are nonetheless subjected to considerable public scrutiny, while for utilities such as natural gas distribution, municipalities sometimes own the distribution network and sell the gas to the consumer and sometimes a gas company sells direct to the consumer. In the US, on the other hand, utilities such as gas, electricity and telephone are dominated by privately owned utilities (Clawson and Hall 1973).

Two basic types of land uses are considered in this chapter. First, there are uses that *facilitate* interaction and are represented by various types of networks composed of linear and nodal elements. One example, the highway network, underlies the very existence and development of the regional city while others serve as life-lines in other respects to urban areas, e.g. energy transmission lines, pipelines, railways, airports and marshalling yards. Second, there are activities that are concentrated in space, i.e. can be regarded as occupying point-type locations or are discrete. There is some overlap between these activities and the nodes within the networks of the first land-use type, e.g. airports. It is possible to call upon a similar range of factors as that used to explain the dispersal of industry and commerce to account for the development of some of these diverse activities, e.g. educational complexes, research facilities and sanitary landfill sites, in the city's countryside.

Networks and interaction in the city's countryside

Transportion

Changes in transportation technology in terms of the automobile and the development of the highway network have combined to produce the essential condition that has permitted the expansion of the regional city form – dispersal of residence, industry and, to a lesser extent, commercial activities. Transportation networks both facilitate and institutionalize interaction, as well as help direct it.

The road network development and associated changes in people's means of transport are essential to understanding the regional city form, although for the larger metropolitan regions, commuter trains and subway extensions have also been of key importance in leading to the expansion of certain nodes in the city's countryside, e.g. around London, Paris, New York and Toronto. Even in such large metropolitan areas where it has been possible to introduce rapid intra-regional transit systems, e.g. in the Paris region, concern has been expressed by the continuing move towards the private automobile (IAURIP 1972). In a survey of 3,000 job holders in 1968 in the Paris region, 30 per cent were found to have changed their means of transport in getting to work in the previous 10 years; 26 per cent of those changing had switched from public transport to private car while only 7 per cent involved a move from private car to public transport. Flexibility, comfort and rationalizing purchase of a car for other motives were among reasons given to explain the net shift to the private automobile. Interestingly enough, this survey did not show any great differences in terms of types of changes between those who had been affected by a change in the workplace – residence link and those who had not changed either workplace or place of residence. Finally, public investment in highway construction has certainly not impeded this move to the automobile, a point that Raup (1975) has made as well for the US.

It is useful to distinguish communication networks at three different scales, related to different geographic scales of interaction, viz. local, intra-regional and interregional. There are often important linking nodes between the different scale levels, e.g. the airport between interregional air routes and intra-regional road and rail networks; the commuter train station and the local highway network; and the expressway interchange between the intra-regional and local highway networks. An important feature of transportation networks is the density of the different scales of network in the city's countryside. Particularly at the intra- and interregional scales, there is a focusing of networks on urban areas, and thus an increasing density in the city's countryside. A glance at any highway map demonstrates this. Furthermore, both the space needs of modern highways (e.g. even a local road in North America of 30 m in total width takes up 3 ha for every kilometre) and the need to service demand for interaction places the city's countryside, especially the inner fringe, in a vulnerable position *vis-à-vis* new road construction; witness the ring roads around many North American cities, e.g. Minneapolis – St Paul, St Louis and Boston. Thus, transportation networks are important in the overall structure of the regional city and are important land uses in the city's countryside, as well as having a number of important effects (see below).

Certain key nodes in transportation networks are also found in the city's countryside, because of being attracted to the urban concentrations of demand as well as being in need of significant areas of land. The railway marshalling yards of Trappes, south-west of Versailles in the Paris region, are a good case in point, serving as a key integrating node between the national French rail network and the regional network for goods movements. Without a doubt, however, the most spectacular and probably the most debated example of the transportation nodal-type of land use in the city's countryside is the airport. Apart from private airstrips, airports are attracted to urban centres of demand, the origins and destinations of most trips, but need extensive space as well as needing to avoid built-up zones for reasons of public safety. Quite apart from any attractive influence they may have on other land uses, airports exert an influence on land use far in excess of the land needed for facilities and runways; because of public safety factors, severe restrictions on building may be made in aircraft flight-path zones.

Proposals for new airports or extensions to existing ones are usually faced with a barrage of protests from one quarter or another, leading frequently to protracted discussions and hearings – a good example of which was the debate over the proposed Third London Airport (Roskill Commission 1970). Sometimes it is an agricultural land-preservation lobby, sometimes it is a protest by residents affected by the proximity of the airport site. Indeed, one of the problems facing many existing airports is the fact that prescriptive measures against building in *non aedificandi* zones have often been waived or enforced but loosely. Consequently, airport authorities faced with a need for expansion have often met opposition from the population of adjacent development which has been allowed despite the prior existence of an airport. The discussions surrounding the extension of Malton Airport, Toronto, in the 1970's and the subsequent abortive attempt to create a new airport at Pickering bear witness to the range of issues that extensions and new airport proposals almost inevitably engender. A major problem in terms of the regional city, and even broader urban regions, is the fact that while a new site seems to be a logical solution when extensions of existing facilities meet with stiff resistance, areas within most urban regions where population densities are low over large areas are rare. Almost any site will produce some resistance from local populations.

The land area required for airports is substantial, underlying the difficulties of finding suitable sites. For example, the proposed site of the new Toronto International Airport at Pickering involved the expropriation of close to 7,300 ha of land and another 16,000 ha were 'frozen' in aircraft flight paths, and Mirabel Airport close to Montréal occupies some 35,000 ha (Porter 1977). The location of the most recent Paris airport, the Aéroport de Charles de Gaulle, north-east of Paris, is one of the exceptions that proves the rule, because it involved an area of very low population density. The site is only about 27 km from the centre of Paris, and only 12 km from the old airport of Le Bourget which had become increasingly urban-bound by the late 1950's. Yet the expropriations for the approximately 3,000 ha that began in 1966 did not encroach upon any settlement, and only one set of farm buildings was removed. The surrounding settlements were mostly small except for a few that had grown due to the presence of commuter train services, and the area had been dominated by large-scale field agriculture right up to the airport's arrival (Bryant 1973a). This site was thus close to Paris, with a low population density and with physical characteristics that facilitated construction and engineering; indeed, even back in 1946, when the agency in charge of planning, running and developing all civil aviation facilities within 50 km of Paris was created, the agency was charged with studying the feasibility of a new airport site in this area when the need arose (Aéroport de Paris 1971).

Utility networks

There are many types of utility networks such as natural gas and water pipelines, hydro or electricity networks and sewage collection networks. Again, it is worth noting the variety of scales at which these networks can exist. At the local or intra-regional level, networks for water distribution, sewage collection, electricity and gas distribution are important in that where the public sector controls them, there is an opportunity to use them to shape urban development. This has not been generally the case in the US, though (Clawson and Hall 1973). At the interregional scale, electricity transmission lines and natural gas pipelines link intra-regional subsystems into the broader networks of bulk transmission of energy. Again, important nodes exist in these networks, either at the source of the product being transmitted (e.g. a thermal electricity generating station or a water well), at the destination of a product being collected (e.g. a sewage treatment plant), or at links between networks of different scales (e.g. electricity substations or switching stations). The focus in this short section is on electricity transmission networks.

As electricity transmission technology has developed, electricity transmission lines have become physically larger and have increasingly made an impact on the landscape. Because the final destination is the consumer – households, industries, institutions and their supporting infrastructure – there is a natural convergence of such lines on urban areas through the city's countryside. While hydroelectric power stations are constrained in terms of sites by the presence of physical environment features, thermal generating stations have a natural attraction for urban areas, and certainly in the early days, this led to the construction of many coal-fired thermal stations close to, or in, urban areas. At the same time, modern thermal generating stations require large quantitites of water for cooling purposes (Porter 1977). Thus, in Ontario, all planned and existing thermal generating stations are sited at water bodies. Furthermore, with the more recent nuclear stations, additional factors of public safety and concern have to be taken into account by the planners of transmission systems; it is clear from the Three Mile Island incident in 1979 that public awareness of the fallibility of technology has been increased. Despite the apparent dangers though, some nuclear stations are sited close to major centres of demand, e.g. Pickering near Toronto, while other more remote ones are being suggested as potentially capable of attracting industrial development, e.g. Douglas Point on Lake Huron.

It is not so much the land-space requirements that are significant for electricity transmission systems, as the range of impacts they can have. The whole of the Ontario Hydro Bulk Transmission system is estimated as involving only 73,000 ha of land (Porter 1977), contrasting with the total land area of Ontario of just over 89 million ha. Yet locally, where lines converge, significant areas can be affected, even though the area of direct purchase by an electricity supply agency may be absolutely small. Where generating stations or substations are involved, descrete areas of varying sizes are involved ranging from the 930 ha of the Bruce Nuclear Power Development (plus the adjacent 9,300 ha subject to regulation of population development) in Ontario (Porter 1977), to the 20 ha area of a 400 kV substation in the UK grid, to a few square metres for a low-voltage substation (Essex County Council 1976). When several utility networks are considered, together with transportation networks, it is obvious that their collective impact on landscape and other activities could be considerable, even from the perspective of landscape requirements. Obviously, concentrating the linear components of various networks into the same corridor can reduce the total area involved or affected, e.g. 'utilidors' or corridors with several utility networks combined, or 'communication corridors' which include transportation networks too. An example of the latter is illustrated in the Standing Conference (1976) report on the London Green Belt.

Impacts of networks in the city's countryside

Apart from the land requirements of the various networks identified above and the impact this may have on land resource inventories, there are other impacts that may affect economic activities, cultural values and especially amenity considerations and land prices. First, these networks may modify the shape of development of the urban form. At one level, the availability of trunk service facilities – water, gas, electricity – can be an important factor in guiding the expansion of the urban area. More importantly, changes to transportation networks affect accessibility patterns and thus help shape the overall regional city form. Key nodal points in transportation networks may also attract clusters of other economic activities, thus serving to create a greater dispersal of employment nodes in the regional city. Airports are good examples, and the clustering not only of hotels and restaurants, but of various industries close to airports serves to illustrate the complex and interacting effects on other economic activities of new airports, and the inevitable changes in road or rail networks that accompany them. The 'barrier' effect of certain communication corridors, e.g. a limited access highway, can also be used positively in shaping the urban form by using them to reduce accessibility in some directions while increasing it in others.

A major impact derives essentially from the linear nature of networks, i.e. fragmentation of the landscape. Fragmentation has many ramifications. First, transportation links can affect agricultural operations negatively (see Ch. 6). New roads, road widening and upgrading of road quality can all lead to greater effective separation between farmstead and fields, problems which are likely to be greater in the urban fringe than elsewhere (Paton, Smith and Gram 1973). Similarly, electricity transmission lines have been commonly regarded as leading to greater costs of farm operation in the right-of-way paths (Priddle *et al.* 1976); the real magnitude of these effects, though, is difficult to determine and thus the whole issue of just compensation is equally difficult. Various solutions to the 'barrier' effect of roads particularly have been tried, e.g. creation of underpasses or overpasses for farm traffic, the redistribution of land between farmers on either side of a new highway to reduce or eliminate the need to cross the highway, or failing this, outright compensation or purchase of the entire farm property. The legislation in France that outlines the obligations of an expropriating agency to farmers provides a good idea of the range of possible forms of compensation (e.g. Bryant 1975).

Another major impact of fragmentation involves the effect of networks on cultural values, especially amenity considerations. Communication corridors tend to attract other uses to them and so the impact of communication corridors on landscape amenity can be considerable at the subregional level. In an analysis of 'damaged' and 'threatened' landscapes in London's Green Belt (Standing Conference 1976), a very high correlation was found between 'damaged' landscapes and the communication corridors that have developed along the river valleys of the Thames and its tributaries; and several of the areas of 'threatened' landscape also coincided with communication corridors. Public utilities were identified as a major factor in areas of damaged landscapes, with overhead electricity transmission lines being a general problem especially where they are concentrated near switching stations.

Responses to such problems include ensuring the problem is concentrated, e.g. concentration of as many linear components in the same corridor as possible, as well as taking care to integrate features such as high-voltage electricity transmission lines into the surrounding landscape. The 1957 Electricity Act of the UK, section 37, requires for instance that the various agencies involved in the planning of transmission routes and substations (Essex County Council 1976: 4): 'take into account any effect which the proposals would have on the natural beauty of the Countryside or on any such flora, fauna, features, buildings or objects' that are of special natural, architectural or historic interest. In the case of electricity transmission, placing cables underground would certainly reduce substantially or eliminate many of the amenity problems in the long term; however, cost considerations remain prohibitive (Porter 1977), the ratio of costs of placing cables underground to overhead lines cited in one UK report ranging from 17 to 1 for 400 kV lines, 12 to 1 for 132 kV lines, down to 2.5 to 1 for low-voltage lines (Essex County Council 1976).

Effects on land values are complex. Accessibility is affected by changes in transportation networks; the positive relationship between accessibility and land values has been discussed earlier (Ch. 4). Another area of potential impact of networks on land values is through the impact on landscape amenity. Protests against electricity transmission lines frequently involves the question of lowering of land values. However, evidence is sparse. In one study (Priddle *et al.* 1976) in which a corridor of land along a 230 kV line in southern Ontario near an urban area was analysed and compared to a parallel corridor of land 1 mile distant from the transmission corridor, no significant differences were found in land transactions (number and type) or land values between the two corridors. The period of analysis of the real-estate data was approximately 15 to 20 years from the date of construction of the line. The conclusion was that the *long-term* effects of this transmission line on land values were negligible to non-existent and that a distinction must be made between short- and long-term effects. In the short term, disturbance in the land market may be substantial but in the long term people adapt and get used to the transmission corridor. This perspective was confirmed in the same study by a survey of residents in both the transmission and the control corridor; indeed, it appeared that the control group was more negatively disposed to the transmission line than those living in the transmission corridor. Of course, the fact that this study was of a single, isolated transmission corridor puts it into a different situation compared to a landscape where several transmission corridors are visible. The configuration of the natural environment would also be of importance presumably in allowing amenity disturbances to be reduced by careful site planning.

Other infrastructural and institutional uses

There are a variety of other activities that are part of the essential infrastructural and institutional framework, ranging from various utilities such as sewage works and sanitary landfill sites to social institutions such as educational and administrative complexes. Some have been attracted to suburban locations and locations in the city's countryside because they need large areas of land while at the same time requiring access to the urban centre or other extra-regional urban centres. Examples include: the campus of the recent University of East Anglia, located on the urban periphery of Norwich, UK, the governmental and university research complex on the Plateau de Saclay on the southern inner fringe of Paris, France, which includes the Centre d'études nucléaires de Saclay and the Centre d'essai des propulseurs as well as several other research institutes (Délégation Générale au District de la Région de Paris 1966); the government and commercial research laboratories in the Washington, DC, area (Hoover 1971); various hospital and administrative complexes; and certain military installations. Other space users that are found in some fringes include cemeteries, especially the private memorial gardens type in which a quiet and pleasant landscape is provided and which are close enough to urban areas for the visiting public; and reservoirs which also often serve several functions including recreation.

Finally, some public uses are 'pushed' out of the urban areas because, just like the sand-and-gravel industry and the auto-wrecking yards, they are 'unwanted'. Locations in the city's countryside represent the path of least resistance. Examples include sewage works and garbage dumps or rubbish tips. Negative externalities are associated with such uses, including pollution problems, potential health hazards and amenity impacts (e.g. aesthetic impact on landscape and odour problems). In the case of garbage dumps and rubbish tips, both planned and unplanned sites may exist. Unplanned cases sometimes reflect lack of property upkeep attracting unofficial dumping; there will undoubtedly always be problems of unlawful dumping of garbage. As the Countryside Commission (1976:30) of the UK put it semi-facetiously: 'The erection of "No Tipping" notices... seems positively to encourage further tipping!'. Planned garbage-disposal sites, or sanitary landfill sites, often generate protests because of the negative externalities involved, especially when toxic waste materials are concerned. Public concern has increased because it has become clear that the history of waste disposal, especially of toxic and dangerous substances, illustrates how inadequate past precautions, if any, have been, e.g. the Love Canal case in Niagara Falls, New York where residential development had occurred in an area in which a trench, an abandoned canal, had been filled with some 20 000 tons of toxic wastes during the 1940s and early 1950s; by the late 70s, seepage had occurred which was eventually linked to various birth defects and serious ailments (Barbarel, 1981). It is clear that a great deal still remains to be learned. It is not surprising, then, that proposals for waste disposal meet with stiff local opposition; a good example has been the recent and ongoing controversy over the Ontario government proposal to use land at South Cayuga, south of Hamilton, that had previously been purchased for a new town that never materialized, as a collection and disposal site for hazardous liquid wastes. It is to be hoped that dealing with the 'mistakes of the past' will provide essential technological experience that can be applied to contemporary proposals.

Summary

The various types of activities that have been considered above under the general rubric of infrastructure and institutions add to the complexity of land uses and activities in the city's countryside. Just because these uses are often organized within the public sector does not mean that their impacts are likely to be any less important. Indeed, because they are often part of the public sector, some problems related to the negative externalities sometimes associated with such uses are brought more sharply into focus. In particular, questions are raised of the moral obligation of the public sector towards the adjacent and previous users and uses that are affected by proposals for new public infrastructure and institutional projects. Clearly, some of the proposals, if not all, are pursued because they are seen as benefiting society generally; at the same time, however, some minority (the local people) is being asked to bear some of the costs involved. This issue is particularly signficant when compulsory purchase is used to acquire the land. Its solution requires a clear identification of priorities, of who pays and who benefits, and might logically involve a whole variety of different types of compensation (see, e.g., Bryant 1975). Our consideration of these frequently publicly provided and controlled uses has thus brought us explicitly into the area of allocation of land between different users and uses. Part III of this book is therefore devoted to a consideration of land management, the issues and the approaches, in the city's countryside.

Further reading

Hoover, E. M. (1971) *An Introduction to Regional Economics* (1st ed), A. A. Knopf, New York.

III Land management in the city's countryside

Introduction

In Parts I and II, the various dimensions, activities and changes occurring within the city's countryside were identified and the 'problems' associated with these changes noted. Next our attention is turned to the issues of management or control of such processes.

It is in keeping with our general view of the city's countryside that *land management* is dealt with in a separate part of this book, rather than treating the problem in turn with each of the specific activities. This is a specific recognition of the systems nature of the complex interrelationships between activities within the city's countryside, and of the fact that management aimed at any one activity is bound to affect other activities. Unfortunately, management has not been characterized by a holistic and regional approach, but rather has often been single activity-oriented.

In Chapter 10, as a prelude to considering land-use management, the various functions that land can perform are discussed. In Chapter 11, a link is made between the geographic structure of the problems that land-use management has to contend with and the geographic structure of the regional city form, while the formal management structures within which solutions are attempted forms the basis of the rest of the chapter. In Chapter 12, the various concerns of land-use management that are important in the city's countryside are discussed, along with the types of tools or approaches that have been used. Finally, in Chapter 13 we offer some conclusions relating to our state of knowledge of the processes and problems involved in the evolving settlement form around our cities, to the urgency of certain of the land resource use conflicts and to certain possible future directions.

10 Land use, function and open space in the city's countryside

The discussion in Part II has centred on various land uses involving the cultural environment (e.g. country residential development) and the economic environment (e.g. industry and agriculture). The field of land-use planning, management and control is, however, concerned with much more than the physical use to which land is put. Planning, by its very nature, is concerned with the future and the broader functions which land can be called upon to perform for society. The argument is made below that a consideration of the functions of land provides a better key to understanding planning strategies than does a consideration of land uses. It is with this in mind that the focus in this chapter is upon 'open space' because the major part of planning considerations in the city's countryside deals with unbuilt-on land and with manipulating the pattern in which the functions of that 'open space' evolve, be they ultimately oriented towards a built environment or the maintenance of 'rural' uses.

The need for management

In Chapter 2, a conceptual framework of the city's countryside was introduced, involving a breakdown of the environment into its various dimensions – natural, economic and cultural. At the intersection of these dimensions can be seen the current landscape and all of the changes and processes occurring within it. The emergence of 'problems' arises from actual and potential conflicts in *values* attached to the elements in these various dimensions. A set of decisions to transform the use or function of a resource or piece of land may be perfectly rational on the basis of one set of values but quite unjustified from another perspective, e.g. the decisions of a builder to buy land and develop against an agricultural conservationist perspective; or the decision to expand a sand-and-gravel operation against a lobby concerned with maintaining safety on roads (against truck traffic) and keeping noise levels to a minimum; or the decision to create a reservoir against a desire to maintain agriculture or an area conducive to the preservation of wild fowl.

Frequently, of course, the situation *seems* to be one in which some *private rationality* based on *individual economic gain* is set against some more *collective rationality* based on *collective economic gain* or some *non-economic values*. But the situation is not as easy as that. It might be a simpler world if our planning problems involved a direct confrontation between a private and a collective rationality! In reality, it is difficult to conceive of a single collective perspective, except perhaps in some form of Utopian world. Many conflicts exist at the so-called collective level – in the debate concerning the reservoir versus the conservation of agricultural land, for instance, collective rationality can be, and is, used to defend both perspectives. The notion of 'collectivity' also lacks precision; for example, a local taxpayers' association fighting to protect the 'environment' (the local environment) against further development may use collective rationality – the 'good' of the area as a whole – against the developer who although also defending his private enterprise, may call upon collective rationality – the satisfaction of a need for housing – to justify development. And the private rationality used by an industrial enterprise for its expansion (e.g. a sand-and-gravel pit operation) may be supported by an equally pressing collective perspective (e.g. the need for construction materials at relatively low costs).

Thus, we are confronted with a situation of an environment containing various resources, each possessing a range of potential and actual uses or functions, and each associated with different values assigned by individuals, groups, and various formal government structures. It is not surprising, then, that conflicts develop, and that the need to resolve them has been felt and recognized. It is also not surprising that the responsibility for dealing with such conflicts should have fallen mainly upon formal government structures to various degrees. This in itself has not been without its problems, for formal government structures have hardly formed a coherent front, being divided geographically, hierarchically and in terms of activity and, furthermore, government can hardly be said to have been an unbiased arbitrator in the resolution of conflicts, being frequently one of the main contenders in the battle!

Use, function and incompatibilities

In the hierarchy of concerns that planning deals with, the *function(s)* of the land resource occupy a key position because function can be most readily identified with the goals of society. Given the priorities that a planning process elaborates, be it on the basis of a broadly based sampling of public opinion or of a more technocratically determined ordering, a logical step is the assignment of broad functions to zones within the particular jurisdiction, e.g. agricultural production, aggregate mineral production, amenity, residential development and so forth. The *use* of land can thus be seen as subsidiary to the *function* of the land; the important point then from a management or planning perspective is that use must be compatible with function.

Let us elaborate. First, the simplest case, is where the physical use of the land is closely identified with the function; hence, agricultural activities (perhaps of specified type' would be closely identified with an assigned agricultural production function. A second case is where a use must be compatible with the assigned function; for example, let us assume that a floodplain zone has been identified as a 'flood hazard zone' in which the main function is to reduce potential damage to both private and public property. Agricultural activities can thus be seen as compatible with the hazard zone designation, as long as structures are not erected which would impede water movement, increase floodwater velocity and thereby increase damage to other necessary structures, such as bridges and roads, as well as increasing erosion potential. Another similar situation is where the main function of a zone has been identified as a scenic or amenity function, e.g. parts of the Niagara Escarpment in southern Ontario (Gertler 1968) or the deeply incised valley of the Biévre south of Paris (Préfecture de la Région d'-Ile-de-France 1976b). Under certain circumstances, agricultural uses could be viewed as entirely compatible with the amenity function of an area, though this might not extend to modern farm buildings and greenhouses, and even certain types of residential development with architectural control over design, materials and tones could be compatible. The third general situation is where a specific use is definitely incompatible with an assigned function, e.g. residential development on top of a significant aggregate mineral resource.

Therefore, identifying the level of compatibility between uses and functions would seem logically to be an important step in a planning process. And to the extent that a parcel of land or an area can perform several functions, all of which are desired, then one must also establish the level of compatibility between different functions. Yet it is no easy matter to establish the real magnitude of compatibility levels between uses and functions, meaning, in effect, that it is by no means easy to establish the degree of conflict between competing uses and functions.

Why is this so? The answer is to be found in the fact that most, if not all, incompatibilities have a *culturally based* origin. While it is conceivable that certain incompatibilities are absolute and have a quantifiable and technical basis, e.g. construction of buildings and effect on floodwater movement in a floodplain or intensive livestock production and health hazards, even these are affected by cultural values in the sense that 'minimum standards' or what people are willing to accept as tolerable varies from place to place. Other types of incompatibilities have an even stronger cultural basis, e.g. the potential incompatibility between the effects of farm operations such as odour and dust and country residential development. This is important, for it implies that questions involving solutions such as multiple use, sequential use and the setting of minimum standards are all subject to change as values are modified. It also, of course, indicates the potential for changing certain values through education and public information and awareness programmes.

Open space

Classification of open space

The term 'open space' means different things to different people (Platt 1972). On the one hand, it can be simply equated with unbuilt-on land which can include both man-made landscapes (e.g. gardens, golf courses, agricultural landscapes) and natural landscapes (e.g. wilderness areas, forest land). Even though some French studies have used the term *espaces naturels* (Latarjet 1972), it is clear that the dominant type of landscape involved is in fact man-made. The definition of open space as unbuilt-on land is not a particularly useful perspective except in so far as it represents a generous definition of all types of open space. It is, of course, possible to classify open space on the basis of activity (agricultural, managed woodland, etc.) or form (large or small, compact or irregular, etc.), but function of open space is a more appropriate basis for our purposes. In terms of functions, open space has often been regarded as land having amenity value. Thus, Williams (1969:17) cites the US federal definition of open space that was contained in the 1961 Housing Act (75 Stat. 149, Title VII, Section 706) as: 'any undeveloped or predominantly undeveloped land in an urban area which has value for (A) park and recreation purposes, (B) conservation of land and other natural resources, or (C) historic or scenic purposes'.

This amenity and conservation perspective on open space is useful in so far as it reflects certain potential functions of land. However, they represent only some of the functions; and various authors have identified a broader range of functions for open space. Clawson (1969) identifies five open-space functions: the provision of light and air to buildings; space to relieve a sense of crowding; recreation; ecological functions; and city-forming functions (shaping of the urban area). Williams's (1969) classification of open space is more detailed and at the same time easier to integrate with the conceptual frameworks that we have utilized for the city's countryside – the three-dimensional environment and the regional city. Each of Williams's six functions (Williams 1969:18–19) contains several classes and subclasses; the six functions are:

1 open space for managed resource production (such as forestry, agriculture, mineral production and water supply), i.e. functions involving activities that are primarily located in the production environment;
2 open space for the preservation of natural and human resources (such as sites of particular geological, biological or cultural values), i.e. functions involving values especially in the natural environment–cultural environment intersection and the cultural environment generally;
3 open space for health, welfare and well-being, involving both 'protection' functions (maintenance of groundwater quality, sanitary landfill functions), 'play' functions (parks, amenity value) and design functions (shaping of urban morphology);

4 open space for public safety, including 'protection functions' against natural hazards (flood control, landslide areas, fires) and man-made hazards (flight paths of aircraft);
5 open space for corridors, involving networks of utilities and transportation;
6 open space for urban expansion.

In an applied context a recent planning study of a rural–urban fringe municipality (Clackamas County, Portland, Oregon), five of these functions were identified in slightly different terms within a framework of priorities (Clackamas County 1980).The primary open-space function was identified as one of satisfying demand for active and passive recreation. Secondary open-space functions were then identified as protection from natural hazards, conservation of critical finite natural resources (farm and forest land), providing an edge for urban development and satisfaction of psychological needs for space. Obviously a particular parcel of land may fulfil more than one function.

An explicit integration of functions and planning considerations is provided in a French study (Latarjet 1972) in which a two-step, hierarchical classification of open spaces in terms of first, broad functions, and second, planning objectives is developed. The functions and objectives are given in Table 10.1.

Table 10.1 Functions and objectives of open space

Functions	*Objectives*
1. Recreational	(a) development of sports complexes
	(b) development of recreational complexes
	(c) encouragement of hiking and other 'diffuse' recreational activities
	(d) permit urbanites access to landscapes and natural resource areas
2. Ecological	(a) management of natural resources and maintenance of natural equilibrium
	(b) management of woodland and outstanding sites
	(c) permit agricultural production in urban fringe zones
3. Spatial organization	(a) maintenance of discontinuous urban form and sharpening of urban/rural landscape contrasts
	(b) creation of land reserves for future infrastructure (e.g. transportation)
	(c) creation of land reserves for unspecified future infrastructure
	(d) increase contact-length between urban and rural areas
	(e) development of land banks to facilitate exchange of land with owners whose initial land is needed for other purposes.

(Source: developed from the text of Latarjet 1972)

It can readily be seen how the functions already noted can be fitted into this system. Obviously, this type of classification becomes quite specific in its objectives since it takes into account particular regional resource configurations and needs. All of these classifications, however, emphasize the multiplicity of roles that open spaces can perform, ranging over the whole spectrum of the values and activities that have been discussed in Parts I and II; hence the use of 'open space' to integrate the activities and the management discussions. While it would appear that interest in the various functions that open space can perform has increased in the past 15 years or so (especially as evidenced by the concern over public welfare, e.g. Williams 1969), this is not really so; witness Platt's discussion (1972) which traces the concept of open space from the Middle Ages onwards. And in the discussion in Chapter 12 where 'green belts' and the like are considered, it becomes apparent that many of the functions we have just attributed to open space were behind, implicitly at least, the creation of various green belts.

Open space and potential

The identification of open-space functions begs the question of how apt is a particular area or environment for fulfilling particular functions, i.e. what is a particular area good for? In terms of planning, this is a critical question; to answer it, an appropriate knowledge, or data base is essential, although this in itself is inadequate for purposes of assigning priorities. Let us take the problem one step at a time.

First, it is possible to take any specific function, e.g. agricultural production and to derive some form of rating system of the 'environment' that will indicate how well that environment will perform that function. In terms of agriculture, a starting point would be an appreciation of the physical quality of the land resource, in terms of soil quality and constraints on cultivation or agricultural management; an example of such data bases is the Canada Land Inventory land capability for agriculture classification (McKeague 1975), similar in most respects to the US capability system (Vining, Plaut and Bieri 1977). However, this in itself is insufficient because other factors affect the potential of an area for supporting viable agriculture (see Ch. 6). Size of total area may be important in terms of the possibility of supporting agricultural infrastructure such as service centres (e.g. Hilchey 1970); level of fragmentation of the farm landscape could be critical; and the existing density of non-farm scattered residential development should also be considered Immediately, the key problem is apparent – most of the criteria which can affect the potential of an area for performing an agricultural production function are *subjective*. The situation becomes even more complex when the state of the existing socioeconomic structure of agricultural production is considered. Clearly, viability of agriculture depends on more than the land resource; people and capital are needed too. Farm size, level of investment, labour supply and many other factors, all can have a bearing upon farm viability and thus must be considered in planning for an area if a pragmatic perspective is taken. At the same time, it is obvious that possible modifications to the socioeconomic structure of production cannot be ignored.

Similarly, it has been argued that one of the prerequisites for rational planning of the sand-and-gravel industry is an adequate data base on the location, quantity and quality of the aggregate resources (Bryant and McLellan 1975b). However, other factors such as nature of adjacent land uses and density of existing residential development affect the real potential of the aggregate resource; again, though, the effects of some of these factors may be modified through changes in attitudes on the part of the public, thus bringing us into the area of subjectivity very explicitly.

One interesting attempt to provide a methodology for evaluating potential of an area is provided by the pre-planning studies that preceded the creation of green belt-like zones (*zones naturelles d'équilibre*) in the Paris region, France (Latarjet 1972). It was suggested that a number of 'fundamental morphological criteria' can be identified which influence the type of function(s) an area can perform and how well the function can be performed. Some of the criteria were based on an analysis of the morphology of open spaces in twenty urban agglomerations around the world, including London (UK), Berlin, Moscow, Rome, Stockholm and Washington. Eight basic morphological criteria were considered important:

1 shape of the area;
2 size of the open space;
3 adjacent development density;
4 degree of openness of the space , e.g. closed versus open spaces;
5 distance from the urban centre;
6 relief;
7 land use;
8 geological–hydrological characteristics.

A ninth criterion was also identified, viz. property structure and land values, but was not utilized in the detailed analysis in this study.

A matrix was then created of the twelve open-space objectives linked to the three broad open-space functions noted on Table 10.1 (see Fig. 10.1); the matrix is filled in by considering the question whether a particular criterion is *very important* in attaining a particular objective, *important* or *not important*. This is very subjective, but the important point is that the subjectivity is made explicit. Analysis of the matrix shows that size of the space under consideration is considered a significant discriminating factor for several objectives, as well as distance from the urban centre (because distance can be taken as a crude surrogate for pressures and intensity of use in the countryside) and adjacent development density. On the other hand, in the

Figure 10.1 Open-space objectives and key criteria for performance of objectives. (Source: developed from Latarjet 1972: 36).

Functions	Objectives*	Criteria							
		size	distance from centre	surrounding density	land use	relief	degree of openness	shape	geological – hydrological features
1. Recreational	a. sports complex								
	b. recreational complex								
	c. hiking and diffuse recreational activities								
	d. access to landscape and natural areas								
2. Ecological	a. maintenance of natural equilibrium								
	b. woodland and outstanding site maintenance								
	c. agricultural production								
3. Spatial organization	a. discontinuous urban form								
	b. land reserves for future infrastructure (transport)								
	c. land reserves for future infrastructure (unspecified)								
	d. increase rural – urban contact length								
	e. land banks for property exchange								

*See Table 10.1 for details

Importance of criterion in attaining objective:

very important

important

neutral/not important

Functions	Objectives*	Size (ha)				Distance from centre (km)		
		<100	100 – 1,000	1,000 – 10,000	>10,000	<7	7 – 20	>20
1. Recreational	a. sports complex	2	2	4	4	2	2	3
2. Ecological	a. maintenance of natural equilibrium	3	2	2	2	1	1	2
3. Spatial organization	a. discontinuous urban form	3	2	1	2	4	1	2

Importance of indicator in attaining objective:

1 very useful in attaining objective
2 useful in attaining objective
3 neutral in attaining objective
4 incompatible with attaining objective

* See Table 10.1 for details

Figure 10.2 Open-space objectives and morphological indicators. (Source: partially abstracted from Latarjet 1972: 37).

ranking of criteria, shape of the area and geological–hydrological criteria are considered significant for a much smaller number of objectives. Conversely, if the rows of the matrix are inspected, it is apparent that the working group undertaking this study considered the maintenance of agriculture in the urban fringe as the most demanding of the open-space objectives while land banks for property transfers and infrastructure land banks are the least demanding.

The final step in the analysis involves asking the question: what types of spaces can best perform particular functions and which spaces have the basic requirements capable of fulfilling several functions? This type of analysis can then provide the basis of some form of typology of open spaces. A second matrix was then established, with the twelve open-space objectives on the vertical axis and thirty indicators representing different values of the eight criteria on the horizontal axis (Fig. 10.2). Examples of the indicators are: for size – 'small' or less than 100 ha; 'average' or 100 to 1,000 ha; 'large' or 1,000 to 10,000 ha; and 'very large' more than 10,000 ha; and for distance from the urban centre – 'near' or less than 7 km; 'medium distance' or between 7 and 20 km; and 'distant' or more than 20 km. Again, a subjective questioning led to each cell being assigned a label indicating how useful (or incompatible) a specific 'value' of a criterion is for supporting a given objective or function. The analysis proceeded with a manual orthogonal resorting of the matrix (moving rows and columns) to produce either groups of indicators which would be capable of performing similar functions or, conversely, groups of functions dependent upon similar indicators.

Interestingly enough, some of the indicator groups actually coincided with types of geographic space. One type of space identified was useful to many functions, i.e. a geographic space typified by a few hundred hectares in size, at medium distances from the urban area, elongated and/or radial in form and having medium to high adjacent development densities. It was suggested that such zones could perform practically all twelve functions very well, excepting the maintenance of natural resource equilibrium and the creation of recreational bases. This multiplicity of roles underlines the difficulties of land-use planning in urban-fringe areas. A second type of geographic space that came out of this analysis was one particularly suited to natural resource maintenance, woodland preservation and recreational functions, as well as the agricultural production function to a somewhat lesser extent. Characteristics of these spaces included: low adjacent development density, and land uses including forest, heath and agricultural uses. Finally, a third type of geographic area was identified as being especially suitable for the spatial organization functions; such areas would be characterized by relatively small sizes, agricultural uses, low or medium adjacent development densities, located at medium distances from the urban area, and either compact or elongated.

While this procedure involves considerable subjectivity at every stage, and even though the assigned levels of utility of the criteria and their indicators may vary according to regional circumstances, it does demand that the reasoning be set down very explicitly. It is rare to find studies of open space where so much effort has been made to analyse the characteristics of the spaces, and indeed, the processes of change within them (MEAR 1971).

Once the potential value of an area has been determined for several uses, the major problem remaining is that of choice between the functions that an area can perform, assuming an incompatibility analysis shows that multiple use or function is ruled out. This is where the difficult task of assigning priorities comes in, which logically must consider the total demand for each particular function, the total possible 'supply' of each function and the value placed on each function by the appropriate 'public'. It would be naive to think that this important process is as highly structured as the above account might suggest. Planning is very much a political process, involving the interplay of many interest groups and individuals, even in a country with a reputation for a highly bureaucratic system of government like France. Trade-offs must be made between many functions of open space, e.g. agricultural production versus amenity function (Davidson and Wibberley 1977), and between open-space functions and urban development functions, e.g. denser urban development and agricultural land conservation.

Summary

A distinction has been made between land uses and the functions of land. Planning is concerned with both function and use, but there is a logical hierarchical ordering of function first, use second. It is useful to consider the planning of open-space functions as representing the major preoccupation of planning in the city's countryside; it may then be appropriate to label as 'management' that part of planning which deals with the coordination of uses or activities with functions. The analysis of potential for open-space functions, the setting of priorities and the determination of acceptable levels incompatibilites between uses and functions is a highly subjective one, but one which is probably best undertaken as explicitly as possible.

Some jurisdictions have tried to introduce the hierarchical ordering of functions and uses explicitly into the planning process. Research described above in the Paris region can be taken as indicative of this effort. Another interesting effort along these lines was undertaken in the County of Huron, southern Ontario (Ontario Ministry of Housing and County of Huron 1976), as part of an investigation into planning policies in rural areas. While the study area is not in an urban-fringe zone, part of the suggested methodology can be applied to such zones. The authors of the study considered that the key to planning in a rural area was to establish a 'perspective' (or, in other words, excluding the urban perspective, a dominant open-space function) for a particular area, e.g. an agricultural production perspective. Then, all other activities in such an area would have to be supportive or neutral (non-conflicting) in relation to this central perspective. In establishing a 'perspective', a planning authority must therefore consider the capability or potential of an area for performing the various functions possible and must then identify priorities. The chosen perspective then provides a reference point, a yardstick against which all other uses must be measured.

This study raises an important question which other open-space planning studies tend to skirt, viz. the particular scale at which it is appropriate to view a given 'perspective' or function. The scale question is implicit in the Paris region study (Latarjet 1972) in the size-of-area criterion used in the matrices, but it ignores how one delineates the geographic units for analysis in the first place; should they be a standard size, a landscape unit, or ...? The Huron County study recognizes that these units must vary in size depending on the perspective or function. Thus, it may well be possible to have a recreational complex developed within a broader scale unit devoted to conservation of woodland and natural environment characteristics. This study recognized five major 'perspectives', viz. agricultural; forestry; recreation (including second-home or cottage areas); urban; and mineral resources. Natural environment considerations were singled out for special treatment, arguing that land-use policies dealing with these are very particular, being protective and restrictive rather than enabling. General environmental standards were noted as being very important, e.g. pollution control, and that two types of open space related to the natural environment should be identified, viz. nature preserves and environmental protection areas (e.g. flood plain protection, landslide-prone areas, high amenity areas).

This approach follows the discussion in this chapter quite closely. However, its simplicity reflects the relatively simple nature of the pressures for land-use change in the County of Huron. In the city's countryside, especially in the urban fringe of relatively mature regional city forms, it would often be difficult to establish a single perspective for any substantially sized area because of the greater pressures and the already greater intermixture of uses and activities. Multiple-use solutions, even 'buffer' transitional zones, within a given geographic zone (as opposed to multiple use only of a particular property) therefore are more likely to be important. The identification of the problems and development of strategies is likely to be more difficult, then, in the city's countryside. With this, we turn to consider the geography of the problems and of management and planning in the city's countryside.

Further reading

Platt, R. F. (1972) *The Open Space Decision Process*, Research Paper 142, Department of Geography, University of Chicago, Chicago.

Williams, E. A. (1969) *Open Space: the Choices before California*, Report to the California State Office of Planning, Diablo Press, San Francisco.

11 The geography of land management

In the previous chapter, an important distinction was made between function and use of land. There is also an important distinction between the location and extent of the spatial 'hot spots' representing areas of greatest competition between land uses and functions, and the legal, and geographically constituted municipalities which have an interest in the organization and management of land and society.

First, then, the geography of the processes and the problems themselves are discussed. This involves the natural division of geographic space into areas possessing a set of similar problems or set of similar environmental concerns, e.g. an area where aggregate extraction conflicts with aesthetic values or country residential development with prime agricultural land. Second, there is a geography of the formal management units, i.e. the administrative structure of municipalities, townships or shires, regions, provinces, or states and special districts. There may be many small municipalities or a few large ones; there may be a centralized structure or a very fragmented one; there may be some coincidence of the legal boundary with natural or economic environment areas but more likely this will be absent. Of particular concern are:

1. the hierarchical organization, the respective responsibilities and resultant problems of each level for land management, and the various issues of self-interest, especially of local governments;
2. the frequently overlapping organizations, both in terms of administrative structures and geographic space, dealing with particular activities;
3. the regional structures based on natural divisions, e.g. water districts in the western US and Conservation Authorities in Ontario.

Clearly, it is inappropriate to base formal management structures purely on a problem-identification basis, since many of the specific problems identified throughout our discussions are linked to each other, being frequently the outcome of a common set of processes. The use of management structures that incorporate many different areas but which are affected by a common set of processes is, therefore, an appealing one, e.g. the urban-centred region; we shall return later to the concept of such unitary management and its alternatives and the sorts of problems created by existing formal governmental structures.

Total management structures can be complex and are certainly diverse. Sometimes there may be two tiers of government with clearly defined responsibilities; sometimes there may be intermeshing special districts which rarely coincide with municipal boundaries yielding considerable complexity in the structure of responsibilities; and sometimes there may be higher levels of governments, state and/or federal or central, which modify the responsibilities of local units. One direct result of the divergence between formal management units and problems has been the emergence of pressures to change municipal and other administrative structures to match them with the processes underlying the evolving regional city form. In Ontario, the outcome was the formation of a number of regional government units in the early 1970s; the mixed success of such apparently logical moves provides food for thought and underlines the complexity of the issues.

The evidence presented earlier relating to the ongoing processes in the regional city form has emphasized the systems interrelationships involved in the use of land around cities in the Western world. Recall that five factors were identified as underlying the developing regional city form (Ch. 1) : population growth and redistribution; free enterprise and competition for land; the acceptance of individual rights – to life styles, territory and property; accessibility, expanding transportation and communications technology; and lack of unitary governmental-administrative planning structures (Russwurm 1980a). These five factors are interwoven within the natural, economic and cultural environments, creating various problems within the city's countryside, which were enumerated in Chapter 3. Again, the influence of these factors surfaced when the activities occurring on the land were discussed in Part II. Now it is time to bring factors, environments, problems, and activities together and lay a framework for looking at the different approaches and techniques applied to land management in the regional city form and all its constituent zones, i.e. the inner fringe, outer fringe and urban shadow zones.

In all the countries from which our major examples are drawn, two common features stand out. One is the emerging regional city form as exurbanite households and urban-oriented land uses spread outward from cities for at least 50 km; the other is a conflict over the protection of property rights including development rights and their attenuation as the recognition of negative externalities has led to collectivized restrictions. In the US, these changes in land management have found expression both as 'The quiet revolution in land use control' (Bosselman and Callies 1971) and the associated concern for the natural environment.

At the same time, it must be recognized that regional differences exist between jurisdictions both between and within countries. Five such differences are worth noting more explicitly:

1. Societal attitudes to the use of land vary primarily in terms of acceptance of restrictions on the bundle of rights associated with property and notions about stewardship of the land.
2. There is great variety in the legislative regulations dealing with land, especially with respect to the mix between the responsibilities of local government and of higher levels of government. Moreover, the readiness to use the legal system varies, its use being undoubtedly most pronounced in the US.

3. The variety in land-tenure patterns plays an important role often not well recognized in planning, e.g. the highly fragmented property structure found typically in Western Europe; the township-range survey system of the western US and Canada compared to the less regular eastern survey systems; or the presence of many small parcels which make country residential development easier to undertake, e.g. the 4 ha parcels granted to railway companies in the Saanich Peninsula north of Victoria, British Columbia, compared with the characteristically large parcels in Australian rangelands.
4. The type of physical environment, its associated resource base, and the historical settlement pattern varies considerably. For instance, water concerns dominate in arid Arizona, southern California, and parts of Australia in contrast to most of Western Europe. Settlement patterns vary in accordance with such differences in the physical environment and the resource base. One could argue that in an area with many more kilometres of road per unit area and with smaller parcels of land, country residential development may be more scattered in contrast to much more isolated 'leap-frog' subdivisions under a township-range land-tenure system.
5. There is great variety in the political organization of territory. While a general trend has been towards fewer and larger political units, the pace of change and the resistance to it varies greatly between jurisdictions.

It is the interconnections between these five areas of differences in the context of the regional city form and the continued importance of private land ownership rights which should be borne in mind as we discuss, in turn, the geography of the processes and problems, then the management units, and finally consider some broader management structures in which an attempt is made to integrate processes and problems at the same scale as management.

Land-use processes and problems in their spatial context

Though regional cities vary, there is a declining intensity of uses outwards which provides the basis for the inner fringe, outer fringe and urban shadow zones (see Fig. 1.2). This simple pattern can be distorted considerably by variation in the five factors noted above, but these zones can be related to different intensities of land-use conflicts. For instance, large-scale continuous subdivision development occurs mainly in the inner fringe as accretionary development and the maintenance of agriculture is beset with more conflicts in the inner fringe; and characteristically, infrastructure networks converge on the city, creating a greater degree of fragmentation effects in the inner fringe. On the other hand, natural hazards, ecologically valuable areas and exploitable resources occur more irregularly. We will isolate some of the more significant variations for the three major zones in the following sections.

The inner fringe

In this zone, the maximum number of conflict-types and thus 'hot spots' occur. This zone is the one most dominated by non-farm land ownership and urban-oriented uses and non-farm households probably outnumber farm households by more than five to one in some parts. Some refer to it as the urban–rural fringe (Andrews 1942) or more generally the city-fringe. Three topics can be used to illustrate processes at work in the inner-fringe context: viz. sand-and-gravel extraction, agricultural activities, and rural-to-urban land conversion. Of course, these phenomena are found in all three zones; the key difference is in the intensity of the conflicts.

The sand-and-gravel industry can be seen as a nuisance activity, an essential but unwanted economic activity. However, unlike other nuisance activities located in the city's countryside (e.g. cement plants, electricity transformer stations), sand-and-gravel extraction is bound to its resource base in terms of site. In areas with intermittent rivers, e.g. southern California and Arizona, resources are taken from river beds which may pose problems associated with water quality. On the Salt River in the Phoenix inner fringe, gravel pits have been converted into waste disposal sites but in a recent '100-year flood' some were washed out with resultant pollution. In glacial areas, potential sites are usually more diffused, being dominantly associated with outwash deposits and spillway terraces. In a glaciated depositional area like southern Ontario and parts of Great Britain, where there is a profusion of outwash deposits, many cities are inevitably found close to such deposits. Usually, this is beneficial given the costs of hauling the material. But as urban development has expanded outward, some deposits have been built over by housing while in other areas, zoning and citizen protests have sterilized effectively other deposits in the inner fringe.

In such circumstances and depending upon the jurisdiction, permits to open new workings often demand expensive public hearings. The industry is thus faced with additional costs and uncertainty, costs which are inevitably passed on to the consumer. Terrace-type deposits often underlie good agricultural land or may be in scenic areas with outdoor recreation potential, which will generate other types of conflict. Moreover, in the inner fringe country residential parcels are more numerous, land ownership is more fragmented, and infrastructure networks more dense as they converge on the city, all of which pose problems for the sand-and-gravel industry. Where pockets of country residential households interface with sand-and-gravel properties, public protests have often made it nearly impossible to expand workings. Such 'hot spots' have, of course, resulted partly from the lack of anticipatory planning and arise from a heritage of reactive and negative planning reflecting a control approach rather than a true management approach.

Agriculture on good farmland also exists check by jowl with urban uses in the inner fringe. It is a myth that large tracts of idle land exist around most cities centred on good agricultural land. Nevertheless, farming adjustments to inner fringe locations are necessary and should be recognized in land management attempts. More land is rented, much machinery movement occurs because operating units tend to be more fragmented, trespass can be a problem, and farm enterprises will often emphasize cash cropping instead of livestock. Yet in some inner fringe areas, intensive agriculture is still maintained, e.g. Phoenix, where subdivisions are interspersed amidst cotton fields, intensive feeder-lot dairy and beef operations and citrus groves. Aerial pesticide spraying and sharing of water supplies between urban and rural demands result in ongoing conflicts. In only a few areas has the needed research been done separating myth from fact about farming at the city edge (but see Fielding 1979; Moran 1978; Auckland Regional Authority, Moran, Neville and Rankin 1980; Metropolitan Council of the Twin Cities Area 1979a; Bryant 1981). A thorough literature search and field experience shows that the inner fringe, though posing difficult problems for agriculture, is anything but a wasteland. There are opportunities for agricultural development in the inner fringe which can be enhanced through management. Of major importance in maintaining the agricultural resource in the inner fringe is the retention of sizeable blocks of land intact and the highlighting of the open-space significance (see Ch. 10) of agricultural land.

Related to this latter point is the spatial form exhibited by the urban land conversion process as it extends outward. Where a city is expanding haphazardly in all directions, chances of retaining large contiguous blocks of agricultural land are slim. If the expansion process is a channelled one, the possibilities are much greater. While evidence shows that productive agriculture can continue even with a sprawling edge like Phoenix and that direct loss of prime agricultural land to urban uses is not critical (Vining, Plaut and Bieri 1977; Shumway 1971), it seems irresponsible to convert the best farmland when lesser-quality land would serve equally well. But this is only possible with channelled growth involving clearly identified urban growth boundaries such as those demanded by the state planning process in Oregon (e.g. Metro Portland Metropolitan Service District 1979).

In addition, it can be expected that land speculation, higher land values, and non-farm ownership will be more widely diffused, the more sprawling and irregular the city edge. Bryant (1982) has shown that around a medium-sized compact Ontario city, the sales between intermediate actors in the land market were highly concentrated in the first 3 km from the built-up edge during his study period. At the same time, it must be recognized that some margin of supply of land for development must be left, otherwise demand can drive land prices excessively upward. Thus, in the Metro Portland Metropolitan Service District (1979) urban growth boundaries, this margin was left at 25 per cent above projected needs to the year 2000.

Land survey patterns are important in any consideration of land conversion ramifications in two ways. Developers often avoid an area which is fragmented with many small parcels, in preference for larger parcels; city annexation proposals may exhibit the same tendency, e.g. Calgary (Russwurm 1977b). Generally, the smaller the parcels and the more irregular the survey pattern, the more tentacular and sprawling is the city edge. Such is the pattern in the Atlantic provinces of Canada and the state of New England in the US. A very regular survey system with large blocks such as the township-range system of the western US and Canada can accommodate either sprawl or compactness. With strong planning controls, e.g. Saskatoon or Regina, a very regular edge occurs. But where such controls are lacking and where a fully developed square mile grid road system exists, e.g. the flat alluvial valley landscape around Tucson and Phoenix, a lead–lag pattern has resulted. Developers (or speculators) bought up tracts of land based on main crossroads and established outlying shopping centres; then, commercial strip development filled in back to the built-up edge and, finally, low-density residential infilling followed. This type of conversion process mitigates against maintaining large blocks of agricultural land intact and leads to a sprawling, low-density metropolis. Thus, Phoenix with 1.5 million people extends 100 km from east to west, compared with Toronto, with its 2.75 million people and an east–west extension of about 50 km. In addition, the larger the built-up areal extent, the greater the inner fringe zone and the greater the possibility for, and range of, potential land-use conflicts.

The outer fringe

This second zone is differentiated from the inner fringe in four key ways. First, no city accretionary urban development is expected in this zone in the easily foreseeable future; thus, the expectation of large-scale urban land development will be extremely low. Second, this zone is often the site of the first main ring of settlements of a size that merit planning attention of themselves. Often, these settlements may have been strong agricultural service centres now facing rapid growth as commuter centres as well.

This nodal component of population in the urban field, while not dealt with in a separate chapter, is nonetheless of considerable importance. Our simple model of the regional city population components based on the Canadian context suggests that about 15 per cent of the population lives in the outlying small cities, towns, villages and hamlets between 50 and 10,000 people (outlying places 10,000 or over were considered cities and their population is included as concentrated urban). All will have their own small sphere of influence and many may be legally established municipalities with their own planning powers. In the US, others will be unincorporated communities within the county municipal structure. Their presence provides another alternative location for households desiring to flee the principal city.

Table 11.1 A typology of common urban-associated land space–resource activities of the fringe

Land space		
City-unwanted	*Space cost-economizing*	*Traffic-oriented*
Dog kennels	Animal hospitals	Cabins
Fur farms	Auction barns	Drive-in eating places
Mushroom farms	Car body repair shops	Fruit and vegetable stands
Poultry	Dance and banquet halls	Motels
Stockyards	Drive-in theatres	Restaurants
Auto wreckers	Farm equipment	Service stations and garages
Animal slaughtering	Farm and garden supplies	
	Fertilizer supplies	
Concrete products	Furniture	
	Lumber yards	
Construction equipment and storage	Marine sales and supplies	
	Meat markets	
Chemical plants	Monuments	
Masonry products	Motorcycle sales and services	
Oil refineries		
Trailer courts	Night clubs and taverns	
Gas and oil pumping stations	Ornamental and building stone	
Railroad switch-yards	Trailers and mobile homes sales	
Incinerators		
Sanitary landfill	Used-car lots	
Sewage lagoons	Wholesale groceries	
Snowmobiling areas	Automobile assembly plants	
Psychiatric hospitals		
	Oil and gas storage	
	Tent, trailer, mobile home manufacturing	
	Trucking terminals	
	Airports	
	Amusement centres	
	Auto racetracks	
	Campgrounds	
	Fish and game clubs	
	Go-cart tracks	
	Horse race tracks	
	Multi-family residential	
	Community colleges	
	Universities	
	Ethnic community halls	

(Source: Russwurm 1980a: 463–4)

Resource	
Export-oriented	*On-site oriented*
Sod farms	Game farms
Flowers	Put-and-take fishing
Market gardening	Riding stables and ranches
Nurseries	Antiques
Water wells	Single-family residential
Ground water	Hydro stations
Sand and gravel pits	Microwave towers
	Radio towers
Stone quarries	Television towers
	Water pipelines
	Water-supply reservoirs
	Sewage treatment plants
	Beaches
	Parks
	Ski resorts
	Swimming resorts
	Swimming places
	Walking trails
	Monasteries
	Schools for emotionally disturbed children

The larger of these nodes are usually located in the outer part of the outer fringe or in the urban shadow zone because historical competition from the principal city made growth difficult adjacent to the competing core city. Clearly their presence disrupts our smooth zonal patterns.

The third way in which the outer fringe differs from the inner is that the number and kind of urban-associated uses will differ. Of the common urban-associated activities occurring in the city's countryside, relatively fewer of the 'unwanted', space cost-economizing and traffic-oriented land-space activities will be present in this zone (see Table 11.1) compared to the inner fringe. Most of these activities demand higher levels of accessibility than do those of the other category, resource activities, and they can pay the higher land prices found in the inner fringe. On the other hand, some of the resource activities such as outdoor recreation activities will likely be more common, and the most significant urban-associated uses will be the country residential uses, an on-site oriented use. Generally their density, unless severely restricted by planning regulations, is only slightly lower than in parts of the inner fringe and can be expected to range between equal numbers of farm and non-farm units up to five non-farm to one farm household, i.e. a semi-urban zone. The inner fringe, however, will contain most of the scattered subdivisions, especially in the US, where leap-frog development has been more common than in the other countries from which our illustrations have been drawn. The fourth difference is that the competition between municipalities for tax-providing industries will be less than in the inner-ring municipalities which in the US and Australia, at least, normally contain part of the built-up urban area.

The outer fringe zone is one in which agriculture can generally be given first priority without too much difficulty, because the pressures on farming are less. In his landholding study around London, Ontario, Troughton (1976) showed the steady increase with distance from the city edge in full-time farmers to a position of dominance over part-time and hobby farmers in the outer fringe at about 15 km from the built-up edge. Thus, in comparison with the inner fringe zone, where full-time, part-time and hobby farming may be almost equally represented, outer-fringe farming is dominated by full-time farmers. Large-scale urban-associated developments may still pose problems at times in some places, e.g. large commercial recreation complexes and airports. In addition, problems will arise from utility rights-of-way such as electricity or gas transmission corridors. Possibly most crucial of all may be the political power potentially held by non-farm households who outnumber farm households.

The urban shadow zone

This zone generally extends outward to the limits of the main daily commuting zone of the core city, although the maximum extent of the commuting zone will go beyond the urban shadow. Depending upon particular configurations of the physical environment, this zone may merge into agricultural lands, forests or highlands, e.g. Vancouver, Los Angeles, Sheffield, Sydney. Unless farming is marginal, it is reasonable to expect non-farm households to be generally fewer than farm households, with ratios ranging from 1 : 5 to 1 : 1, i.e. a 'semi-rural' area.

Even though this zone is relatively distant from the urban core of the regional city, there may still be some difficult land-management issues, which are sometimes related to use of this zone as a seasonal and/or leisure life-space by urban populations. For instance, the Blue Mountain area of the Niagara Escarpment, southern Ontario's major ski resort, lies in the urban shadow zone of Toronto. Considerable land subdivision has taken place in surrounding hills and adjacent apple orchard areas for ski chalets and second homes. Concern over servicing costs, impact on agricultural lands and loss of potential recreational lands had led to firm provincially directed subdivision controls by the early 1970s. Similar types of problems have surfaced in the western US over so-called 'remote' subdivisions (Parsons 1972; Vaux 1977).

The land-use conflicts stemming from the processes at work in the urban field of the regional city have been schematized as occurring in three simple zones using distance bands. The key assumption underlying this framework is that intensity of pressures and competition for land exhibits a distance-decay relationship from the urban edge. Obviously, the real world is not so neatly compartmentalized; indeed, the differences between regions that were related to the five factors earlier in this chapter also operate at the subregional scale.

As an illustration of discontinuities in the city's countryside, Fig. 11.1 shows the ratio of non-farm to farm households categorized along a rural-to-urban continuum around Stratford, a small (25,000) southern Ontario city located on prime farmland (Neice 1977). Note the smooth distance-decay effect apparent when distance bands are used compared with a grid system which gives a more broken pattern.

The importance of the conceptual models used above is in understanding complexity; but as soon as key relationships can be identified, other variables must be recognized and introduced. It should be expected that particularly around larger cities, identifiable 'hot spot' situations of different types will occur within these zones. It might be a country residential–sand and gravel conflict, a market gardening–leap-frog subdivision interface, or a mixed residential–commercial ribbon development. In other parts of a zone, even in the inner fringe, agriculture may be the sole activity. The combining of simple zonal concepts with discrete-type situations is one means of clarifying the complexity in the city's countryside. This approach has been illustrated by work in the Paris region, France (MEAR 1971; Bryant 1974).

Arguing that agriculture is the major land use in the rural areas of the

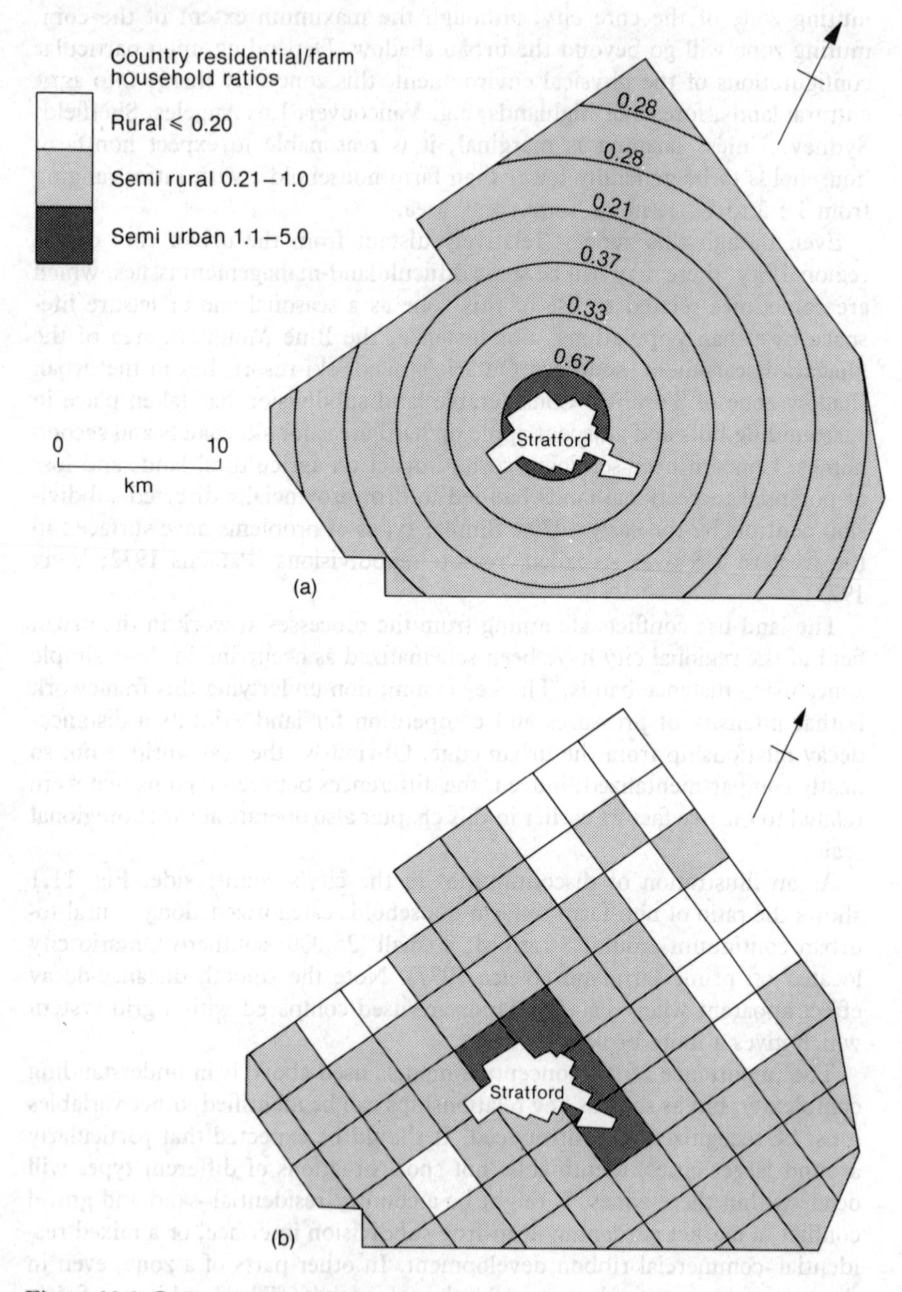

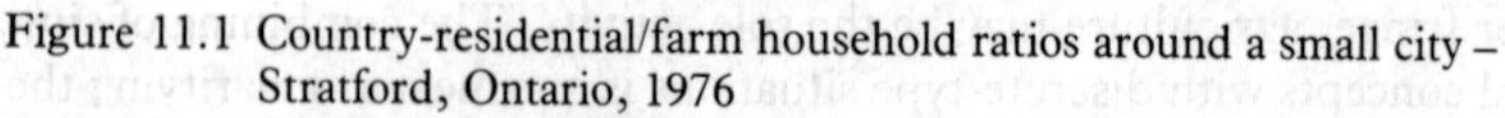

Figure 11.1 Country-residential/farm household ratios around a small city – Stratford, Ontario, 1976
(a) By distance bands
(b) By a square grid. (Source: compiled from data in Russwurm 1980a: 488 from an original map drawn by Neice 1977).

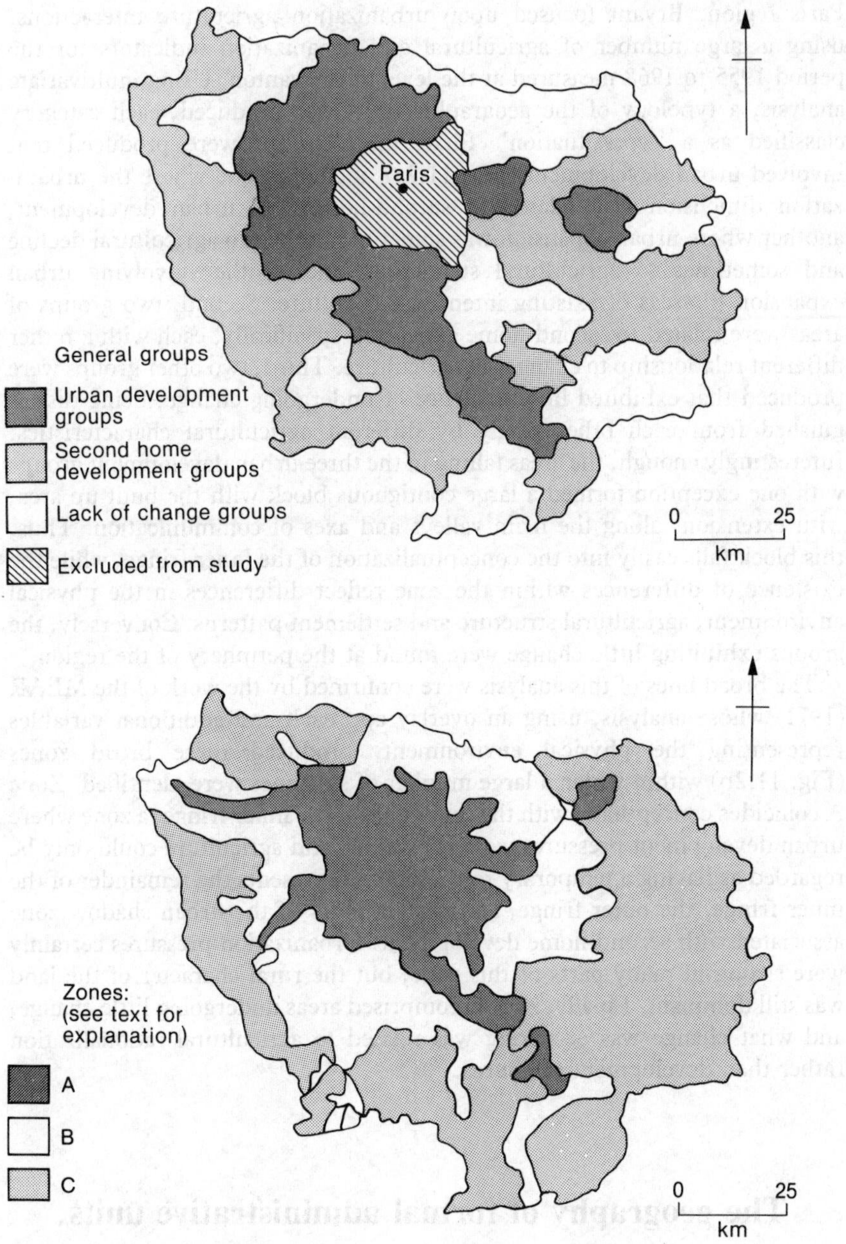

Figure 11.2 Geographic situations in the Paris region
(a) Typology of urbanization–agriculture situations in the Paris region. (Source: generalized from Bryant 1974: Fig. 6a, p. 22).
(b) Typology of situations in the Paris region (MEAR 1971). (Source: Bryant 1974: Fig. 7, p. 25).

Paris region, Bryant focused upon urbanization–agriculture interactions, using a large number of agricultural and urbanization indicators for the period 1955 to 1968 measured at the level of the canton. Using multivariate analysis, a typology of the geographic units was produced, each category classified as a 'type-situation'. First, three groups were produced that involved urban development (Fig. 11.2a), including one where the urbanization dimension was related to second-home and urban development, another where urban expansion was sometimes linked to agricultural decline and sometimes to agricultural stagnation, and another involving urban expansion in areas of existing intensive agriculture. Second, two groups of areas were related to second-home expansion specifically, each with a rather different relationship to changes in agriculture. Third, two other groups were produced that exhibited little evidence of undergoing change, being distinguished from each other partly by different agricultural characteristics. Interestingly enough, the areas falling in the three urban development groups with one exception formed a large contiguous block with the built-up area, with extensions along the main valleys and axes of communication. Thus, this block falls easily into the conceptualization of the inner fringe, while the existence of differences within the zone reflect differences in the physical environment, agricultural structure and settlement patterns. Conversely, the groups exhibiting little change were found at the periphery of the region.

The broad lines of this analysis were confirmed by the work of the MEAR (1971) whose analysis, using an overlay approach and additional variables representing the physical environment, produced three broad zones (Fig. 11.2b) within which a large number of subzones were identified. Zone A coincides conceptually with the inner part of the inner fringe, a zone where urban development pressures were substantial and agriculture could only be regarded as having a temporary role. Zone B represents the remainder of the inner fringe, the outer fringe, and certain parts of the urban shadow zone associated with second-home development. Urbanization pressures certainly were strong in many parts of this zone, but the rural character of the land was still dominant. Finally, zone C comprised areas undergoing little change, and what change was occurring was related to agricultural rationalization rather than development pressures.

The geography of formal administrative units

The interacting processes underlying changes in the economic, cultural and natural environments of the regional city have now been ordered spatially into three gradational zones at a fairly general scale. At a more detailed scale, 'hot spots' of land use-land management situations occur irregularly within each zone as a result of differences in natural resources, accessibility and land-tenure patterns. At the same time, land space has been carved up into legal home territories administered by various types of municipal bodies. Once established, the rights of municipalities within their boundaries are often guarded with the same zeal as private property rights. In the vast majority of cases, these entities have been in place long before the forces that created the regional city came into play. Then, economies changed, people adopted the technology of the automobile, rural areas became exurbanized, agriculture highly mechanized, and cities thrust ever outward. It can hardly be expected that the geographically defined municipalities, territorially enshrined, would continue to match, if they ever did, the evolving land-use activity patterns and the new geographic functional units of the socioeconomic system.

No attempt is made here to detail the various types of administrative structure by which territorial space is managed, but some of the geographical aspects of the common structures in the Western world are highlighted. A major factor in the development of structural problems in management is the division of the city's countryside into many different jurisdictions at one level or another. The fundamental issue is really how the power and responsibilities for land-use planning are divided up between different levels of government. In France, for instance, five levels of an administrative hierarchy can be identified, viz. the *commune* (both rural and urban), the *canton*, the *département*, the *région de programme* and the state. This hierarchy provides a formal link between local land-use planning and national and regional development planning; however, the *canton* level has little significance any more in the ordering of people's lives in terms of land-use planning so that at the lower level the link is more properly one between the *commune* and the *département*.

It is useful to think of a threefold division of administrative structures, centralized, decentralized and mixed, a categorization that borrows from hierarchy theory, a part of systems theory (Pattee 1973; Whyte *et al.* 1969). Centralized structures in regard to land management involve strong participation from the national governmental level, with both the UK and France providing good examples. The more centralized, the fewer the responsibilities of lower levels of government for decision-making, and the more directly articulated are the management goals of the top level which are passed down for implementation (UK Government White Paper 1976). On the one hand, such structures have the potential for matching management strategies to changing land-use processes more readily at the appropriate scale. On the other hand, it is also more remote from the people and resources being planned and runs the considerable risk of not being in tune with all the significant dimensions of a problem locally or regionally. A centralized structure is not without coordination problems either, especially when responsibility over land-use planning matters is divided vertically between different agencies, e.g. a Ministry of Agriculture, of the Environment, of Housing, of Communications, and so forth, although this type of coordination problem exists in both centralized and decentralized structures. When each national agency has its own internal jurisdictional structure, problems of coordination at a local scale are even more difficult. Thus, a major step in the development of the regional planning framework in France was the central government decree in 1960 that all internal ministerial jurisdictional structures conform to the twenty-one planning regions (Boudeville 1966).

Decentralized structures are perhaps more commonly associated with the US, in which maximum responsibility in land-use planning matters has fallen to local government units. The states have the reserve of power but have often delegated powers to local government bodies; thus, in most states of the US, subdivision regulations and zoning ordinances are a local responsibility (Clawson and Hall 1973). However, 'local control' can lead along rather different paths: it can mean maximum rights of individuals to use their properties as they wish; or maximum rights of individual municipalities to manage their territories; or maximum control by local decision-makers collaborating within a larger framework (Healey and Rosenberg 1979). Which of these three paths of local 'home rule' is dominant will have a profound effect upon how land-use management proceeds. One consequence, however, that may result from a decentralized structure is perhaps a greater readiness to accept special-purpose agencies, e.g. the Water Districts in California and Arizona, or the Metropolitan Service District of Metropolitan Portland, or the California Coastal Commission, or the British Columbia Land Commission.

Mixed structures involve various combinations of centralized and decentralized structures. Thus, in Ontario, a number of local governments have been amalgamated into regional government units which provide unitary government in several areas; at the same time, subdivision regulations and zoning by-laws require provincial approval and special agencies are also maintained, e.g. School Boards and Conservation Authorities (the latter based on watersheds). In some ways, the mixed structure has become more common as a concern about environment, land and urban development has evolved. In decentralized structures, more regional coordination has become apparent, e.g. the regional government units in Ontario, while in centralized structures, greater efforts seem to be aimed at taking account of local needs and wishes, e.g. the development of the *Plan d'aménagement rural* in France (Commissariat Général du Plan 1971) which is based on cooperation between several adjacent rural communes that collectively identify goals and objectives, and the role advocated for 'positive' management in the UK (Davidson and Wibberley 1977) involving working with land owners and people at the local and individual scale. In the city's countryside, then, a multitude of structures and adjustments affecting land management have been attempted, and in the next section, an overview is given of the move towards the more unified approaches to management structures in the city's countryside.

Some attempts at more unified management structures

Given the resultant lack of congruence between government structures and the problems they faced during the 1960s and 1970s, it is not surprising that attempts were made to shore up the holes. Six different types of structures are reviewed here from Canada and the US, selected for their innovative approach. In Canada, the Regional Governments of Ontario and the Regional Districts in British Columbia are discussed, while in the US, the Metro Council of the Twin Cities (Minneapolis–St Paul), the Metropolitan Services District (MSD) of Metropolitan Portland (Oregon), the Oregon Land Conservation and Development Commission (LCDC), and the California Local Area Formation Commission (LAFCO) are considered. These responses represent mainly decentralized structures moving toward the mixed mode. Additional comments on trends in management in the more centralized structures of the UK and France are made in the following chapter.

Regional government in Ontario

Urban growth in Ontario was pronounced between 1951 and 1976, with the population in places over 10,000 doubling (Russwurm 1980b). Most of this growth was centred in the southern parts of the province containing the best farmland. The existing governmental structure dated back to 1848; cities, towns and villages constituted the urban-governing entities and townships the rural-governing entities. With rapid growth in the 1950s and 1960s, many rural townships adjacent to towns and cities became urbanized and found themselves on a treadmill as far as land-use management was concerned. Initial responses involved city annexations of township land, often involving contentious hearings arbitrated and decided upon by the provincial government.

It was in this context that it was recognized that the scale of the socioeconomic growth processes underlying the evolution of the settlement system could probably be handled better by larger governmental units in a regional-city context. After detailed studies, already foreshadowed by the formation in the early 1960s of Metro Toronto (when thirteen municipalities were amalgamated into six), eight regional government units were formed by the mid-1970s with several counties being given the status of regional government units. Prior to this time, counties, unlike their US counterparts, had very limited governmental power. Under this restructuring which centred mainly on the more urbanized areas, cities, towns and villages were put back into a shared-government structure with the townships.

Each regional municipality was created separately by the Ontario Legislature and has roughly similar powers. Usually the number of municipalities has been reduced by about half, sometimes involving amalgamation of urban and rural municipalities. For instance, in the Regional Municipality of Waterloo, six contiguous urban municipalities were reduced to three, and four outlying towns and villages were amalgamated with their surrounding rural township. Generally, regional municipalities have one regional council and a local council for each member municipality; the regional council consists of a Chairman appointed by the municipalities and members appointed from the elected local councils roughly in proportion to population with the usual bias to overrepresentation of the less populous rural municipalities. Regional Council is responsible for region-wide services such as planning, policing, utilities and the regional transportation network.

Inevitably in such structures, the distrust that rural municipalities will be dominated by the urban centres surfaces from time to time but regional government reviews instituted by the provincial government have shown this problem not to be based on fact (e.g. Mayo 1976), even though their success in the public eye has been mixed. One study in the Waterloo region showed that urban and rural regional councillors did not differ in responding to issues concerning agricultural land, country estate development, water supply and industrial land problems (Honsberger 1979). Despite some problems, these governmental units appear to have been reasonably successful and certainly provide one approach to the unitary planning needed in an urban-centred region, providing a formal forum where elected rural and urban politicians deal with each other. Carefully developed and firmly controlled official plans have resulted which are eliminating many of the problems noted in Chapter 3.

Regional Districts in British Columbia

This situation differs from that in Ontario in that the districts are not governmental units strictly speaking, that almost no amalgamations have resulted and that the entire province is covered by twenty-eight Regional District units created by the Municipal Act of 1965. These districts combine rural and urban communities and are generally based on an urban centre and its trade area. Under the original statute, they are responsible for two functions, viz. land-use planning and hospitals, although additional regional-level functions can and have been delegated to them by member municipalities. As in Ontario, this regional type of management unit grew out of intense urban pressures, especially around Vancouver and Victoria in the early 1960s, a trend followed later around the interior cities. While much haphazard development has occurred as elsewhere, and while financial support for the Regional Districts could be stronger, regional planning efforts are mitigating regional-scale problems partly by developing comprehensive land-use plans.

Closely linked to urban-growth pressures and the Regional Districts was the creation of the British Columbia Land Commission (see Ch. 12). Its main goal is the preservation of agricultural land by establishing Agricultural Land Reserves (Rawson 1976) in the context of the Regional Districts. Changes to a land use other than agriculture within the Reserves must now be approved by both the Regional District and the BC Land Commission. Since the inner boundary of the Agricultural Land Reserves (ALRs) is the outer urban growth boundary and since firm control exists within the ALRs, the framework for control of the future regional city form clearly exists for both the concentrated and dispersed parts. The combination of a provincially appointed special body and a regional body whose council, as in Ontario, consists of members nominated from the elected local councils, is a promising land-management alternative combining a provincial-wide agricultural zoning with approved local comprehensive plans.

Metropolitan Council of the Twin Cities Area (Minneapolis–St Paul)

The Metropolitan Council (MC) serves a seven-county area with a 1980 population of 2.1 million, covering 8,000 sq km, roughly 90 km across. The free-standing Minneapolis–St Paul metropolitan area is the dominant urban centre in Minnesota, containing over half the state's population. The MC was created by the state in 1967 to ensure orderly and economic development over a sprawling, spreading low-density urban area that had been fostered by fragmented and competing municipal units. Accountable to the State Legislature, the MC consists of sixteen members appointed by the state for four-year terms for sixteen districts of equal population. The Chairman, the seventeenth member, represents the region as a whole and serves at the pleasure of the governor (Metropolitan Council of the Twin Cities Area 1979b; Bosselman and Callies 1971; Baldinger 1971).

The MC essentially serves as a regional coordinating entity. It is responsible for preparing and maintaining a Metropolitan Development Guide whose land-use planning Development Framework provides the basis for policy plans on sewers, transportation, water management, housing, open space and parks (Metropolitan Council of the Twin Cities Area 1975). It is this Development Framework (Fig. 11.3) that is supposed to ensure that local developments are congruent with each other. Currently the two major concerns are:

1. to reduce leap-frog suburbanization and scattered rural development, preserve prime agricultural land, protect the environment (a lake-studded one) and minimize public service costs;
2. to maintain or strengthen the older, developed portions in order to use existing public investments more efficiently (Munson 1980).

Seven geographic areas with their own development policies were established (Metropolitan Council of the Twin Cities 1975). Four are in the Urban

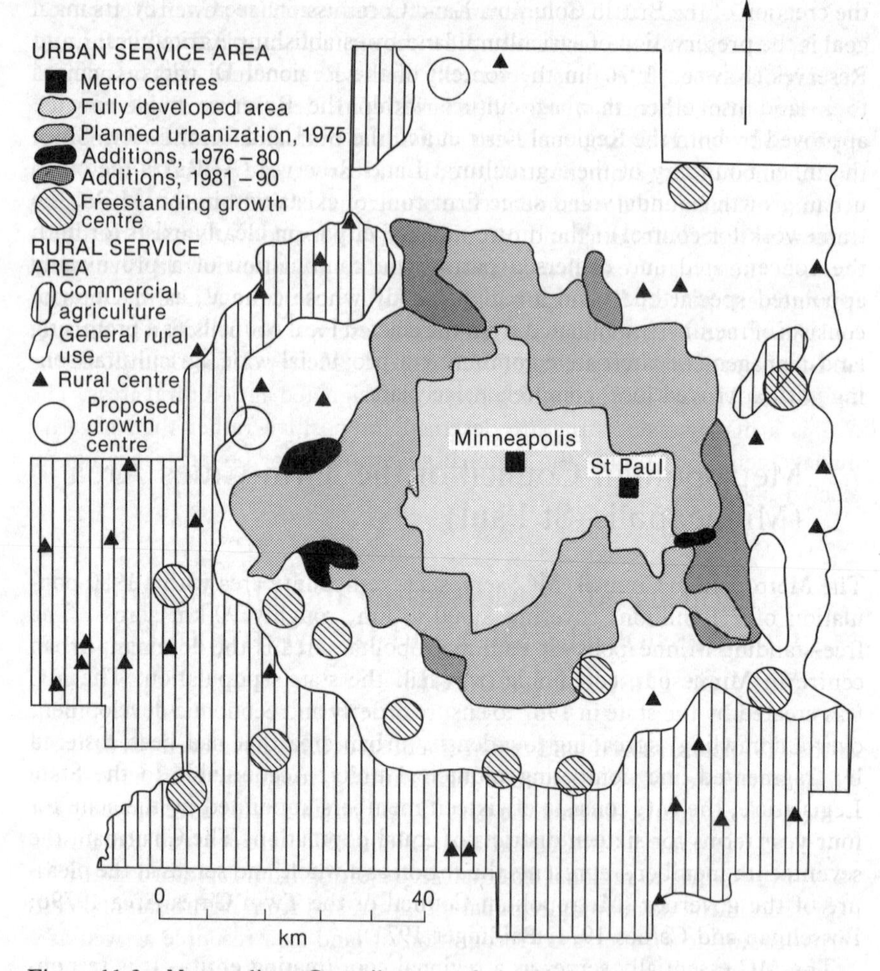

Figure 11.3 Metropolitan Council Area of the Twin Cities of Minneapolis–St Paul, 1980: Development Framework Plan. (Source: generalized from Munson 1980: 10).

Service area: the Metro Centres, the downtown cores of Minneapolis–St Paul; the Fully Developed Area; the area of Planned Urbanization (largely serviced but not completely developed); and fourteen Freestanding Growth Centres, physically separate but intended to be fully serviced and at the small-city scale. The Rural Service area covers the remaining area and is divided into a General Rural Use region (equivalent to the inner fringe) and a Commercial Agriculture Region (the outer urban fringe and urban shadow) in which almost no residential development will be permitted except in the Rural Centres, whose other role is to provide agricultural services.

Since its creation, the MC has played a significant role in shaping the landscape of the seven-county region. While not possessing subdivision and zoning controls which remain local government functions, it has power over capital budgeting, region-wide services and for requiring local plans to conform to the regional one. It is thus a centrally imposed structure with appointed members from districts whose boundaries coincide with or divide municipalities but which do not represent individual municipalities. Evolving out of a Council of Government structure, it is clearly more powerful now than the many Council of Government-type of regional entities; the latter are supported by federal funding and can only try to persuade voluntary members through their many excellent planning studies because they lack any real management power. One example of the influence of the MC is the passing in 1980 of the Metropolitan Agricultural Preserves Act which was directly based on its Rural Area Task Force Report (Metropolitan Council of the Twin City Area 1979a) and which protects designated agricultural areas. The MC is a management structure designed for positive rather than negative management. But unlike the regional governments of Ontario, it is not an elected body.

Oregon Land Conservation and Development Commission (LCDC) and the Metropolitan Service District (Metro)

In the US, decentralized land management structures have been particularly strong since the 1920s when state legislatures gave authority over land use to local governments. During the past 15 years many states have moved back into land-use control (Bosselman and Callies 1971; Healey and Rosenberg 1979) in response to regional externalities resulting from rapid urban growth expressed in the developing regional city form and from environmental concerns leading to an increased recognition of land as a resource as well as a commodity.

At the state level, aside from Hawaii (Myers 1976), Oregon has taken the strongest state-wide approach beginning in the 1960s (Little 1974), and highlighted in 1969 when all cities and counties (the only two types of municipalities in Oregon) were required to prepare comprehensive plans and zoning to meet statutory standards. Then in 1973 Senate Bill 100 created the Land Conservation and Development Commission (LCDC) to raise the quality of local planning (1000 Friends of Oregon 1980). The LCDC was given the authority for establishing mandatory state-wide goals to refine the broad standards established in 1969. After many public hearings, nineteen comprehensive goals with broad guidelines for implementation were approved between 1974 and 1976 (Table 11.2). Three of the more critical goals for the city's countryside are: the maintenance of agricultural lands; conservation of open space and the protection of natural and scenic resources; and the provision of an orderly and efficient process of conversion from rural to urban

Table 11.2 Oregon: areas affected by state-wide planning goals

1. Citizen involvement	9. Economy of the state
2. Land-use planning	10. Housing
3. Agricultural lands	11. Public facilities and services
4. Forest lands	12. Transportation
5. Open spaces, scenic and historic areas and natural resources	13. Energy conservation
	14. Urbanization
6. Air, water and land resources quality	15. Willamette River Greenway
7. Areas subject to natural disasters and hazards	16. Estuarine resources
	17. Coastal shorelands
8. Recreational needs	18. Beaches and dunes
	19. Ocean resources

uses (Oregon LCDC 1978). Senate Bill 100 seems assured of a continued life as support on a citizens' initiative to repeal it in 1978 showed 61 per cent support compared with only 57 per cent support in a similar initiative in 1976.

The local comprehensive plan contains the data analysis and policy decisions required by the state goals with which it must comply. All local land-use decisions involving zone changes, variances and subdivision approvals must conform to the plan, which is mandatory and authoritative rather than advisory. All municipalities were to submit their plan for LCDC approval by mid-1980. Once the LCDC acknowledges that the local plan complies with the state goals, then it becomes the controlling power in local land-use development, i.e. 'home rule' would again reign but now with a definite set of rules integrated into a state-wide framework.

Much credit for the consistent application of state goals in the comprehensive plans must be given to the 1000 Friends of Oregon, a voluntary group which is largely citizen-funded. This group began work in early 1975; has three full-time staff attorneys and an influential advisory board and board of directors with an annual budget of about $110,000 (1000 Friends of Oregon 1980). The group has taken a watchdog role to ensure that Senate Bill 100 would be a success by taking legal and advisory action on matters such as inadequate urban growth boundaries, the application of the exclusive farm-use zoning in the agricultural lands goal, and many other issues. Consequently, broad state-wide goals have been clarified so they can be applied rigorously at the local scale.

Geographically, a key aspect of the LCDC is the division of land into three zones: urban, urbanizable and rural, involving an urban growth boundary (UGB): 'The urban growth boundary process is at the heart of Oregon's land use program and the primary tool which local governments must use to manage growth.' (1000 Friends of Oregon 1980: 8.) This is so because Goal 14 relating to urbanization requires that all new urban growth occur inside the UGB. Urbanizable lands are the readily serviced lands inside the UGB surrounding existing urban land, which are needed for projected urban use to the year 2000; a 25 per cent surplus has been accepted as reasonable to allow the land market to function normally (Metro Portland Metropolitan Service District 1979). Orderly growth inside the UGB is required by the comprehensive plan. Finally, rural lands are those outside the UGB. Within the rural lands are the exclusive farm-use zones (EFU) arising out of Goal 3, associated with agricultural land having US Soil Conservation Services capability classes I to IV (I–V in Eastern Oregon). Some flexibility in permitting non-agricultural uses is included. In terms of the zonal framework used early in this chapter, the urbanizable land zone would include much of the inner fringe. In Oregon the most critical UGB is that of Metropolitan Portland, which with about 1 million people contains over two-fifths of Oregon's population.

To cope better with various regional land-use pressures that had arisen in the Portland Metropolitan area, a Council of Governments, the Columbia Regional Association of Governments (CRAG), was formed in the early 1970s. Such associations exist in most states and are provided with considerable federal funding for planning purposes but must rely on voluntary membership and persuasion to implement plans. This body was unable to develop a UGB acceptable to the LCDC. Under state pressure, CRAG and a voluntary Metropolitan Service District were combined on 1 January 1979 into the current Metropolitan Service District (Metro) consisting of three counties and twenty-four cities. Having roughly the same functions as the Metropolitan Council of the Twin Cities Area, Metro is unique in having a managing council of publicly *elected* members serving districts roughly equal in population but not based on municipal boundaries. It is the first directly elected regional government in the US, and has managed to get its twenty-seven member municipalities to establish an acceptable UGB, also considered to be the first of its type to be put in place in the US. In its first-year report (Metro 1980), Metro points out that the importance of such a regional body, especially a directly elected one, is in addressing specific regional issues and in working cooperatively with local governments to reach solutions. The crucial point is that in contrast to Councils of Governments (COGS), Metro has implementing powers in that local land-use plans must dovetail with an overall Metro plan required to meet state-wide planning goals. Consequently, a management structure now exists that combines urban and rural interests in an attempt to cope effectively with both the needs for urban development and the maintenance of the resource base in the immediate urban surroundings.

A UGB, if respected, can be an important tool in land management at the regional scale. Our final example of management structure adaptations looks at one aspect of the California situation.

California land-use planning and the Local Agency Formation Commissions (LAFCOs)

Unlike the much more direct state intervention characterizing Oregon, California has essentially adopted a special district or sectoral approach with the creation of various agencies to deal with extra-local issues, e.g. the Coastal Commission which cuts across many regional cities (Healey and Rosenberg 1979). In a much larger state with 94 per cent of the population classified as urban and with almost ten times the population of Oregon, greater complexity results especially when decentralized 'home rule' has been, and is, a vital ongoing force (California Office of Planning and Research 1978). The complex situation for land-use management is illustrated by Table 11.3. Fourteen hundred local governments exist, each requiring a general plan consisting of nine elements (somewhat comparable to Oregon's goals) dealing with land use, circulation, housing, conservation, open space, seismic safety, noise, scenic highways and safety (California Office of Planning and Research 1980). The first element, land use, has been required since 1955 with the others being added by 1971. After commenting on the many local government units, special districts, and regional, state and federal agencies involved, the authors of a recent study (California Land-Use Task Force 1975: 13) write:

> There are cases of inter-agency 'coordination', but in fact planning in California is not coordinated. Some plans do not fit with other plans, some controls do not match other controls, some controls are not based upon plans at all. Sometimes one agency does the work of another, and sometimes one undoes the work of another. There are many pieces to the picture: but they do not add up to a single whole that landowners, business interests, public officials and citizen groups can relate to with the secure knowledge that it represents California land use policy.

One element of the complex land-use management structure of California highlights a management issue that has long occurred in the inner urban fringe – annexation. For many years, as cities have grown beyond their boundaries, they have taken land from surrounding rural municipalities. In Ontario, in areas where regional governments occur, this issue has now been largely eliminated. In some states, e.g. Texas and Oklahoma, cities are able to add to their limits almost without hindrance. Elsewhere, bitter legal proceedings may occur if the municipality whose lands are being annexed resists, e.g. the costly two-year case in Edmonton, Alberta (Batey and Smith 1981). In the US, it is common for urban municipalities to be able to annex areas under immediate development pressures as long as a reasonable case is shown. But, what greatly complicates the situation in the US is the fragmentation of units, the situation in California being a typical example. As a result, many strangely shaped boundaries occur, including enclaves and strips along roads.

Table 11.3 California land-use and planning agencies

A. State-level planning

1. *State comprehensive planning agencies*
   (a) Office of Planning and Research
   (b) Council on Intergovernmental Relations

2. *State development planning agencies*
   (a) Department of Transportation
   (b) Department of Housing
   (c) Public Works Board

3. *State resource planning agencies*
   (a) Air Resources Board
   (b) State Water Resources Control Board
   (c) California Coastal Zone Conservation Commission
   (d) Energy Resources Conservation and Development Commission
   (e) Department of Fish and Game
   (f) Department of Parks and Recreation
   (g) Department of Water Resources
   (h) Department of Navigation and Ocean Development
   (i) Solid Waste Management Board
   (j) University of California

4. *Related regulatory agencies*
   (a) State Lands Commission
   (b) Public Utilities commission

B. Regional-level planning

1. *Councils of Government*

2. *Statutory regional agencies*
   (a) Metropolitan Transportation Commission
   (b) Bay Conservation and Development Commission
   (c) Tahoe Regional Planning Agency

C. Local-level planning

1. *The Local General Plan*
2. *Implementation of the General Plan*
   (a) Zoning
   (b) Subdivision Regulations
   (c) Urban Renewal
   (d) Housing
   (e) Growth Management
   (f) Property Taxation
   (g) Environmental Impact Assessment
   (h) Local Agency Formation Commissions
   (i) Airport Land Use Commissions

(Source: California Land-Use Task Force 1975)

In California, Local Agency Formation Commissions (LAFCOs) established by the state legislature in 1971 govern the boundary changes of all local governments (including all special districts except school districts). Each county

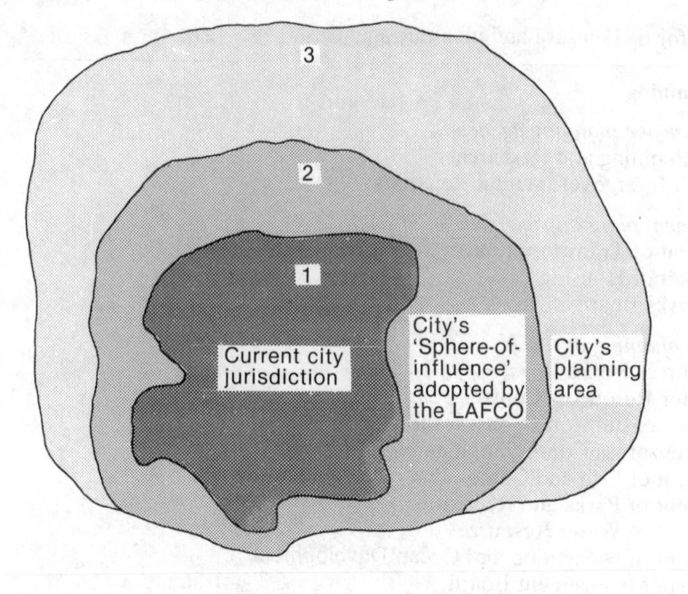

1. Incorporated Territory: land use controlled by the city.

2. Unincorporated Territory: to be ultimately annexed and served by the city. Land use controlled by county in formal consultation or by joint action with the city.

3. Unincorporated Territory: not to be annexed and served by the city, but bearing some relation to the city's planning. Land use controlled by county in consultation with the city.

LAFCO: Local Agency Formation Commission

Figure 11.4 Theoretical relationship between a city's planning area and sphere-of-influence, California. (Source: California Office of Planning and Research 1980: 15).

has a state-funded LAFCO with powers to deal with annexations, incorporations, formation of special districts and consolidations, mergers, and dissolutions of local government (California Office of Planning and Research 1980). They are also responsible for establishing the 'sphere-of-influence' of each local agency within a county; the theoretical relationship for a city is shown in Fig. 11.4. Eight factors must be considered in determining the sphere-of-influence: maximum possible service area; range of possible and existing services; projected future population; level and type of projected development; present and future service needs; agencies providing services; social and economic interdependence; and agricultural preserves. They must be reviewed every five years and projected twenty years into the future.

LAFCOs are, thus, potentially a crucial state agency in the development of California regional cities with a strong potential regional planning influence. While not possessing power to initiate change, LAFCOs can direct urban growth through their determination of boundary changes of incorporated municipalities and special districts, especially servicing districts. In fact, two general goals are to discourage urban sprawl and to ensure the orderly formation and development of cities and special districts. For instance, two stated objectives (out of twelve) for the Fresno–Clovis metropolitan area involve discouraging urban sprawl and leap-frog development to keep servicing costs down and encouraging the continued farming of prime agricultural lands (Fresno County LAFCO 1974).

Selected examples have been used to illustrate some of the adaptations in land management structures that have arisen to cope with the regional-city issues which extend beyond the ability of existing governmental structures. It appears that most commonly some mixed mode is developing rather than either centralized or decentralized modes. It is essential that a systems view be developed that recognizes under one conceptual framework the many interacting economic, cultural and economic environment processes at work. It is not necessarily a question of no controls (the extreme form of decentralized structures) or absolute control (the extreme centralized structure) but the right controls for the particular concern and region (Bjork 1977).

In the next chapter the important ongoing concerns of land management in the city's countryside are sketched out and illustrated, and examples of specific tools that have been developed by various management units and structures are commented upon. There is inevitably some overlap between the consideration of formal management units and structures of this chapter and the concerns and tools of land-use management of the next chapter because the structures have been evolving, as the concerns have been recognized, in order to utilize existing and anticipated tools more effectively.

Further reading

Bosselman, F. and Callies, D. (1971) *The Quiet Revolution in Land Use Control*, US Government Printing Office, Washington, DC.

Bryant, C. R. (1974) An approach to the problem of urbanization and structural change in agriculture: a case study from the Paris region, 1955 to 1968, *Geografisa Annaler*, 56, B(1), 1–27.

Clawson, M. and Hall, P. (1973) *Planning and Urban Growth: an Anglo-American Comparison*, The Johns Hopkins Press, Baltimore, London.

Whitby, M. C. *et al.* (1974) *Rural Resource Development*, Methuen, London.

12 The tools and concerns of land-use management

In this chapter, we identify the principal concerns of land-use management in the city's countryside and relate these in a general way to the various types of tools and approaches that have been developed. Our aim is not to produce a catalogue of tools, because many more detailed accounts exist (e.g. Geay 1974; MEAR 1971; Listokin 1974), but rather to suggest a framework within which the tools and concerns can be viewed. In keeping with our geographic perspective of the regional city, the concerns of land-use management are discussed first in terms of those proper to the expansion of the built-up area, which deals essentially with the major portion of the inner fringe, and second, in terms of those related to the open countryside, the outer fringe and urban shadow zones. Inevitably, the two areas of concern overlap. Indeed, while the built-up area itself is not of direct concern to us, the manner in which the built-up area expands has direct implications for what happens in the remainder of the city's countryside, e.g. land consumption rates and degree of dispersal of urban-associated uses. Planning for development in some areas logically should be associated with planning for non-development in other areas. Our treatment of concerns and tools in the context of the open countryside is nonetheless undertaken in more detail, which is only proper given the focus of our book.

Expansion of the built-up city in the inner fringe

Expansion of the built-up city into the inner fringe affects the land of the more open countryside at different levels. This expansion takes place partly through processes exhibiting a regular distance-decay effect and accessibility considerations generally, as well as more irregular resource location effects. The regular distance-decay effect has been characterized as a wave-like process reflecting a dynamic equilibrium between centrifugal and centripetal forces (Blumenfeld 1954; Boyce 1966). The growing edge of the built-up city is seen as a tidal wave engulfing all before it; the area where inner and outer fringes merge is characterized as a precession wave presaging the tidal wave. This smooth wave-like process is of course disrupted, just as waves are on a rocky shore, by less regular infrastructure and resource location patterns.

Each regional city develops its own external spatial form resulting from the general outward growth of land-use activities, population distribution and service networks. Only four distinct alternative external spatial forms seem possible: concentric, multinodal, linear and dispersed (Fig. 12.1).

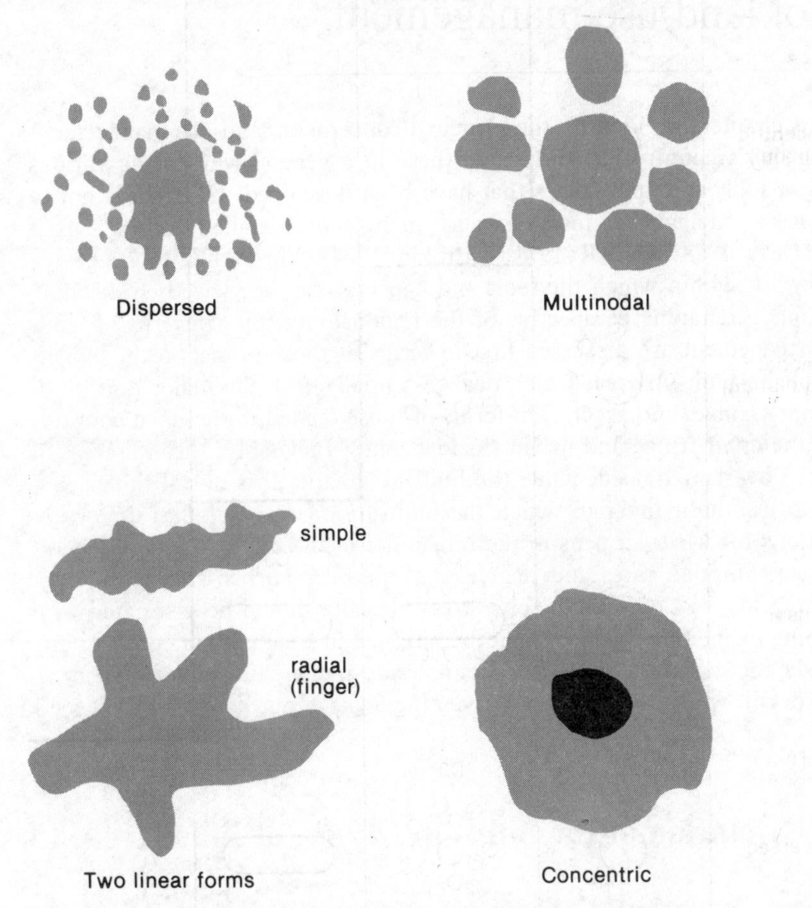

Figure 12.1 The four basic external urban forms. (Source: Russwurm, 1980b: Fig. 20, p. 319).

On the basis of existing evidence, we have characterized the overriding evolving form of the regional city as a concentrated–dispersed one. Superimposed on this concentrated–dispersed form and varying from city to city are imprints of multinodal and linear forms (Russwurm 1980b). These form variants, illustrated by Fig. 12.2, are largely independent of population density. The concentrated–dispersed perspective can be regarded as reasonable for most countries because of the relative infancy of planning controls; however, in the UK, given the commonly accepted view of the sharper contrast between urban and rural landscapes resulting from the Town and Country Planning Act of 1947 (Strachan 1974), the concentrated–multinodal pattern seems more appropriate in the British context.

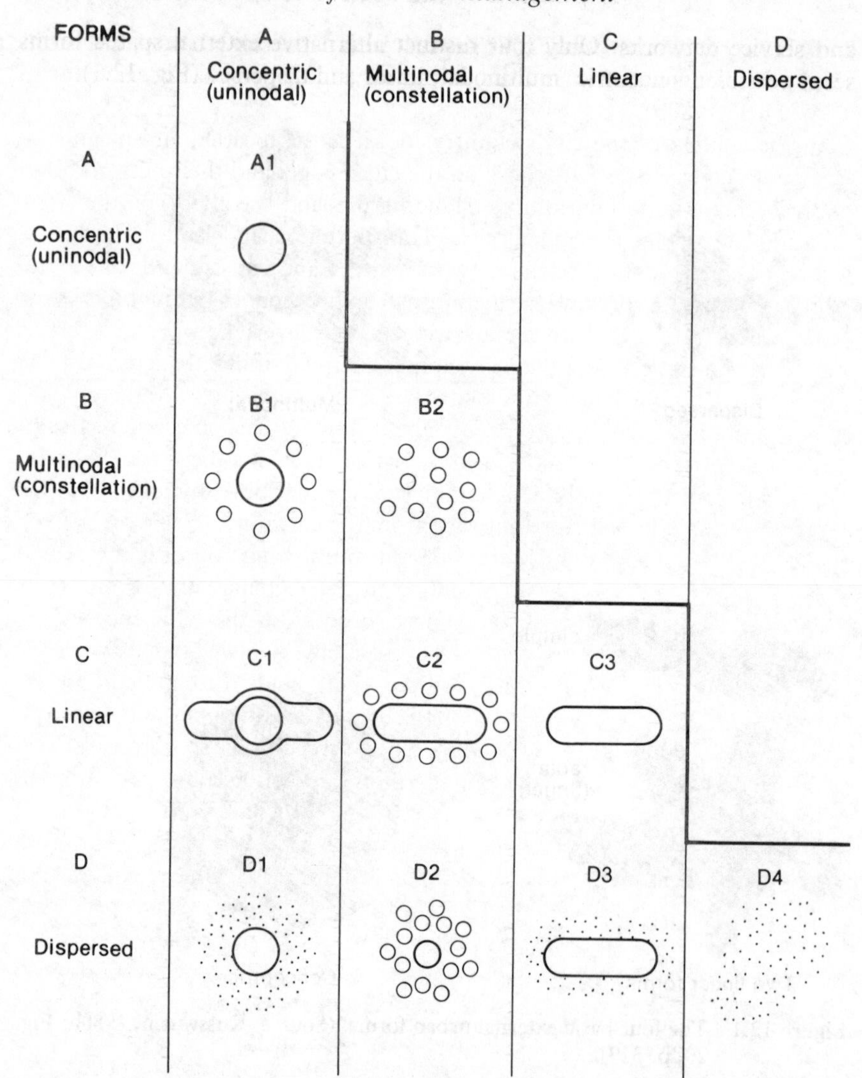

A classification of urban macro-forms. Pure forms are along the diagonal.

Figure 12.2 Combinations of alternative external spatial urban forms. (Source: Russwurm 1980b: Fig. 21, p. 321).

Any particular city will possess an internal and external spatial form historically conditioned by seven form-generating factors: population growth; competition for land; property rights; developers' activities; planning controls; technological developments; and the physical environment (Russwurm 1980b). Resulting from the interplay of these seven factors is the development of activity nodes which organize the urban flow of people, goods and information. Seven areal types of nodes are especially prominent: the downtown; shopping centres; industrial areas; institutional areas; prestige residential areas; apartment concentrations; and open-space leisure areas (Russwurm 1980b).

In the context of the city's countryside, it is the location and magnitude of activity nodes, especially those on the city's edge, and their network linkages which are important in understanding the land-use effects on the countryside of a particular regional city. Transportation and land-use planning efforts in concert reinforce the network pattern and consequently the external spatial form. Expressways, the ultimate expression of automobility, have both concentrating and dispersing aspects. However, networks associated with communications and the provision of energy dominantly act as dispersing forces (Ch. 2). Thus, an airport that is not contiguous to the city demands a linking expressway (e.g. Mirabel, Montréal). Soon economic forces lead to a corridor of activities. At the same time, if other road links are allowed to join the expressway, country residential development and other urban-associated uses diffuse outward from the corridor.

Keeping this background framework in mind, what concerns are critical and promise to be ongoing for planning in the regional city? In our view, they can be subsumed under the general heading of the 'efficiency' of the expansion process, which includes concerns about development patterns, land consumption rates and the use of the 'right' land. Absolute efficiency is a difficult concept to define, including, as it does, notions of what, for whom, and at what costs to whom. Obviously, this is a problem greater than we can handle here. Some economists have disposed of the difficulty by giving it to the 'market'. As a compromise, efficiency can be taken in a relative sense to mean some improvement in land-use patterns resulting from the application of various methods of land management, leading to a lower input of energy (costs and disutility) for the same or greater output with the benefits shared over a broader section of society. From both the perspectives of urban development and of the land resources in the city's countryside, it means striving to develop the 'right' land in the 'right' place at the 'right' time, the term 'right' reflecting concern for efficiency; land management can thus be seen as an attempt to achieve such efficiency.

Land management and urban development

Land management methods can be categorized broadly as negative-regulatory, persuasive-regulatory or positive-regulatory. A fourth category, perhaps an ideal one, might be labelled integrated or comprehensive. Regulations over land until 1945 were largely negative in scope and were intended primarily to protect individual property or public welfare and safety. This is a fair statement even in the context of the UK which has had a considerable head-start into land-use planning over most countries (Strachan 1974), for even though the 1932 Town and Country Planning Act extended planning control to most classes of land, it was hampered by a mechanism that was too unwieldy to be effective. The bundle of rights of ownership in land potentially includes mineral, air, and surface (development) and access rights. However, the rights that have been attributed to private landholders have never been absolute (Bryant 1972), and the public body has long circumscribed the rights of private landholders.

Nonetheless, the assumption that the market can allocate land fairly and that restrictions should be absolutely minimal and as local as possible has persisted in the public mind, albeit more strongly in some countries (e.g. the US) than in others (e.g. the UK). Even in the US though, the establishment of zoning as legal and not necessarily compensatable by 1926 weakened this assumption, and the rapid and often chaotic urban growth of the 1960s led to increasing regulations. Normally the most critical problem areas occurred in the inner fringe. As long as land was viewed primarily in terms of a commodity allocated by the supply-and-demand mechanism, negative regulations prevailed. As criticism of development patterns related to fragmented local planning systems became more pronounced in North America, persuasive-regulatory approaches at a broad regional scale became prominent. Local planning was seen to have four flaws:

1. short-term political reactions;
2. local plans conflicted with each other;
3. negative externalities were not recognized;
4. too many local governments made it impossible to develop effective long-range policy (Hawkins 1975).

Something had to be done by higher-level governments. A similar situation existed in Great Britain prior to the 1947 Town and Country Planning Act; prior to that Act, nearly 2,000 district councils were involved, presenting an enormous variation in the standards of planning and difficulties in preparing any long-range plans because of the rivalries between local authorities (Strachan 1974).

But as long as the traditional lay view of private property remains dominant, whereby development rights are implicit in land ownership, the conflict between individuals and the public body is pronounced. Thus, in North America attempts at persuasive-regulatory approaches evolved based on voluntary associations of adjoining municipalities at least partly supported by federal, state or provincial funds. Examples are the joint planning boards in Ontario and the regional planning commissions in Alberta in the 1960s and the Councils of Governments in the US in the 1970s, e.g. the South-East Michigan Council of Governments (Detroit) or the Association of Bay Area Governments (San Francisco). While some collective regulations arose and coordination improved considerably, the emphasis remained on local and, by extension, individual rights. One result can be a cumbersome, bureaucratic planning process (e.g. Ontario and California) as persuasion is increasingly clothed in layers of regulations administered by a multitude of agencies.

Gradually a new principle, already recognized in Great Britain since 1947, emerged for the US and Canada. This collective principle is the idea that development rights are: 'created and allocated to the land by society', and that 'development potential, on any land and in any community, results largely from the actions of society' (Reilly 1973: 143). Recognition of both the individual and collective principles leads to an equity dilemma, with individual land owners conflicting with efficient collective land-use regulations.

Resolution of this dilemma could be called positive-regulatory, characterized by broader-scale, more centrally directed regulation. It is being attempted in Oregon where state-wide planning goals are being merged with local plans, with the legal system serving as the mediator. Crucial to the Oregon approach is the funnelling of land-use controls through the Land Conservation and Development Commission (see Ch. 11). In positive-regulatory approaches, the three key assumptions are that somehow both individual and collective rights can be accommodated, that a better (more efficient) use of land is possible, and that governmental direction will result in more efficient land-use patterns. Certainly, these assumptions can be and are challenged by some economists: 'it would be a serious mistake to subject the allocation of land use to the caprice of governmental direction when a more efficient alternative – the market – is available' (Gramm and Ekelund 1975: 128). The general tenure of the market–based arguments is that market failure has not been demonstrated (Frankena and Scheffman 1980), that there is more evidence of 'government' botching up the job than performing it efficiently, and that externalities can be accommodated by the market. More specifically, Gardner (1977) argues that market failure can only occur when a desired collective good is not provided (e.g. police services), when uncompensated negative externalities exist, when a monopoly or monopsony exists, when 'merit' goods (e.g. a right of everyone such as pure air) are at stake, and when public policies distort prices. In terms of agricultural land preservation, Gardner then argues that only the 'merit good' argument can be demonstrated, i.e. agricultural land provides an open space and amenity good. But even so, he argues that if such 'merit' goods are proven lacking, they can be provided directly.

Inefficiencies associated with urban development

How do these regulatory approaches relate to the efficiency of development patterns in the inner fringe? To tackle the question, perceived inefficiencies must be noted. Two broad areas of possible inefficiency can be identified. First, there is the lacerated edge of the city and its associated sprawl. This lacerated edge is seen to create inefficiences through the fragmentation of land uses and parcels and the resulting higher costs of urban development. The fragmentation of land and land uses makes it more difficult to ensure an orderly development process, increases the costs of servicing development and creates negative externalities for surrounding and adjacent land uses. As an external spatial form of the city, it is an uncoordinated, dispersed one. Undoubtedly, two key reasons for this lacerated edge in many regional cities are the land conversion problems associated with the land market and land speculation noted in Chapter 3, and, at a broader scale, the frequently fragmented municipal structures, with each municipality striving for growth.

In the US, the external spatial form of most cities is less compact and more lacerated than even in Canada. This is partly related to the common phenomenon of 'leapfrog' subdivisions, and perhaps even more so to the pattern of shopping centres being built in advance of residential development outside the legal boundary of the city involved. These shopping centres may be in the right place, e.g. crossroads of main arterials or expressway interchanges, but may be developed at the wrong time. Usually this problem relates to fragmented municipal jurisdictions striving for an enlarged tax assessment base. Ramifications are felt in the expansion of urban sprawl and in competing effects on the centre and may in time contribute to lower population densities as more people move out from an increasingly poorly serviced inner city. The recognition and incorporation of such concerns into planning in the UK effectively dampened such developments until the mid-1960s at least (Dawson 1974).

Furthermore, low-density sprawl is unnecessarily costly for servicing even with relatively continuous development (Real Estate Research Corporation 1974). And as was noted in Chapter 6, those who benefit from the services may not be carrying a 'fair' share of the costs involved. Also related to the fragmentation pattern are negative externalities. Thus, an asphalt plant may belch smoke over neighbouring residences, or traffic resulting from a highway commercial ribbon development may interfere with commuters, or farmers may be afflicted by urban trespassers.

The second broad area of inefficiency is the impact on the resource base, especially agricultural land, expressed through the unnecessary use of good land, the occasional idling of land, fragmentation of land, and high values of land related to speculative ownership. Unnecessary loss to the private sector of potential recreational land and development on hazardous or otherwise unsuitable development land can also be cited. As noted in Chapter 6, agriculture is the major land user in the city's countryside so that most concern in terms of impacts on the resource base has been related to the agricultural land resource. Rates of land loss for several countries were noted in Chapter 6; both growth and lower densities of development (cf. Neutze 1977; Yeates 1975) have contributed to the loss of agricultural land. What trends will develop in the future are uncertain to the extent that population growth and its demographic structure are subject to change. However, it seems quite likely that future land conversion rates at the city edge will be at somewhat higher densities given the concerns over more efficient land use, the promoting of infilling, and the elimination of low-density and haphazard sprawl (California Office of Planning and Research 1978). Certainly, if the experience of Great Britain in the post-war period can be used as an example, this is almost bound to happen (Best 1976).

Concerns about land resources clearly include recreational, sand and gravel and water-recharge lands as well as agricultural lands. It may be that a block of good agricultural land is developed first when it could have been retained in production for 20 years by using less productive agricultural land. It may be that an area of potential public recreational land falls into private hands eager to develop and is converted to large-lot residential estates for the wealthy and lost to the community except for open-space viewing. It may be that a valuable sand-and-gravel deposit is unknowingly built over when the residential use could have been a sequential one. Or it may be that an important groundwater recharge area is built-over when it should be part of the open-space land. We will return to some of these land resources issues in our discussion of concerns in the open countryside. Only by positive-regulatory approaches based on a comprehensive and flexible plan supported by a thorough inventory of the resource base and integrating local and broader concerns, can such problems be ameliorated. Positive regulation demands a longer-term and a systems view. It does not necessarily mean more regulations (Oregon has fewer than California) but it does mean that the highest level of government involved must be prepared to act when necessary (Clawson and Hall 1973).

Thus, the various inefficiencies mentioned above have been, and are being, moderated in many regional cities by various persuasive-regulatory and positive-regulatory approaches. The mix of approaches at any one place partly reflects prevailing attitudes with respect to the role of government intervention and to the degree to which privately held rights to land should be restricted. In relation specifically to the land development process, a wide range of tools have been utilized to address some or all of the questions relating to the efficiency of urban development, including questions of price and adequate land supplies. The range of tools has included taxation of capital gains on land, public land assembly, price controls, and public planning. Over the greater part of its history, public planning, involving official land-use plans of various types, zoning and subdivision controls and the like, and manipulation of public investment, has been perversely unsuccessful in ensuring an orderly development process – the development of the right land, at the right time in the right location. Official land-use plans and zoning ordinances have not been able to cope with land supply and land price problems for urban development. In most instances, these approaches evolved under a prevailing negative-regulatory perspective, and detailed zoning, and even some broader plans (e.g. the Development Plans in Great Britain under the 1947 Act) create monopolistic conditions for land owners that can lead to restrictions in land supply and further price increases in the absence of a mechanism to recapture unearned increments in land values

(Bryant and Martin 1976). Essentially, such approaches still work within the context of a strong attachment to individual property rights and, as well, of the jealously guarded powers of local municipalities and authorities.

Once people begin to perceive the inefficiencies and the inequities involved, it is easier for them to be persuaded of the necessity to surrender some rights and powers, either in a persuasive-regulatory or a positive-regulatory vein. The promotion of transferable development rights through the private sector in the US is a good illustration of a persuasive-regulatory approach, in which voluntary participation is a key (James and Gale 1977). This still works within the context of private rights in land, but manipulation of the distribution of the development rights potentially allows some collective goals to be achieved more readily too. Moves placing more responsibilities for planning at higher levels of government can be seen as part of a trend towards more positive-regulatory approaches, e.g. the reorganization of planning responsibilities under the 1947 Town and Country Planning Act in the UK, regional government units in Ontario, and the development of the regional planning framework in France from the mid-1950s onwards (Boudeville 1966). At the same time, to the extent that a meaningful dialogue is maintained between lower and upper levels of government, strong elements of the persuasive-regulatory approach may remain. Attitudes towards land ownership thus appear as critical in determining what mix of approaches can be successfully utilized in a given national, or even regional, context. Thus, the system for the public assembly of land and the monitoring, even arbitration, of land prices in France in designated development zones involves a particular positive-regulatory approach (positive because designation of development areas is undertaken at a broad regional level and the land market therein is monitored and controlled for the benefit of the public purse, even though a market in land still exists) that would be difficult to introduce in North America because it touches land ownership rights in a direct way.

The open countryside

Within the open countryside, four broad areas of concern for land-use management can be identified, their level of expression varying considerably from country to country. First, there is a set of issues related to economic resource conservation and development, i.e. a concern for the maintenance of the *production function* of resources in the city's countryside. The two principal activities involved are agriculture and the aggregate industry. For agriculture, the issues are those of agricultural land conservation and of maintaining viable farming operations in the face of a potential threat from incompatible land uses. For the aggregate industry, the issues involve maintaining access to aggregate resources and reducing the level of negative externalities associated with the industry's operations. Second, there is a concern regarding the function of the city's countryside as a place to live. What sort of residential development should be permitted in the city's countryside? What densities? And under what conditions? Again, the concern is with reducing the level of any negative externalities associated with this use. Third, there is a set of concerns that relate to the play and protection functions of land in the city's countryside. These concerns can be identified with conservation of the landscape, either because of the amenity function of landscape, the heritage of the past contained in the landscape, or because of the natural environment elements that landscape incorporates, e.g. hedgerows, woodlots, swamp areas (Delavigne *et al.* 1970). Finally, a noticeable concern, particularly in the past decade or so, has been the need to incorporate or be responsive to public desires. This last concern cuts across the other three; it is beyond the scope of this book to treat this concern, except in so far as it is implicit in our concluding statements concerning a more integrated or comprehensive form of management and control.

The level of expression of these various concerns and the collective response to each has varied considerably from country to country. For example, general concern over the agricultural land resource base has had a long history in the UK (e.g. UK (HMSO) 1942). In the US, this concern was not widespread until the mid-1960s, while in France a concern for the conservation of agricultural land resources has never been coherently articulated. Yet concern for the amenity function of landscape has been much more developed in Western Europe than in North America, and landscape considerations are more firmly embedded into land-use management strategies in Western Europe. In our general survey of the approaches used to tackle each of the major planning concerns, this international variation must be kept in mind.

Resource conservation and development concerns

Agriculture

Planning for agriculture in the city's countryside requires ideally two prerequisites:

1. The realistic delimitation of urban growth boundaries so as not to precipitate unnecessary disinvestment in agriculture (Bryant 1973a).
2. The existence of a sound data base (Moran 1980). The data base would theoretically involve both information on the quality of the land resource (e.g. Vining, Plaut and Bieri 1977) as well as on the viability of the existing socioeconomic system of production.

The public response to agricultural concerns in the city's countryside can be placed into three categories: geographic prescription (largely negative-regulatory); easing the financial burden of farming; and more integrated approaches, usually at a broad geographic scale. Geographic prescription includes zoning and severance control, and, in so far as it involves maintaining separation between urban-associated and agricultural uses, is largely a negative-regulatory control approach. Zoning has for long been the traditional land-use control in North America (Listokin 1974; Nelson 1977), while similar approaches exist in several other countries, e.g. the *Plan d'occupation du sol* (POS) in France (Berteloot 1972; Geay 1974), the tool being largely developed at the local municipal level. International differences exist, though, in the processes of zoning formulation and the approval and review processes. Theoretically, zoning and the like represent the implementation of a broader planning document, such as an official plan, but the relationship between zoning and plans has been tenuous historically (cf. Listokin 1974).

Zoning involves several features, including delimitation of an area for a specific use, identifying permitted and prohibited uses, and sometimes specification of regulations for particular uses (Berteloot 1972; Solberg 1967). The exclusive agricultural zone is a rather illusory concept, since a variety of other uses are often permitted in agricultural zones (e.g. residential development associated with the farm operation and sand-and-gravel operations). Different types of agricultural zones may be identified, sometimes based on differences in the quality of the agricultural land resource so that priority agricultural zones would be protected more stringently than secondary agricultural zones, where country residential development might be acceptable. Zoning in relation to agriculture has, however, not had a particularly successful history (cf. Whyte 1968; Nelson 1977; Listokin 1974), partly because of the lack of congruence between zoning documents and longer-term planning documents. It has been too easy in most instances to move from an agricultural use designation to a 'higher and better' economic use, a move that local municipalities have frequently been unwilling to halt owing to the implications for local revenues in many jurisdictions.

Severance control represents another prescriptive measure that has been used, especially in North America, to attempt to control development within agricultural areas. A severance is created by the legal division of a property parcel into two separate parcels; sometimes, more than one additional parcel is created, but the creation of multiple lots at one time is generally referred to as a subdivision and often involves a different approval process. Terminology varies, however; in western Canada, a severance of land is referred to as a subdivision of a property while in the UK, the term 'lotting' has been used to refer to multiple parcel creation (Munton 1979) and in the US the term 'splitting' is often used.

Severances have many purposes, such as road widening, farm boundary adjustment and building lots. The appearance of severances in an agricultural zone has been generally regarded as the first step towards urbanization of an area. This is particularly so in North America where the land survey system is still youthful compared to Western Europe and large property parcels are still the rule in most agricultural areas. Thus, while control over country residential development can also be exercised potentially through zoning and the granting of building permits, control over severances, and subdivisions, has been regarded in many parts of North America in the last fifteen years or so as the obvious way to nip the process of country residential development in the bud, thus eliminating the potential incompatibilities between agricultural and residential development before they arise.

Control over severances has various forms. The setting of minimum parcel sizes, e.g. the minimum 10 acre lot (about 4 ha) in many municipalities in Ontario, Canada, in the early 1960s, represented one attempt; smaller parcels would then require approval. However, in Ontario this simply resulted in severances being created that were slightly greater than the minimum; raising the minimum to 25 acres (about 10 ha) led to similar results. Consequently, all severances now require approval.

While not relating to severance control, the use of the *coéfficient d'occupation du sol* (COS) in French land-use plans (Berteloot 1972) has an effect on the parcel sizes that are developed. The COS expresses the relationship between net built floor space and property size and has the effect for a given size of house of specifying minimum parcel sizes. Thus, a COS of 0.1 in a zone means that a structure with a residential floor space of 100 square metres must be built on a minimum parcel size of 1,000 square metres (minimum parcel size = 100 divided by 0.1 = 1,000 square metres). The lower the COS, the less dense the possible development; the COS can thus serve as a method of almost eliminating development in a particular zone.

In the North American context, severance control has usually been the domain of the municipality, either local, county or regional, although various guide-lines (often a persuasive-regulatory approach) have been established by upper levels of government (e.g. Ontario Ministry of Housing 1976; Government of Ontario 1978) and in the process of approval of zoning plans and land-use plans, some involvement by upper levels of government is not uncommon, e.g. Ontario, representing more positive-regulatory approaches. In some situations, where residential development can be permitted, minimum distances between residences and intensive livestock operations are strongly suggested in order to reduce the potential for complaints as well as reduction of any health hazards (e.g. Ontario Ministries of the Environment and of Agriculture and Food 1973). Residential development for farm-related purposes characteristically have been permitted even in top-priority agricultural zones, e.g. for farmers' sons or daughters, or workers or for farmers' retirement homes (cf. Berteloot 1972; Government of Ontario 1978). However, in the long term and given the continuance of the trend towards larger farms and labour rationalization, such houses eventually become 'surplus' and end up in non-farm hands. Even permitting such residential construction without granting a severance is not likely to prevent this process in the long term.

The property taxation problem for agriculture has received considerable attention in North America, where property taxation provides a significant portion of municipal revenues. The problem, as noted in Chapter 6, arises because of:

1. The tendency for agricultural land to be overestimated in value in the urban fringe, even when value 'in use' is the rule;
2. The extra municipal costs that have to be borne resulting from the demands of exurbanites for additional services.

Regionalization of assessment of property values (e.g. Walrath 1957) and of certain public costs (e.g. through the creation of school districts or boards) has certainly eliminated part of the problem by spreading the burden over a wider geographic area. A variety of other techniques has been attempted, ranging from the single rebate of 50 per cent of the property tax on farmland for farmers with a minimum volume of farm-produce sales in Ontario currently, to preferential assessment whereby agricultural properties pay taxes on the basis of agricultural values rather than market land values, to more complex 'roll-back' systems. Under the latter, taxes are paid on the basis of agricultural land values, but upon sale of land involving land-use conversions, the difference in taxes between what was paid and what would have been paid if market values were used for a specified number of years becomes due, sometimes with interest. The techniques are reviewed elsewhere with specific examples of jurisdictions using them (Hady and Stinson 1967; Hady and Sibold 1974; Whyte 1968; Gloudemans 1971; US Council of Environmental Quality 1976; Roberts and Brown 1980).

Of course, the techniques noted above begin to make much more sense when they are part of an integrated package. For instance, if an agricultural zone is credible, then land values will be more likely to reflect agricultural use values, which can be reinforced by some form of preferential assessment. All of these techniques have suffered historically from the important role ascribed local municipalities in the plan formulation and approval processes. Clearly, such problems are more significant in decentralized structures than in centralized ones. The belief that individual municipalities will take decisions that necessarily reflect the evaluation of global costs and benefits in the conversion of agricultural land is a naïve one. Increasingly, then, both as the geographic scale of the processes underlying the regional city form and the regional and national importance of agricultural land resources have been recognized, there have been moves to broader scales of agricultural land-use management. While some programmes also have objectives relating to functions of land other than agricultural production, they do not provide the potential for an integrated countryside-management framework in the context of the regional city form as does the green belt.

In the US probably the best-known programme is that administered under the California Land Conservation Act (Williamson Act) of 1965 (Snyder 1966; Williams 1969; Gustafson and Wallace 1975; Carman 1977; Gustafson 1977) although the North Carolina experience is an interesting one, too. The land-use objectives of the California Act were to maintain a maximum area of prime agricultural land and indirectly to maintain open-space areas. Under the Act, contracts may be made between owners of agricultural land and local governments voluntarily (thus placing it in the persuasive-regulatory category), either within designated 'agricultural preserves' or upon application by the land owner. The contract outlaws any use of the land other than open space and other compatible uses for a minimum of 10 years in return for a use-value assessment for property taxation. The contract is also renewable annually, unless one of the parties files notice of non-renewal in which case taxes increase progressively over the remaining life of the contract. By 1976, 40 per cent of California's farmland and 33 per cent of its prime land was under contract (Carman 1977) but very little contract land was found in the urban-fringe area where pressures are greatest. The programme has been criticized because it is voluntary and therefore leads to a fragmentary pattern of contracted land, because the financial inducements are inadequate and because it has not been coordinated sufficiently with other land-use planning measures (Gustafson and Wallace 1975). In both 1976 and 1977 proposed Acts which would have prohibited the conversion of prime land to non-agricultural land uses except under special conditions were debated (Gustafson 1977).

The 1971 Agricultural District Laws of New York State, combining farm value assessment of property and state-wide zoning, is similar in some ways to the California situation (Bryant and Conklin 1975). Responsibility resides mainly at the local government level, although the State must review the agricultural districts to ensure conformity to state-wide plans. However, a minimum area of land must be set aside to qualify for 'agricultural district' designation, and a roll-back provision on deferred taxes is part of the programme. By 1975, agricultural districts covered 50 per cent of the full-time farmland in New York state, although once more, there were none in the agricultural areas closest to New York City.

Other examples exist of agricultural land conservation programmes at a scale broader than the local municipality or even the region. The British Columbia Land Commission Act of 1973 has already been discussed in Chapter 11 in relation to the Regional Districts of British Columbia. It can be regarded as more of a positive-regulatory approach than its US counterparts just discussed because the Commission has province-wide powers over the administration of the Agricultural Reserves established by each Regional District and it is thus more insulated from the vagaries of local pressures. A recent US exception not yet well-tested is the Oregon approach which combines exclusive farm-use zones, urban growth boundaries and preferential assessment (Oregon LCDC 1978; Banta 1980).

We have not exhausted the range of techniques that can be used to help conserve agricultural land resources. Naturally, many of the approaches used to deal with residential development in the city's countryside can also help in promoting agricultural land conservation. Furthermore, techniques developed for other purposes can have beneficial effects for agricultural land conservation, e.g. capital gains taxation or speculation taxes which may reduce the incentive for non-farm interests to hold agricultural land as an investment; the various forms of transfer of development rights (Rose 1975) have potentially great significance for the maintenance of agriculture, at least, in limited areas; and public servicing policy may serve to guide development away from key agricultural areas. Finally, even though it may not be realistic over large areas, public ownership of agricultural land has some potential. Institutionalized agricultural activities, e.g. agricultural research stations, may sometimes be the safest way to ensure the maintenance of agricultural land, although no examples of the deliberate use of this as a strategy are known to the authors. However, quite extensive public agricultural land holdings do exist in the London Green Belt, in which the Greater London Council owns over 4,000 ha of agricultural land which is rented to farmers and overseen by the Land Agency Group of the Greater London Council (Blessley, undated).

Aggregate mining activities

Land-use management strategies for the aggregate industry are faced with two types of problems. First, the industry produces essential commodities for the process of economic growth yet certain components of that process, especially residential development, conflict with the operation of the industry and can even lead to the sterilization of valuable resources (Bryant and McLellan 1975a). This is particularly serious where reserves of the resource base are becoming physically exhausted in any case, as in parts of the London Green Belt (Verney Committee 1976). Second, partly because of the locational matrix in which the industry often finds itself in the city's countryside and partly because of the inherent nature of its operation, the aggregate industry generates significant negative externalities. Increasingly, protests by local residents affected and by amenity-conscious groups have made it more and more difficult for the industry to gain approval for new workings; examples of these problems are found throughout Western countries where the aggregate industry has a significant presence in the city's countryside, e.g. south-east England.

The land-use management and planning challenge is to ensure the industry has access to adequate raw materials and that current development patterns do not sterilize reserves, while minimizing the impact of negative externalities. This implies that a two-pronged strategy is necessary, one dealing with the location and timing of development of the industry and the other dealing with the conditions under which the industry should operate. The early phase of dealing with the industry was characterized by a negative-regulatory approach, e.g. up to the early 1970s in North America, and public responsibility for the industry rested largely with local municipalities and local authorities. This early phase of management was essentially unsucessful, for a number of reasons.

First, the locational aspect to management of the resources demands a substantial data base on the location, volume and quality of the resource base, as well as information on the industry's needs. Local municipalities and authorities have frequently, if not usually, had inadequate financial resources and technical staff to undertake the necessary surveys (Bryant and McLellan 1975b), even if the need for such information had been realized. Second, with mounting public opposition to the industry during the 1960s, local municipalities and authorities reacted in various ways reflected in different approaches contained in local planning documents such as land-use or development plans, and zoning ordinances. In one detailed study of several municipalities in a region in southern Ontario (Bryant and McLellan 1975a), three different approaches to locational planning of the industry were noted. In the first approach, the industry could be a prohibited use, either by expressly prohibiting it or by not including it as a permitted use. The industry continued to exist in such situations only as a non-conforming use. In the second approach, the industry was sometimes classed as a permitted use within, e.g., an agricultural zone. In the third approach, specific extractive industry or gravel pit designations may exist, elevating the industry to the same level as uses such as agriculture and residential use in planning. The first approach is inadequate because it does not recognize the importance of the industry and the second approach seriously needs some form of licensing system to maintain any type of control at all; and both the second and third approaches need a solid information base before any claims to achieving a sound resource and land-use management strategy can be made.

In terms of regulating the operation of the industry, once established, the early phase of negative-regulatory control was characterized by lack of success too. In the above case study, some municipalities had regulating by-laws which dealt with such things as set-backs and hours of operation, while others had none at all (Bryant and McLellan 1975a). In one instance, there were even statements made about ensuring some sort of rehabilitation. However, they were all characterized by one feature – lack of enforcement and inspection, except if specific complaints were made. The level of resources of many of the local municipalities and authorities involved clearly would not permit the maintenance of the necessary staff. Munton (1979) notes that planning officers in the London Green Belt, too, were often sceptical about the ability of local authorities to ensure that conditions on the operation of the industry were carried out.

It is against this background of lack of success in management and control of the early phase that movements towards a more positive-regulatory approach in several jurisdictions in the 1970s must be viewed, e.g. Ontario and Colorado. On the one hand, efforts were made to undertake systematic inventories of resources and needs across broad regions (e.g. Bryant and McLellan 1974; Proctor and Redfern 1974; Colorado Division of Mines 1973), and on the other hand, movements have been made to strengthen the involvement of upper levels of government in managing the resources and industries in several jurisdictions. In Ontario, the Pits and Quarries Control Act (Ontario 1971) represented a major thrust in this direction in an attempt to establish operational standards and ensure rehabilitation of the land through a system of issuing mining permits. Applications for a mining permit from the Division of Mines of the Ontario Ministry of Natural Resources must first, however, conform to local by-laws and regulations regarding aggregate extraction. The applications comprise plans of the existing site and adjacent land uses, a proposed plan of operations including plant and buildings and a plan of rehabilitation for after-use; approval of an application also requires a security deposit (a bonding system) to ensure progressive rehabilitation, since it is refundable as costs for rehabilitation are incurred; and the regulations are policed by regional officers of the Ministry.

The approach in Ontario encountered many problems in the 1970's, not least of which was the absence of a strong provincial statement on mineral extraction policies. While the Pit and Quarries Control Act represented a move towards a positive-regulatory stance, responsibility for identifying key resource areas is still very much a local or regional matter and therefore the relationship between lower and upper levels of government is essentially a persuasive one. Furthermore, the appeals procedure open to the public through the Ontario Municipal Board provided a forum in which local public opposition to the industry continued to be heard and very largely respected. Another problem area concerns questions about the effectiveness of the requirements regarding rehabilitation. On the one hand, some of the requirements of the original Act are almost silly, e.g. permissible slopes of rehabilitated land are often too steep for most types of aggregate materials. Furthermore, it appears that the initial security deposit did not really encourage progressive rehabilitation and that it was simply regarded as an extra cost by the industry rather than as an inducement; interestingly enough, it appears that the attitude in the UK does not favour a security deposit system (Stevens Committee 1976; Verney Committee 1976). Finally, there remain many questions about the real possibilities of restoring the agricultural capability of the land in cases where residential and recreational after-uses are not reasonable uses (e.g. Lowe *et al.* 1977), which cannot help but frustrate attempts to manage this industry rationally. Nonetheless, some enlightened municipalities, e.g. Waterloo Region, southern Ontario, have made significant strides in reserving aggregate resources and attempting to control any other development that might sterilize them.

As a final example, the State of Colorado (Colorado Division of Mines 1973) has moved also towards a more positive-regulatory approach. First, recognizing the necessity and value of aggregate resources, a directive was given to the Colorado Geologic Survey to inventory all reserves by 1 July 1974, and another to the county planning commissions to analyse how such reserves could be made accessible. Second, statements were made about the need for rehabilitation, but progressive rehabilitation was not promoted.

From this point of view, no progress was made over the Ontario situation.

Even though the nature of the problem faced by the aggregate industry has been identified now, and the necessity of planning this use of land resources recognized, the movement towards a more positive-regulatory approach has not yet been characterized by substantial success. This is partly because an adequate data base still remains absent in most jurisdictions, partly because upper levels of government have been more reticent about using their powers to protect an activity that, although necessary, has not endeared itself to the public, and partly because there still appear to be technical uncertainties to be resolved about certain types of rehabilitation. In all of these respects, then, there are considerable differences between this experience and the moves to a more positive-regulatory approach for agriculture noted above in some jurisdictions in the 1970s.

Residential development

Residential development is at the heart of two sets of concerns in land-use management. First, the geographic pattern of residential development, both in terms of location and density, has created concerns for the servicing costs of development and its impact on the resource base, the latter being more recent. Second, the degree to which residential development is integrated into the surrounding landscape – within existing settlements and in the open countryside – has generated concerns for 'rural character', essentially an amenity concern. Both the timing and the level of articulation of these concerns has varied from country to country and even within countries. In France, for instance, the 'official' position on urban development has been dominated for some time by a perspective favouring concentration in the larger and medium-sized urban centres. Bauer and Roux (1976) argue that most French regional land-use plans have adopted this approach because of the assumed efficiencies of servicing and the greater range of facilities possible with large urban centres. Either suburban expansion or, around the largest agglomerations, the development of satellite New Towns seem to have been the preferred option of the French, even though the actual experience in the 1960s and 1970s has continued to show that the more dispersed patterns have been occurring, e.g. dispersed single-family dwellings, expansion of smaller villages, and the parachuting of entire 'new metropolitan villages' into the countryside (Préfecture de la Région d'Ile-de-France 1976a; Poupardin *et al.* 1971). However, changes were beginning to appear in the 1970s in some regional land-use plans, in which the more dispersed types of development, especially the clustering approach, are gaining favour. Furthermore, there has been more concern expressed over potential impact on the natural and economic resource base in the 1970s, while the concern over rural character, although fairly recent in some ways, can be traced back to the much older concern over the preservation of historic sites.

In Britain, these concerns go back much further than elsewhere (Strachan 1974); the excesses of urban development in the inter-war period led to the Town and Country Planning Act of 1932, the Restriction of Ribbon Development Act of 1935, and a number of other measures early on which culminated in the Town and Country Planning Act of 1947 which was to guide the planning system in Britain for over two decades (Whitby *et al.* 1974). Concerns for the orderly development of urban areas found bed partners for themselves with concerns for preserving prime agricultural land and protecting the rural character of the countryside.

In contrast, these concerns in the US and Canada have been expressed in a much more fragmented manner because of the higher degree of decentralization of planning responsibilities. However, in an increasing number of jurisdictions in North America, as we have already seen, mounting concern with the impact of development on the resource base as well as servicing costs has given rise to more and more restrictions on development, with some form of clustering and infilling approach being commonly favoured. However, the concern for rural character is a much less articulated concern in North America than in Western Europe; it is found sometimes in areas with major scenic resources or in the dormitory-type villages where the newcomers organize themselves to maintain the character of the small settlement against further development (e.g. Sinclair and Westhues 1975), but this has not reached the proportions of the amenity-conscious groups that have become established in the metropolitan villages in Britain (Connell 1974).

Approaches to controlling and managing residential development in the city's countryside have been dominated by negative-regulatory systems and techniques, with movements towards a more positive-regulatory stance being made where there is some broader regional involvement in planning and control. Control over the location and density of residential development has been largely one of geographic prescription. Various types of zones catering for residential development can be found in the local municipality zoning of North American jurisdictions (cf. Solberg 1967) and their counterparts in other countries where it exists, e.g. the POS of France.

In the French POS, urban zone designations are centred on existing settlements and contiguous areas for relatively immediate expansion; in rural zones, dispersed development is permissible under certain conditions; in agricultural zones, only agriculturally-related construction is permitted; and in rural-amenity zones designed to protect special scenic or historic sites, single-family residential development may sometimes be permitted under certain conditions (Berteloot 1972).

Such zoning-type control can be used to encourage clustering of development, either in existing selected nodal settlements or in small rural-estate subdivisions and can be encountered both in the plan proper and the control device, e.g. the zoning by-law. Characteristically, where residential development is permitted, additional regulations often specify density of development through minimum lot size requirements (e.g. Calgary Regional Planning Commission 1977), sometimes linear frontage minima, minimum floor space and sometimes the specification of a minimum ratio between net floor space constructed and lot size (e.g. the *coéfficient d'occupation du sol* of the French POS). Particularly where subdivisions are possible, additional requirements may relate to servicing, such as water and sewage disposal. In North America, another major prescriptive tool has been through the exercise of control over severances, the division of properties, a topic already discussed under the agricultural concerns.

In the UK, the intimate relationship established since 1947 between plan formulation and implementation or control through the granting of planning permission led to a very tight control over urban encroachment into rural areas; county plans, dealing with the rural areas, were characterized by large 'white' areas in which the intent was that existing uses should continue undisturbed. Through the exercise of statutory development control, development was successfully controlled during the next two decades (Whitby *et al.* 1974). Although the effort was largely negative-regulatory in stance, there were elements of a more positive-regulatory approach in that overall policies were established at the central government level and the latter exercised approval over the 1947 Development Plans and, more recently, the 1968 Structure Plans.

Performance zoning, a recent variation of traditional zoning, is worthy of mention also (Stockham and Pease 1974; Pease and Morgan 1979). This zoning modification provides controls to regulate the effects or impacts in the surrounding area instead of separating uses into various zones. Thus, uses sometimes labelled incompatible, like country residential development in an agricultural zone, could be permitted if designated standards of performance are met. In a sense this device can be compared with the Ontario Agricultural Code of Practices, but it would be flexible and tailored to individual situations.

A key problem with all the negative-regulatory approaches and the broader-scale positive-regulatory mechanisms has been their acceptability. While there is some variation in the acceptability of these regulatory approaches, ranging from a relatively high level of tolerance of government intervention in Great Britain to quite low levels in the US (Clawson and Hall 1973), all attempts at geographic prescription represent in a sense the institutionalization of inequities in wealth. Attempts to solve this have ranged from trying to recapture for the public purse the increments in development values conferred on some land by planning activity, e.g. the chequered attempts in Britain since 1947 (Clawson and Hall 1973), to holding down land prices in specified development zones as in the French *zones d'aménagement différé* (Bryant and Martin 1976).

In North America, planning has often lacked credibility; in the US, the separation between planning and implementation or control is considerable and so the promises of planning have had difficulty being carried out. Thus, in any context where private property rights are jealously guarded, solutions that permit private land owners the continued enjoyment of development values while still guiding or controlling development are likely to be interesting alternatives in the future. Examples that come to mind include the schemes relating to transfer of development rights in the US (Rose 1975) and the possibilities of concentration of permitted densities of development under Article 19 of the French *loi d'orientation foncière* of 1967 (France 1968). Under the latter arrangement, municipalities could acquire land for, say, park space by allowing a property owner whose COS was, say, 0.02 to increase the density of development to ten times the initial density (a COS in this case therefore of 0.2) on one-tenth of the property, the remainder being donated to the municipality; it was envisaged that a similar procedure could be developed for a whole group of property owners.

Amenity concerns related to residential construction in the city's countryside or a concern for 'rural character', despite differences between countries, is increasingly found in planning documents throughout the Western world, e.g. British Columbia (cf. Okanagan – Similkameen Regional District 1974), the US (cf. Metropolitan Council of the Twin Cities Area 1979a), Australia (cf. Australian Department of Urban and Regional Development 1975; McQuinn 1978) and France (cf. Préfecture de la Région d'Ile-de-France 1976b). In some instances, the landscape concern is very explicit; for instance, in the Areas of Outstanding Natural Beauty and other areas designated as having a high landscape value in the UK, development control has been carefully enforced to ensure developments will harmonize with the landscape (Strachan 1974). In other cases, amenity considerations are merged and confused with other concerns such as the location of development in agricultural areas, so that specific control mechanisms cannot readily be identified with the amenity concern.

Where there are specific regulations regarding the exterior characteristics of residential development (e.g. in the French POS), there has usually been little guidance for local municipalities in terms of how criteria are to be interpreted or even created. This element of subjectivity in the area of landscape amenity emphasizes the impossibility of ever reaching a definitive solution to such issues.

Recreation and nature

The amenity concerns just noted are closely interwoven with concerns for nature and outdoor recreational opportunities in the city's countryside. Setting aside recreational concerns that can be accommodated, partially at least, through the private sector or through the provision of facilities for intensive outdoor recreational uses (e.g. swimming, tennis courts) in near-urban parks, the principal concerns have to do with the demand for open space for active outdoor recreational activities, e.g. hiking and cross-country skiing and for more passive activities, e.g. countryside-viewing, in turn related intimately to the conservation of the environment.

The recreational supply–demand relationship can be summed up for the city's countryside as a divergence between the supply and demand for space for short-term recreational need (day-use and weekend use dominantly). Intensity of demand is greatest closest to the urban area, but the supply of space is limited; the reverse is the case in areas more removed from the urban areas. One solution to this has been the greater degree of institutionalization or formalization of recreational open space close to urban areas in an attempt to channel pressures and cater for demands, e.g. near-urban park. There is a limit, however, to the extent to which formal park spaces can provide the range of outdoor recreational experiences demanded by some segments of urban populations. Indeed, it has been argued, even in the North American context, that private property will have to play a much more important role in the provision of recreational opportunities than hitherto (Cullington 1980). This raises difficult issues of access, both in physical terms and in legal terms; realization of such difficulties lies behind recent changes in the laws in Ontario relating to liabilities of property owners for damages incurred by users of their properties (Cullington 1980), which should increase the potential for multiple use of the land resource.

The whole concern for landscape amenity overlaps with concerns for 'protection' or conservation of the natural environment, even though the latter in some instances relates to public health and safety considerations, e.g. safeguarding groundwater recharge areas, protection of floodplain land and prevention of development in environmentally unstable areas such as steep slopes. From the perspective of landscape amenity, 'natural environment' elements in the landscape such as treelines, woodlots and hedgerows, are important because they provide relief from a landscape which is otherwise dominated around most cities by the economic production system and they provide a habitat for flora and fauna which are of scientific and general educational value. While landscape amenity is an elusive concept for measurement, it is important to note that: 'Man does not live by bread alone' (Nature Conservancy Council 1977: 7), so that it is still important. Interestingly enough, in the West European context, it is modern agriculture that is seen as being increasingly in conflict with landscape amenity and natural environment conservation (Nature Conservancy Council 1977; Davidson and Wibberley 1977; Centre National d'Etude et de Recherche du Paysage 1975), rather than urban-associated land-use development.

The simplicity with which we have presented the concerns relating to outdoor recreation and nature hides a multiplicity of demands in fact, which is reflected in the variety of approaches that have been used. Many responses have been elicited, involving many different agencies. Sometimes, the negative-regulatory approach through geographic prescription in plans and development control (e.g. Areas of Outstanding Natural Beauty in Great Britain) or plans and zoning by-laws (e.g. the designation of Environmentally

Sensitive Areas in some regional plans in Ontario) has been used to protect specially valued areas. Where the resources have been easily recognized for their broader regional and even national significance, attempts at larger-scale intervention have been attempted, e.g. the more positive-regulatory system of National Parks created under the 1949 National Parks and Access to the Countryside Act in Britain or the more persuasive approach adopted by the French in their *parcs régionaux*.

Public purchase of land has sometimes seemed the only way to achieve certain results, either because of the difficulties of evaluating the qualities inherent in landscape and the natural environment (e.g. the nature reserves owned by the Nature Conservancy Council in the UK) or because of the presumed need to control absolutely certain types of areas (e.g. the land owned and managed by Conservation Authorities in Ontario in their effort to manage water supplies). Sometimes recreational goals are secondary to natural environment preservation, sometimes vice versa.

In land acquired by public purchase, there is a positive-regulatory thrust where the threat of expropriation is used to attain broader societal goals. Because of problems of cultural acceptability of acquiring land in this way in countries such as the US, other proposals may allow public acquisition of land while still respecting private land ownership traditions, e.g. transfer of development rights (Rose 1975) and easements or the purchase of development rights alone (Whyte 1968), thus representing a more persuasive type of approach.

In the landscape amenity debate, difficult issues are being posed, especially in a West European context. Landscape amenity and 'rural character' present almost impossible measurement problems, yet increasingly actions are being taken to consider them. Maintenance of landscape values in terms of architectural control, both over existing buildings of special significance and over new development, is not foreign to many countries. However, one major source of landscape change which affects both amenity value and access to landscape has largely remained outside the domain of land-use management and control, viz. agricultural change. Agricultural buildings have generally escaped much scrutiny in most countries. Thus, agriculture has generally enjoyed considerable protection in Britain because of the dispensation accorded agricultural buildings in acquiring planning permission in most instances (Whitby *et al.* 1974). Similarly, in the 1971 Agricultural District Laws of New York State, local governments were not permitted to introduce regulations affecting farm structures, except for health and safety reasons (Bryant and Conklin 1975).

Furthermore, modern agriculture presents considerable conflicts with landscape and the natural environment, e.g. chemical fertilizers and pesticides and field enlargement. Indeed, in the case of France, the pursuit of agricultural modernization through reorganization of the fragmented cadastral and field structure in many regions by the process known as *remembrement* has modified many landscapes beyond recognition; only recently have the amenity and technological benefits of such features as windbreaks and hedgerows been reincorporated into this agricultural modernization process. The general conflicts between modern agriculture and natural environment and amenity have been identified very vocally in Britain as well (cf. Nature Conservancy Council, 1977; Davidson and Wibberley 1977; Westmacott and Worthington 1974). Furthermore, modern agriculture is often not particularly well adapted to multiple-resource use, so that modernization of agriculture can be seen as restricting access to the amenity resources of the city's countryside.

Because neither negative- nor positive-regulatory approaches have been geared to handle these types of situations, and because of the almost inevitably cumbersome system that would evolve if direct regulatory control were extended to these conflicts, more and more attention has been aimed at developing *persuasive approaches at the microscale* in which aims might be achieved through an active dialogue between land owners and public representatives. The countryside management projects of the Countryside Commission in Britain (Davidson and Wibberley 1977), some of the thrusts being taken in the French *zones naturelles d'équilibre* (Préfecture de la Région d'Ile-de-France 1976a,b; Chassagne 1974) and the efforts of the Fondation de France to introduce the farming community to the variety of structures and materials available for farm buildings (Centre National d'Etude et de Recherche du Paysage 1976) are all indicative of this mounting concern in Western Europe.

Green belts and the like: a more integrated perspective?

It should be clear by now that the various concerns that exist about the direction the city's countryside is moving in are interdependent. This follows almost automatically from the point argued earlier, that land as a resource performs many different functions. It is in this light that we have to view the movements towards a more positive-regulatory approach, involving broader regional responsibilities and control in plan formulation and implementation that were touched upon in Chapter 11. Here we review briefly the contribution of green belts and similar devices because, potentially at least, they represent the geographic designation of an area called upon to perform a multiplicity of functions in the city's countryside which might therefore be expected to permit a greater degree of integration of the functions.

However, such has not been the experience, even though certain thrusts in the 1970s hold out some hope for a better use and management of green belts in the future. Green belts and green wedges are most readily conceived of in terms of a regional city orientation. Green belts can perform a variety of functions, e.g. shaping the urban form and urban containment, maintenance of the agricultural land resource, preservation of the rural character of the countryside and providing recreational opportunities for urban residents. Almost inevitably, however, there rarely seems to be a consensus as to which functions such zones must perform and what the priorities are. Let us look briefly at two examples, the English Green Belts, especially the London one, and the more recent *zones naturelles d'équilibre* of the Paris region.

There were 4,800 square kilometres of green belt land either approved or under consideration by the central government in England and Wales in 1974 (Davidson and Wibberley 1977). By far the best known one is that centred on London, where the originally submitted and approved green belt covers about 2,260 square kilometres (Standing Conference 1976). The first positive moves towards the development of the London Green Belt came in 1935; plans were developed for the London County Council, working together with surrounding counties, to purchase land. Statutory support for this venture came in 1938 with the Green Belt Act and by 1944, 112 square kilometres had been purchased. Abercrombie's (1945) Greater London Plan of 1944 involved a much larger area, much too large for systematic public purchase. Thus, the Green Belt as we know it today subsequently came into being though the submissions contained in the local authority development plans under the 1947 Act and the use of development control through the granting of planning permission.

Abercrombie had seen the Green Belt not only in terms of urban containment but also as an area in which farming would be the main landscape feature while recreational functions would be of major significance too (Countryside Commission for Scotland 1976). However, while the move towards a more positive-regulatory stance is apparent in the 1947 Act permitting the designation of Green Belts generally, the objectives of green belts have evolved in a less systematic manner. It is clear, however, that the central government by the mid-1950s had come to take a relatively narrow perspective on the purpose of green belts (e.g. UK Ministry of Housing and Local Government 1955; Strachan 1974) in which the urban containment function was paramount and the more positive roles associated with countryside such as recreational opportunities were regarded as quite secondary.

In the case of the London Green Belt, despite the rather fragmented administration of Green Belt policy through local authorities, there is a general consensus that the policy of urban containment has worked (e.g. Thomas 1970), even though it has led to a dispersal of development pressures beyond the Green Belt (Davidson and Wibberley 1977) and may have had other far-reaching negative effects (Clawson and Hall 1973). Furthermore, there has been mounting criticism of the lack of attention paid to the other functions, especially in relation to the London Green Belt; hence, some recent studies have been devoted to the amenity issue, a concern as we have seen that is related to outdoor recreational activities (cf. Munton 1979; Standing Conference 1976). A major problem has evidently been the inability of a physical planning system geared to *land use* to allow for different *interests* in the use of the resources contained in the land. Thus, multiple functions are difficult to handle under a physical planning system dominated by a negative control approach; this is exacerbated by the fact that landscape appearance has essentially escaped any sort of systematic scrutiny and has remained the responsibility of the individual property owner.

It is in light of these criticisms that more persuasive strategies have been called for at the local level – Davidson's and Wibberley's (1977) 'positive' management – by which representatives of public interests would work individually with land owners and farmers to achieve many of the noneconomic functions of the countryside. The urban-fringe land management projects of the Countryside Commission provide very interesting steps towards this more persuasive microscale strategy that can still fit within a broader positive-regulatory framework (Countryside Commission 1976). A project area often would cover several jurisdictions, and receive joint funding from the local authorities and the Countryside Commission. The task of the Project Officer is to work with a Steering Committee and individual land owners and farmers to produce management plans for local authority consideration; and the Project Officer also has been able to finance small projects for improvements, e.g. re-routing of paths and better fencing, in order to try to reconcile farming, recreational and amenity objectives.

At a general level, it can be argued that the strong adherence to the policy of urban containment has created problems by encouraging development to leap-frog across the green belt. From this perspective, green wedges as opposed to green belts would seem to have much to offer since development pressures can be channelled into axial patterns along the main axes of communication into the concentrated built-up area. Thus, room for growth would exist while wedges of countryside alternate with the urban zones. Suggestions that the Ottawa green belt be turned into a series of wedges reflect this partly (Mayo 1976) and the *zones naturelles d'équilibre* of the Paris region can be seen in this light. The history of these latter zones can be traced to the 1966 publication of the master plan for the Paris region (Délégation Générale au District de la Région de Paris 1966; Chassagne 1974), in which the lack of attention to the city's countryside provoked a surge of unrest and research on the rural parts of the region. Following intensive study (e.g. MEAR 1971), a strategy of a series of discontinuous rural zones evolved. Initially labelled *zones de discontinuité*, by 1973 they were renamed *zones naturelles d'équilibre* (ZNE) to catch the combined ideas of countryside and harmony between rural and urban. By 1974, extensive work was under way to identify their boundaries, and in 1976 they took their place in the new master plan for the Paris region (IAURIF 1976) as a positive and integral element in the whole development of the region.

In some respects, the functions of the ZNE smack very much of those which different people have associated with the English Green Belts – structuring of the urban form, maintenance of agriculture and forest management under normal conditions, preserving rural character and facilitating the development of outdoor recreational activities (Préfecture de la Région d'Ile-de-France 1976a,b). Yet there are differences. Note, for instance, the subtle distinction between structuring the urban form as opposed to restraint and containment. Even within the ZNE, while some forms of development are to be outlawed theoretically, other developments are seen as acceptable. Perhaps of more significance is the fact that, although the ZNE fit within the broader positive-regulatory mechanisms of the whole region, the key to success of each ZNE is seen to rest on a consensus between regional administration, local elected officials and the various interests that exist in the countryside (Chassagne 1974; Préfecture de la Région d'Ile-de-France 1976a), with the regionally appointed *chargé de mission* for each ZNE playing a major role in ensuring a continuing dialogue, i.e., a persuasive stance. The accent then is on *process*, a welcome breath of fresh air at a time when planning systems are so often characterized by the establishment of goals and objectives without adequate thought being given to how one achieves them. The promises of the French ZNE are great – but only time will tell whether an acceptable balance between the positive-regulatory and the persuasive-regulatory stance can be achieved to provide a more integrated management system.

Further reading

Davidson, J. and Wibberley, G. P. (1977) *Planning and the Rural Environment*, Pergamon, Oxford, England.

Gardner, B. D. (1977) The economics of agricultural land preservation, *American Journal of Agricultural Economics*, **59**(5), 1027–36.

Listokin, D. (ed.) (1974) *Land Use Controls: Present Problems and Future Reform*, Center for Urban Policy Research, Rutgers University and State University of New Jersey, NJ.

Nelson, R. H. (1977) *Zoning and Property Rights: an Analysis of the American System of Land Use Regulations*, MIT Press, Cambridge, Mass.

Rose, J. G. (1975) *Transfer of Development Rights: a New Technique of Land Use Regulation*, Center for Urban Policy Research, Rutgers University and State University of New Jersey, NJ.

Strachan, A. (1974) The planning framework for modern urban growth: the example of Great Britain, Ch. 4, pp. 53–76 in Johnson, J. H. (ed.), *Suburban Growth*, John Wiley and Sons, London.

13 Overview and future directions

The evolving settlement system

We have tried to provide a series of frameworks with which to analyse what we see as the dominant settlement form emerging during the middle half of the twentieth century and its relationships with the city's countryside. This evolving settlement form, the regional city, was seen as the result of powerful forces, notably population growth and/or redistribution, people's desires to move into a countryside or rural environment, and transportation developments. We can summarize our view of this process schematically (see Fig. 13.1).

Industrialization and urbanization generated patterns of polarization of the space economy, which continue even today at a macroscale (Fig. 13.1(a)). The two hypothetical urban centres attract flows of population and capital from other regions, even from the smaller towns and villages surrounding them, and the urban cores grow in an accretionary fashion, perhaps with certain radial patterns being emphasized. Then with continued urban growth and size, with attendant problems of congestion, transportation developments – including the automobile, highway construction and public transport – permit a greater dispersion of urban functions than had hitherto been possible (Fig. 13.1(b)). This is the early formative stage of the regional city, with a greater dispersal of residential functions taking place both to the nodes of the city's countryside and as a more scattered component too. This is what has been referred to as a microscale explosion within a continuing macroscale implosion (Bauer and Roux 1976). At this stage, we might expect a relatively simple zonation of inner fringe, outer fringe and urban fringe to develop as pressures on the land are more likely to exhibit simple distance-decay characteristics than later on.

With continued growth (suburban, dispersed nodal and dispersed), other processes develop that feed the dispersal of urban functions throughout the city's countryside. Manufacturing tends to develop in suburban nodes and the nodes embedded within the city's countryside in its quest for cheaper space and greater accessibility, both to regional and extra-regional markets and, although more belatedly, some commercial activities follow this pattern. The peripheral shopping centres are particularly characteristic of the North American scene. In this fashion, activity nodes are strengthened, which then act as centres of smaller-scale explosions of residential functions, spreading the web of interactions of the regional city over a broader segment of countryside (Fig. 13.1(c)). Any simple zonation of land-use patterns and conflicts

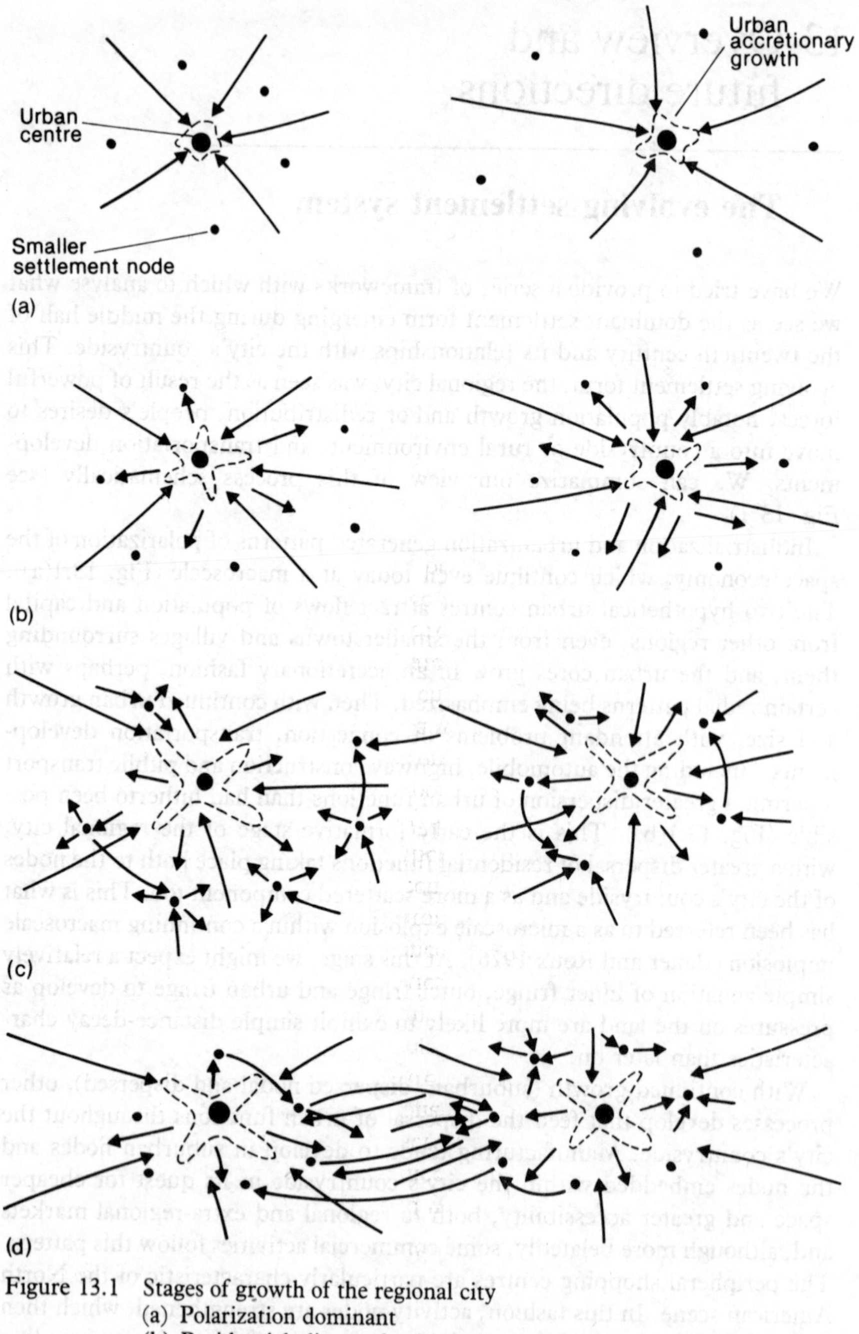

Figure 13.1 Stages of growth of the regional city
(a) Polarization dominant
(b) Residential dispersal with urban growth and transportation developments
(c) Dispersal of economic activities – nodal, axial, suburban
(d) Integrated megalopolitan structure

that may have existed will begin to break down; conceptually they still exist, but empirically they are represented by significant geographic discontinuities. As this process continues, the settlement system begins to lose more and more the perspective of an orientation to a central core; activity nodes in the city's countryside become more self-sufficient as they grow larger although they still exist in an interacting settlement system with the initial core settlements for some types of functions. The web of interactions developing from one regional city system overlaps and merges with those of adjacent systems. Our regional city loses its clearly separate identity and merges into the broader urban-industrial region, the megalopolitan structure (Fig. 13.1(d)). Of course, this stage necessitates a relatively rich urban system in the first place, and will not develop rapidly, if at all, where the initial urban core is truly isolated from other large urban cores, e.g. Regina and Saskatoon in the Canadian Prairies.

Among the forces underlying this simplified descriptive stage model are some that may be historically specific. In the first place, the evolving settlement system has depended upon particular developments in transportation, especially the widespread use of the automobile helped by massive public expenditure on highway construction as well as public transportation, though to a much lesser extent. Implicit then to this interaction have been several decades of 'cheap' energy. How will the energy crisis that began in the early 1970s affect this? Will there be a return to concentration of the urban form? Will public transport play a much greater role?

There are no simple answers to these questions, since if there is any certainty about attempts at painting the future, it is that assumptions will be rendered inaccurate by major unexpected changes. Our comments thus must remain speculative. Much depends on people's attitudes towards car-owning and especially the elasticity of demand for the many functions that cars can be used to perform.

On the one hand, it is worth noting that the much higher energy costs in Western Europe do not deter people from buying cars or using them. They may take fewer trips, for instance, but they will still take trips for discretionary purposes, e.g. recreation and leisure (cf. Travis and Veal 1976).People may substitute shorter-distance trips for longer ones eventually in terms of recreation, but so far the time period during which energy costs have been increasing has been too short to provide any easily interpretable evidence. For commuting, largely a nondiscretionary activity, the rush-hour traffic coming into major cities like Paris and London again demonstrates how people have been slow to adapt, if adapt they will, to changing accessibility costs; it may be, of course, that the costs are still not sufficient to force any substantial change, especially given the rising costs still associated with housing.

On the other hand, it is important to note that even were energy costs to increase very substantially, the level of inertia in existing regional cities, especially the mature ones, in terms of residential and industrial construction and infrastructural development means it is unlikely that reversal towards concentration would take place. What seems more likely is a crystallization of the existing dispersed structure, with concentration occurring at the various nodes and in axial patterns. What this implies is that the regional city as it exists today will likely be a feature of the landscape for a long time, though infilling of one type or another will lead to some modifications.

Another force that may be historically specific is that of population growth since there has been a characteristic slowing of growth occurring in many Western countries in the 1970s. Slowing of overall population growth, of course, does not mean that polarization does not continue, thus feeding the regional city formation process within specific regions. However, other trends noted in our discussion of industrial development indicate that some of the industrial growth in non-metropolitan regions is more than spread forces extending the effective boundaries of urban-industrial regions or megalopolis. Some of this growth has been occurring in truly nonmetropolitan areas (e.g. Lonsdale and Seyler 1979; Summers and Selvik 1979) so that we may be witnessing a turnaround of some of the established patterns of the consequences of industrialization. This might lead to a reduction in pressures in some regions, but an increase elsewhere; whether the settlement system of the new metropolitan regions of the future will follow the patterns we have described in this book remains to be seen. The contradictions are many, with one set of forces, e.g. rising energy costs, encouraging centralization and an increase of pressures in, e.g. the inner fringe or around various nodes, and others, e.g. the slowdown in population growth, leading to a reduction in pressures.

All of these statements must be qualified by the substantial variations that exist in the overall environment between different regional cities, variations that are reflected in the natural, the economic and the cultural environments. Attitudes and perceptions embedded in the cultural environment affect the identification of problems as 'issues' to be resolved and, to a large extent, influence the form of the collective response to such issues through management and planning. The economic environment contains the production system which may be strongly differentiated regionally on the basis of various specializations. Some of this specialization results from variations in the resource base contained in the natural environment, which also can influence in a general way the external spatial form of the urban area and the settlement system.

The activities

Our focus in looking at the activities was to show how their evolution was part and parcel of the evolving settlement system, and simultaneously, to show how they have been influenced by that changing system. Often, we adopted a problem-oriented perspective; however, this perspective can sometimes obscure any positive aspects of a process and we tried to point out some of the potential that land in the fringe has. For instance, we argued that agriculture is alive and well in most parts of the city's countryside, partly because of the frequently good resource base, partly because of the symbiotic relationships between urban centres and agriculture, and partly because part of the farming community has been able to adapt to, and benefit from, the urban-fringe environment.

During our discussion of various activities, it was pointed out that many of the assumptions upon which land-use planning and management are based lack an empirical data base. This is true of such issues as the impact of urban development on agriculture, the phenomenon of land speculation and the idling of land in the urban fringe. Hopefully, various research endeavours that have been pursued in the 1970s will continue and lead us to a better understanding of the real extent and magnitude of the problems. Some of the problems may be critical in some regions, requiring rapid action to 'save' valuable resources; but where our intervention is based on the righteousness of conventional wisdom, we may be committing serious social mistakes that have yet to be appreciated. One response to this would be to do nothing because it will be argued that we never know enough; however, it seems reasonable to develop a 'safe' or conservationist approach to these issues together with a constant readiness to question assumptions.

Management and planning

We argued that in the early phases of public intervention in the substantive concerns identified with the evolving settlement system, a negative-regulatory stance was commonly taken. A prime example of this sort of approach was the use of zoning and associated regulations. Characteristically, this phase was associated with a relatively local scale of application, lack of coordination with any guiding principles or goals and being firmly entrenched within a value system in which private property rights remained practically unassailable.

However, as the scale of the processes involved became more and more appreciated, a recognition that materialized at different times in different countries, other types of approach evolved. In some instances, movements towards a positive-regulatory stance took place, particularly where the formal administrative structure was relatively centralized. The 1947 Town and Country Planning Act of the UK is a good example of such a move, one that was also associated with moves towards a more centralized system. Such positive-regulatory moves often retained some of the shortcomings of the negative-regulatory approach, such as the control aspect and lack of flexibility because they were still oriented towards land use rather than resource interests in land. However, they were – and are – positive in the sense of involving a broader geographic scale of appreciation of the consequences of the ongoing processes and an attempt to develop a coherent set of policies for particular issues. They were still characterized though by an *ad hoc* approach as opposed to a more comprehensive type of approach.

In the US, on the other hand, where the formal system of administration was much more decentralized and local powers perhaps even more jealously guarded, the movement was rather towards a more persuasive-regulatory stance, resting upon cooperation and voluntary association, e.g. the Councils of Governments, the California Land Conservation Act, and so forth. More recently, positive-regulatory movements have also occurred, e.g. in Oregon. Within the persuasive vein we can also include the various property-tax programmes, public acquisition of land in the free market and some of the more recent transfer of development rights programmes.

The move towards both the positive-regulatory and persuasive-regulatory approaches noted above have both gone hand in hand with the development of broader-scale geographic management structures, e.g. the 1947 Town and Country Planning Act and the more recent administrative reforms in the UK (even though the statutory recognition of a specific regional level in the administrative structure remains elusive (Davidson and Wibberley 1977)), the regional government units created in the late 1960s and 1970s in Ontario, and the French regional planning framework that goes back to the mid-1950s. Highly decentralized structures have been associated with the worst examples of land competition, fragmentation of responsibilities and lack of coherency; yet highly centralized structures, while there is apparently more potential for coherent policy-making, lend themselves to abuse and may become out of touch with local and/or regional issues and nuances. Thus, from a pragmatic perspective, it is not surprising that mixed structures appear to be gaining ground, e.g. in Ontario and France. Thus, for example, broader regional units incorporating positive-regulatory functions might maintain a closer dialogue with lower-tier municipalities, acting as much in a persuasive-regulatory vein as in a positive-regulatory vein.

It is clear, though, that these structures will not answer all the problems. It is, of course, essential that in our type of society a persuasive component be present at the macroscale between the various levels of government involved; attention to process necessitates the constant dialogue implied in such cooperative modes of operation if for no other reason than to give the positive-regulatory component a better chance of being accepted. However, programmes of land-use planning require much more to make them successful. Indeed, this is why we have continually talked about land-use planning as practically synonymous with management, although management in our view goes considerably further than land-use planning traditionally has. To start with, management implies coordination between the different types of intervention; the lack of this partly underlies, for instance, why programmes involving property-tax modifications in North America were frequently unsuccessful in attaining their presumed goals. Coordination requires not only the integration of different policies on different issues because of the interrelatedness of the system evolving in the city's countryside, but also involves questions of timing and implementation on the ground.

Furthermore, physical planning systems have often failed to live up to hopes and expectations because they have been too inflexible. The emphasis has been on land use, much too narrow a perspective when we are effectively dealing with businesses and people. And many of the emerging issues have, in any event, involved concerns that have gone beyond the traditional domain of land-use planning, e.g. amenity considerations related to agricultural modernization and informal use of private land for recreation and leisure pursuits. Physical planning systems have thus fallen short of a total management approach. It is in this context that we have noted the increase in interest in persuasive-regulatory approaches at the microscale, e.g. the countryside management projects of the Countryside Commission in the UK and the work of the project leaders (*chargés de mission*) in the French ZNE. These approaches, working within more positive-regulatory and macro persuasive structures, involve dealing directly with the individual land owners, farmers and businessmen, including various professional and nonprofessional organizations. They recognize the continuing importance attached to private interests in land ownership and the impossibility of constructing a bureaucratic planning system that would handle difficult issues such as property upkeep, multiple use of private property, and so forth. While such approaches are not widespread, they represent in our view a glimmer of light at the end of a tunnel, offering the hope that a balance of control and persuasion at macro- and microscale levels will allow us to integrate effectively both people and resource perspectives in the city's countryside.

References

Abercrombie, P. (1945) *Greater London Plan 1944*, HMSO, London.
Aéroport de Paris (1971) *Rapport du Conseil d'Administration: Exercise 1971*, Aéroport de Paris, Paris.
Alberta Land Use Forum (1974) *Parkland County Country Residential Survey*, **Alberta Land Use Forum**, Report 4A, Edmonton.
Alonso, W. (1964) *Location and Land Use: Toward a General Theory of Land Rent*, Harvard University Press, Cambridge, Mass.
Amos, C. D. (1979) *Impacts of Exurbanites upon Small Rural Communities*, MA thesis, Department of Geography, University of Waterloo, Waterloo, Ontario.
Andrew, R. B. (1942) Elements in the urban fringe pattern, *Journal of Land and Public Utilities Economics*, **18**, 169–83.
Archer, R. W. (1973) Land speculation and scattered development: failures in the urban fringe land market, *Urban Studies*, **10**, 367–72.
AREA (Atelier de Recherche et d'Etudes d' Aménagement) (1973) *La Campagne Suburbaine vue par les Citadins, l'Exemple d'une 'Zone de Discontinuité': la Plaine de Versailles*, Report prepared for the District de la Région Parisienne, Paris.
Association Ville–Campagne (1975) *Coopération Ruraux – Citadins*, France, Ministry of Agriculture, Paris.
Auckland Regional Authority, Moran, W., Neville, W., and Rankin, D. (1980) Agriculture and productivity of small holdings, *Rural Small Holdings in the Auckland Region*, **4**, Auckland Regional Authority, Auckland, New Zealand.
Auckland Regional Authority, Moran, W., Neville, W., Rankin, D. and Cochrane, R. (1980) Summary of conclusions and project design, *Rural Small Holdings in the Auckland Region*, **1**, Report to the Planning Division, Auckland, New Zealand.
Australian Department of Urban and Regional Development (1975) *Rural Retreats*, Australian Government Publishing Service, Canberra.
Baldinger, S. (1971) *Planning and Governing the Metropolis, the Twin Cities Experience*, Praeger, New York.
Banta, J. (1980) Legal and administrative implementation, pp. 71–91 in Roberts, N. A. and Brown, H. J. (eds), *Property Tax Preferences for Agricultural Land*, Allanheld, Asmun and Co., Montclair, NJ.
Barbarel, J. (1981) Love Canal, pp. 368–9 in *1981 Year Book (Annual Supplement to Collier's Encyclopaedia)*, MacMillan Education Corporation and P. F. Collier, Inc, London, New York.
Barker, A. J. (1949) *Urban Drones in Rural Hives: the Township's View of the Urban Fringe*, Report to the London and Suburban Planning Board, London, Ontario.
Barker, M. L. (1978) Recreation hinterlands: a metropolitan call on the environmental base, pp. 135–55 in Evenden, L. J. (ed.), *Vancouver, Western Metropolis*, Western Geographical Series 16, Department of Geography, University of Victoria, Victoria, British Columbia.
Barlowe, R. (1978) *Land Resource Economics: the Economics of Real Estate* (3rd edn), Prentice-Hall, Englewood Cliffs, NJ.
Batey, W. L. and Smith, P. J. (1981) The role of territory in political conflict in

metropolitan fringe areas, pp. 199–217 in Beesley, K. B. and Russwurm, L. H. (eds), *The Rural–Urban Fringe: Canadian Perspectives*, Monograph Series, Department of Geography, Atkinson College, York University, Toronto.

Bauer, A. (1970) *A Guide to Site Development Rehabilitation of Pits and Quarries*, Industrial Mineral Report 33, Ontario Department of Mines, Toronto.

Bauer, G. and Roux, J.-M. (1976) *La Rurbanisation: ou la Ville Eparpillé*, Les Editions du Seuil, Paris.

Baxter, D. (1975) *Battle for Land Conference Report*, Community Planning Association of Canada, Ottawa.

Becker, A. P. (1969) Principles of taxing land and buildings for economic development, Ch. 1, pp. 1–47 in Becker, A. P. (ed.), *Land and Building Taxes: their Effect on Economic Development*, University of Wisconsin Press, Madison, Wisconsin.

Bell, D. (1973) *The Coming of Post-Industrial Society*, Basic Books, New York.

Berry, B. J. L. (1973) *Human Consequences of Urbanization*, The MacMillan Press, London.

Berry, B. J. L. (1976) The counter-urbanization process: urban America since 1970, in Berry, B. J.L. (ed.), *Urbanization and Counter-Urbanization*, Urban Affairs Annual Reviews 11, Sage Publications, Berkely Hills, California.

Berteloot, F. Y. (1972) *Les Plans d'Occupation des Sols*, Chambre d'Agriculture de Loire Atlantique, Nantes, France.

Best, R. H. (1974) Building on farmland, *New Society*, 31 Oct., 287–8.

Best, R. H. (1976) The extent and growth of urban land, *The Planner*, Journal of the Royal Town Planning Institute, **62**, 8–11.

Best, R. H. (1977a) Agricultural land loss – myth or reality? *The Planner*, Journal of the Royal Town Planning Institute, **63**, 15–16.

Best, R. H. (1977b) Urban growth and the countryside, Seminar presented at the University of Guelph, 19 Oct. 1977.

Best, R. H. and Ward, J. T. (1956) *The Garden Controversy*, Studies in Rural Land Use 2, Wye College, Wye, England.

Bielkus, C. L., Rogers, A. W. and Wibberley, G. P. (1972) *Second Homes in England and Wales*, Studies in Rural Land Use 11, Wye College, Wye, England.

Bjork, G. (1977) Life, liberty and property: Oregon's challenge in land use planning, pp. 1–18 in Institute for Policy Studies, *Challenges for Oregon 1977–79 Proceedings*, Institute for Policy Studies, Portland State University, Portland, Oregon.

Blessley, K. H. (undated) *London and the Green Belt*, Valuation and Estates Department, Greater London Council, London.

Blumenfeld, H. (1954) The tidal wave of metropolitan expansion, *Journal of the American Institute of Planners*, **20**, 3–14.

Bogue, D. J. (1956) *Metropolitan Growth and the Conversion of Land to Non-Agricultural Uses*, Scripps Foundation Series in Population Distribution, Oxford, Ohio.

Bosselman, F. and Callies, D. (1971) *The Quiet Revolution in Land Use Control*, US Government Printing Office, Washington, DC.

Bossenmaier, E. F. and Vogel, G. G. (1974) *Wildlife and Wildlife Habitat in the Winnipeg Region*, Manitoba Department of Mines, Resources and Environmental Management, Winnipeg.

Boudeville, J. R. (1966) *Problem of Regional Economic Planning*, Edinburgh University Press, Edinburgh.

Bourne, L. S. (1977) Choose your villain: five ways to oversimplify the price of housing and urban land, *Urban Forum*, **3**, 16–24.

Bowen, M. J. (1974) Outdoor recreation around larger cities, Ch. 11, pp. 225–48 in Johnson, J. H. (ed.), *Suburban Growth*, John Wiley and Sons, London.

Boyce, R. R. (1966) The edge of the metropolis: the wave theory analog approach, pp. 31–40 in British Columbia Geographical Series 7, Department of Geography, University of British Columbia.

Brigham, E. F. (1965) The determinants of residential land values, *Land Economics*, **45**, 325–35.

Brunet, Y. and Lepine, Y. (1981) Exurbanisation dans la région de Montréal entre 1971 et 1976, pp. 121–35 in Beesley, K. B. and Russwurm, L. H. (eds) *The Rural–Urban Fringe: Canadian Perspectives*, Monograph Series, Department of Geography, Atkinson College, York University, Toronto.

Brush, J. E. and Gauthier, H. L., Jr. (1968) *Service Centers and Consumer Trips: Studies on the Philadelphia Metropolitan Fringe*, Research Paper 113, Department of Geography, University of Chicago, Chicago.

Bryant, C. R. (1970) *Urbanisation and Agricultural Change since 1945: a Case Study from the Paris Region*, PhD thesis, University of London, London.

Bryant, C. R. (1973a) L'agriculture face à la croissance métropolitaine: le cas des exploitations de grande culture expropriées par l'emprise de l'Aéroport Paris-Nord, *Economie Rurale*, **95**, 23–35

Bryant, C. R. (1973b) The anticipation of urban expansion: some implications for agricultural land use practices and land use zoning, *Geographia Polonica*, **28**, 93–115.

Bryant, C. R. (1974) An approach to the problem of urbanisation and structural change in agriculture: a case study from the Paris region, 1955 to 1968, *Geografiska Annaler*, **56**, B(1), 1–27.

Bryant, C. R. (1975) Metropolitan development and agriculture: the SAFER de l'Ile de France, *Land Economics*, **51**(2), 158–63.

Bryant, C. R. (1976a) Some new perspectives on agricultural land use in the rural–urban fringe, *Ontario Geography*, **10**, 64–78.

Bryant, C. R. (1976b) *Farm-Generated Determinants of Land Use Change in the Rural–Urban Fringe in Canada, 1961–1975*, Technical Report, Lands Directorate, Environment Canada, Ottawa.

Bryant, C. R. (1980) Manufacturing in rural development, Ch. 5, pp. 99–128 in Walker, D. F. (ed.), *Planning Industrial Development*, John Wiley and Sons, Chichester, England.

Bryant, C. R. (1981) Agriculture in an urbanizing environment: a case study from the Paris region, 1968 to 1976 *The Canadian Geographer*, **21**(1), 27–45.

Bryant, C. R. (1982) *The Rural Real Estate Market: an Analysis of Geographic Patterns of Structure and Change within an Urban Fringe Environment*, Publications Series, Department of Geography, University of Waterloo, Waterloo, Ontario.

Bryant, C. R. and Fielding, J. A. (1980) Agricultural change and farmland rental in an urbanising environment, *Cahiers de Géographie du Québec*, **24**(62), 277–98.

Bryant, C. R. and Greaves, S. M (1978) The importance of regional variation in the analysis of urbanisation–agriculture interactions, *Cahiers de Géographie du Québec*, **22**(57), 329–48.

Bryant, C. R. and McLellan, A. G. (1974) *The Aggregate Resources of the Waterloo–South Wellington Counties: Towards Effective Planning in the Aggregates Industry*, Open File Report 5100, Ontario Ministry of Natural Resources, Division of Mines, Toronto.

Bryant, C. R. and McLellan, A. G. (1975a) Towards effective planning and control of the aggregate industry in Ontario, *Plan Canada*, **15**(3), 176–82.

Bryant, C. R. and McLellan, A. G. (1975b) The methodology of inventory: a practical technique for assessing provincial aggregate resources, *Bulletin of the Canadian Institute of Mining and Metallurgy*, October, 113–19.

Bryant, C. R. and Martin, L. R. G. (1976) Public land assembly and land price monitoring: the case of the ZAD in the Paris region, *Plan Canada*, **16**(3, 4), 177–89.

Bryant, C. R. and Russwurm, L. H. (1979) The impact of nonagricultural development on agriculture: a synthesis, *Plan Canada*, **19**(2), 122–39.

Bryant, C. R. and Russwurm L. H. (1981) Regional differences in the evolution of the Canadian regional city, 1941 to 1976, Covrnerbrook, Newfoundland: Paper presented to the annual meeting of the Canadian Association of Geographers, August 13th, 1981.

Bryant, R. W. G. (1972) *Land: Private Property, Public Control*, Harvest House, Montreal.

Bryant, W. R. and Conklin, H. E. (1975) New farmland preservation programs in New York, *Journal of the American Institute of Planners*, **41**(6), 390–6.

Bunce, M. (1981) Rural sentiment and the ambiguity of the urban fringe, pp. 109–20 in Beesley, K. B. and Russwurm, L. H. (eds), *The Rural–Urban Fringe: Canadian Perspectives*, Monograph Series, Department of Geography, Atkinson College, York University, Toronto.

Bunting, T. E. (1980) Style of living in the city: a study of household behaviour systems, pp. 367–92 in Preston, R. E. and Russwurm L. H. (eds), *Essays on Canadian Urban Process and Form II*, Publication Series 15, Department of Geography, University of Waterloo, Waterloo, Ontario.

Bureau of Outdoor Recreation (1973) *Nationwide Outdoor Recreation Plan–First Draft*, Bureau of Outdoor Recreation, Washington, DC.

Burton, T. L. (1967a) *Windsor Great Park: a Recreation Study*, Studies in Rural Land Use 8, Wye College, Wye, England.

Burton, T. L. (1967b) *Outdoor Recreation Enterprises in Problem Rural Areas*, Studies in Rural Land Use 9, Wye College, Wye, England.

Burton, T. L. and Wibberley, G. P. (1965) *Outdoor Recreation in the British Countryside*, Studies in Rural Land Use 5, Wye College, Wye, England.

Butler, R. W. (1979) Government attitudes to the promotion of private land for recreation: a critique, *Geographical Inter-University Resource Management Seminars*, **10**, 25–31, Department of Geography, Wilfrid Laurier University, Waterloo, Ontario.

Calgary Regional Planning Commission (1977) *Calgary Region Growth Study: Land Use*, Report A. 5, Calgary Regional Planning Commission, Calgary, Alberta.

California Department of Parks and Recreation (1972) *California Outdoor Recreation Plan*, The Resources Agency, Sacramento.

California Land-Use Task Force (1975) *The California Land*, The Planning and Conservation Foundation, Sacramento and Wm. Kaufman, Los Altos.

California Office of Planning and Research (1978) *An Urban Strategy for California*, California Office of Planning and Research, Sacramento.

California Office of Planning and Research (1980) *General Plan Guidelines*, California Office of Planning and Research, Sacramento.

Carman, H. F. (1977) California landowners' adoption of a use-value assessment program, *Land Economics*, **53**, 276–87.

Centre for Resources Development (University of Guelph) (1972) *Planning for Agriculture in Southern Ontario*, ARDA Report 7, Department of Regional Economic Expansion, Ottawa and Ministry of Agriculture and Food, Toronto.

Centre National d'Etude et de Recherches du Paysage (1975) *Bâtiments Agricoles et Paysages*, Fondation de France, Paris.

Champion, A. G. (1972) Agriculture and New Towns in Great Britain, *Geographia Polonica*, **24**, 127–39.
Champion, A. G. (1975) *An Estimate of the Changing Extent and Distribution of Urban Land in England and Wales, 1950–1970*, CES RP 10, Centre for Environmental Studies, London.
Chapman, G. P. (1978) *Human Environmental Systems: a Geographer's Appraisal*, Academic Press, London.
Chassagne, M. E. (1974) La politique des Zones Naturelles d'Equilibre en région parisienne, *Bulletin d'Information de l'Atelier d'Etudes d'Aménagement Rural*, **3**(22), France Ministry of Agriculture, Paris.
Chassagne, M. E. (1977) Peri-urban agriculture in the Plain of the Ain, *Conference: Peri-Urban Agriculture*, OECD, Paris.
Childe, G. (1942) *What Happened in History*, Penguin Books, Harmondsworth, England.
Clackamas County (1980) *Parks, Open Space, Historic Sites*, Planning Background Report, Planning Division, Clackamas County Department of Environmental Services, Portland, Oregon.
Clawson, M. C. (1962) Urban sprawl and speculation in suburban land, *Land Economics*, **38**, 99–111.
Clawson, M. (1969) Open (uncovered) space as a new urban resource, pp. 139–75 in Perloff, H. S. (ed.), *The Quality of the Urban Environment*, The Johns Hopkins Press for Resources for the Future, Baltimore.
Clawson, M. (1971) *Suburban Land Conversion in the United States: an Economic and Governmental Process*, The Johns Hopkins Press, Baltimore.
Clawson, M. (1972) *America's Land and its Uses*, The Johns Hopkins Press, Baltimore.
Clawson, M. and Hall, P. (1973) *Planning and Urban Growth: an Anglo–American Comparison*, The Johns Hopkins Press, Baltimore.
Clay, R. (1978) *Properties of the National Trust*, Chaucer Press Ltd for the National Trust, UK.
Colorado Division of Mines (1973) *Colorado Open Mining Land Reclamation Act*, Colorado.
Commissariat Général du Plan (1971) *Rapport de la Commission Espace Rural: Préparation du V1 Plan*, La Documentation Française, Paris.
Conklin, E. and Dymsa, R. (1972) *Maintaining Viable Agriculture in Areas of Urban Expansion*, Report to the Office of Planning Services, New York State.
Connell, J. (1974) The metropolitan village: spatial and social processes in discontinuous suburbs, Ch. 5, pp. 77–100 in Johnson, J. H. (ed.), *Suburban Growth*, John Wiley and Sons, London.
Conservation Council of Ontario (1976) *Private Land, Public Recreation and the Law*, The Conservation Council of Ontario, Toronto.
Council on Rural Development Canada (1979) *A Rural Information System for Canada*, Council on Rural Development Canada, Hull.
Countryside Commission (1976) *The Bollin Valley: a Study of Land Management in the Urban Fringe*, Countryside Commission CCP97, HMSO, London.
Countryside Commission for Scotland (1976) *A Situation Report on Green Belts in Scotland*, CCS Occasional Paper 8, Countryside Commission for Scotland, Battleby, Scotland.
Craddock, W. J. (1970) *Interregional Competition in Canadian Cereal Production*, Special Study 12, Economic Council of Canada, Ottawa.
Crerar, A. D. (1963) The loss of farmland in the growth of the metropolitan regions of Canada, pp. 181–96 in *Resources for Tomorrow: Supplementary Volume*, The Queen's Printer, Ottawa.

Cripps, J. (1976) Introductory remarks, pp. 19–22 in Travis, A. S. and Veal, A. J. (eds), *Recreation in the Urban Fringe: Conference Proceedings*, Centre for Urban and Regional Studies, University of Birmingham, England.

Cullington, J. M. (1979) Attitudes to the promotion of private land for recreation, *Geographical Inter-University Resource Management Seminars*, **10**, 1–24, Department of Geography, Wilfrid Laurier University, Waterloo, Ontario.

Cullington, J. M. (1980) *The Public Use of Private Land for Recreation*, MA thesis, Department of Geography, University of Waterloo, Waterloo, Ontario.

Davidson, J. (1974) Recreation and the urban fringe, *The Planner*, Journal of the Royal Institute of Town Planners, **60**(9), 889–93.

Davidson, J. (1976) The urban fringe, *Countryside Recreation Review*, **1**, 2–7.

Davidson, J. and Wibberley, G. P. (1977) *Planning and the Rural Environment*, Pergamon, Oxford, England.

Dawson, J. A. (1974) The suburbanization of retail activity, Ch. 8, pp. 155–75 in Johnson, J. H. (ed.), *Suburban Growth*, John Wiley and Sons, London.

de Farcy, H. (1976) Les emplois non agricoles aux Etats-Unis, *Bulletin d'Information de l'Atelier Central d'Etudes d'Aménagement Rural*, 2(5), France Ministry of Agriculture, Paris.

Delavigne, R. *et al.* (1970) *De la Conservation des Paysages à la Mise en Valeur du Milieu de Vie*, Planning and Urbanism Branch, France Ministry of Housing and Infrastructure, Paris.

Délégation Générale au District de la Région de Paris (1966) *Schéma Directeur d'Aménagement et d'Urbanisme de la Région de Paris*, La Documentation Française Illustrée, Special No. 216, Paris, France.

Denman, D. R. and Prodano, S. (1972) *Land Use: an Introduction to Proprietary Land Use Analysis*, George Allen and Unwin, London.

Dennis, M. and Fish, A. (1972) *Programs in Search of a Policy: Low Income Housing in Canada*, Hakkert, Toronto.

Donnelly, T. G., Chapin, F. S., Jr., and Weiss, S. F. (1964) *A Probabilistic Model for Residential Growth*, Centre for Urban and Regional Research, Institute for Research in Social Science, University of North Carolina, Chapel Hill, NC.

Duffell, J. R. and Goddall. G. R. (1969) Worcestershire and Staffordshire recreational survey 1966 – use of the motor car for leisure purposes, *Journal of the Town Planning Institute*, 55(1), 16–23.

Duffell, J. R. and Peters, C. M. (1971) Recreational travel in rural areas: Hertfordshire countryside survey, *Traffic Engineering and Control*, 31–5.

Dunn, E. S. (1954) *The Location of Agricultural Production*, University of Florida Press, Gainsville, Florida.

Earney, C. F. (1975) *Mining, Planning and the Urban Environment – an Annotated Bibliography: 1960–1975*, Council of Planning Librarians, Monticello, Ill.

Essex County Council (1976) *Essex Landscape No. 2: Electricity Lines and Substation Sites*, Essex County Council, Chelmsford, England.

Etherington, F. and Anderson, M. (1974) Kitchener–Waterloo: locking up housing land, *City Magazine*, Preview, 16–20.

Fédération Française des Marchés d'Intérêt National (1969) Le Marché d'Intérêt National de Rungis, pp. 180–225 in *Album des Marchés d'Intérêt National*, Fédération Française des Marchés d'Intérêt National, Paris.

Ferguson, M. (1975) *The Pre-Development Land Market and the Initiation of the Rural-Urban Land Conversion Process: a Case Study in the Former Township of Waterloo, 1966–71*, MA Thesis, Department of Geography, University of Waterloo, Waterloo, Ontario.

Ferguson, M. J. and Munton, R. J. C. (1979) Informal recreation sites in

London's Green Belt, *Area*, **11**(3), 196–205.
Fielding, G. J. (1962) Dairying in cities designed to keep people out, *Professional Geographer*, **141**, 12–17.
Fielding, J. A. (1979) *Farmland Rental in an Urbanising Environment: the Fringes of Kitchener, Waterloo and Cambridge, 1971–1978*, MA thesis, Department of Geography, University of Waterloo, Waterloo, Ontario.
Firey, W. (1946) Ecological considerations in planning for rurban fringes, *American Sociological Review*, **11**, 411–23.
Firey, W. (1960) *Man, Mind and Land: a Theory of Resource Use*, Free Press, Glencoe. Ill.
Fitton, M. (1976) The urban fringe and the less privileged, *Countryside Recreation Review*, **1**, 25–34.
Fitzgerald, S. (1977) *Outdoor Recreation Behaviour Patterns of Rural Residents in Woolwich Township, Waterloo*, BES thesis, Department of Geography, University of Waterloo, Waterloo, Ontario.
Found, W. C. and Michie, G. H. (1976) Rural estates in the Toronto region, *Ontario Geography*, **10**, 15–26.
Found, W. C. and Morley, C. D. (1972) *A Conceptual Approach to Rural Land Use – Transportation Modelling in the Toronto Region*, Research Report 8, University of Toronto-York University Joint Program in Transportation, York University Transport Centre, Downsview, Ontario.
Found, W. C. and Morley, C. D. (1973) A behavioural typology of land uses for metropolitan rural space: the case of Toronto, pp. 295–313 in Reeds, L. G. (ed.), *Agricultural Typology and Land Use*, Proceedings of the IGU Agricultural Commission Meetings, Department of Geography, McMaster University, Hamilton, Ontario.
France (1968) Loi d'orientation foncière, *Journal officiel de la République Française*, Reprint No. 68–1.
France Ministry of Industry (1979) *Etude des Sables Fins (de Fontainebleau et de Beauchamp) de la Région d'Ile-de-France*, Ministry of Industry and Institut d'Aménagement et d'Urbanisme de la Région d'Ile-de-France, Paris.
Frankena, M. W. and Scheffman. D. T. (1980) *Economic Analysis of Provincial Land Use Policies in Ontario*, Ontario Economic Council, Research Studies 18, University of Toronto Press, Toronto.
Fresno County Local Agency Formation Commission (1974) *Spheres of Influence Report*, Fresno County LAFCO, Fresno, California.
Friedmann, J. (1973a) The future of the urban habitat, Ch. 3, pp. 57–82 in McAllister, D. M. (ed.), *Environment: a New Focus for Land-Use Planning*, National Science Foundation, Washington.
Friedmann, J. (1973b) *Retracking America: a Theory of Transactive Planning*, Anchor Press, Garden City, NY.
Friedmann, J. and Miller, J. (1965) The urban field, *Journal of the Institute of American Planners*, **31** (4), 312–20.
Friedmann, J. R. (1966) *Regional Development Policy: a Case Study of Venezuela*, MIT Press, Cambridge, Mass.
1000 Friends of Oregon (1980) *Four-Year Report 1975–1979*, 1000 Friends of Oregon, Portland, Oregon.
Fuller, A. M. and Mage, J. A. (eds) (1976) *Part-time Farming: Problem or Resource in Rural Development*, Geo. Abstracts, Norwich, England.
Fulton, M. (1974) Industry's viewpoint of rural areas, pp. 68–78 in Whiting, L. R. (ed.), *Rural Industrialization: Problems and Potentials*, The Iowa State University Press, Ames, Iowa.
Gardner, B. D. (1977) The economics of agricultural land preservation, *American Journal of Agricultural Economics*, **59** (5), 1027–36.

Gasson, R. M. (1966) *The Influence of Urbanization on Farm Ownership and Practice: Some Aspects of the Effects of London on Farms and Farm People in Kent and Sussex*, Studies in Rural Land Use 7, Wye College, Wye, England.

Gasson, R. M. (1977) *The Place of Part-Time Farming in Rural and Regional Development*, Seminar Paper 3, Centre for European Agricultural Studies, Wye College, Wye, England.

Geay, Y. (1974) *L'Utilisation des Terres Agricoles en Matière d'Urbanisation*, Ph. D thesis, University of Paris I, Paris.

Gertler, L. O. (1968) *The Niagara Escarpment Study*, The Queen's Printer, Toronto.

Gertler, L. O. (1972) *Regional Planning in Canada*, Harvest House, Montreal.

Gertler, L. O. (1978) *Habitat Settlement Issues I: Habitat and Land*, University of British Columbia Press in association with the Centre for Human Settlements, University of British Columbia, Vancouver.

Gertler, L. O. and Crowley, R. (1977) *Changing Canadian Cities: the Next Twenty-Five Years*, McClelland and Stewart, Toronto.

Gertler, L. O. and Hind-Smith, J. (1962) The impact of urban growth on agricultural land, pp. 155–80 in *Resources for Tomorrow*, Background Papers, Supplementary Volume, Queen's Printer, Ottawa.

Gierman, D. M. (1977) *Rural to Urban Land Conversion*, Occasional Paper 16, Lands Directorate, Environment Canada, Ottawa.

Gloudemans, R. J. (1971) *Use Value Farmland Assessment: Theory, Practice and Impact*, International Association of Assessing Officials, Chicago.

Golledge, R. G. (1960) Sydney's metropolitan fringe: a study in urban-rural relations, *Australian Geographer*, 7(6), 243–55.

Gottman, J. (1961) *Megalopolis: the Urbanized Northeastern Seaboard of the United States*, The Twentieth Century Fund, New York.

Government of Ontario (1978) *Foodland Guidelines: a Policy Statement of Ontario on Planning and Agriculture*, Toronto.

Gramm, W. P. and Ekelund, R. B., Jr. (1975) Land use planning: the market alternative, pp. 127–40 in *No Land is an Island*, Institute for Contemporary Studies, San Francisco.

Greaves, S. (1975) *Severance Development: a Micro-Study of Albion Township*, M A thesis, Department of Geography, University of Waterloo, Waterloo, Ontario.

Greenspan, D. B. (1978) *Down to Earth*, Federal/Provincial Task Force on the Supply and Price of Serviced Residential Land, 2, The Queen's Printer, Ottawa.

Greer, T. and Wall, G. (1979) Recreational hinterlands: a theoretical and empirical analysis, pp. 227–46 in Wall, G. (ed.), *Recreational Land Use in Southern Ontario*, Publication Series 14, Department of Geography, University of Waterloo, Waterloo, Ontario.

Gustafson, G. C. (1977) *California's Use-Value Assessment Program: Participation and Performance Through 1975–76*, Economic Research Service, US Department of Agriculture, Corvallis, Oregon.

Gustafson, G. C. and Wallace, L. T. (1975) Differential assessment as land use policy: the California case, *Journal of the American Institute of Planners*, **41**, 379–89.

Hady, T. F. and Sibold, A. G. (1974) *State Programs for Differential Assessment of Farm and Open Space Land*, Agricultural Economics Report 256, Economics Research Service, US Department of Agriculture, Washington.

Hady, T. F. and Stinson, T. F. (1967) *Taxation of Farmland on the Rural–Urban Fringe: a Summary of State Preferential Assessment*, Agriculture Economics Report 119, US Department of Agriculture, Economic Research Service, Washington.

Hall, A. (1976) Management in the urban fringe, *Countryside Recreation Review*, **1**, 8–13.
Hall, P. G. (ed.) (1966) *Johann Heinrich von Thünen: Isolated State*, Pergamon Press, Oxford, England.
Hardwick, W. G. (1974) *Vancouver*, Collier-MacMillan, Toronto.
Haren, C. C. (1974) Location of industrial production and distribution, pp. 3–26 in Whiting, L. R. (ed.), *Rural Industrialization: Problems and Potentials*, The Iowa State University Press, Ames, Iowa.
Harker, P. T. (1976) *The Impact of Non-Resident Ownership on Farm Patterns in Egremont and Glenelg Townships: a Case Study for an Area Outside the Commuting Range of Major Ontario Cities*, MA thesis, Department of Geography, University of Waterloo, Waterloo, Ontario.
Harrison, A. (1975) L'agriculture à temps partiel en Angleterre et au Pays-de-Galles, *Economie Rurale*, 31–6.
Harrison, P. (1976) *A Study of the Rural Character and Changing Functionalism of our Rural Villages: Mount Albert, Ontario, a Case Study*, B E S thesis, Department of Geography, University of Waterloo, Waterloo, Ontario.
Hart, J. F. (1976) Urban encroachment on rural areas, *Geographical Review*, **66**, 1–17.
Hauser, P. M. and Schnore, L. F. (eds) (1965) *The Study of Urbanization*, John Wiley, New York.
Hawkins, R. B., Jr. (1975) Local land use planning and its critics, pp. 101–112 in *No Land is an Island*, Institute for Contemporary Studies, San Francisco.
Healey, R. G. and Rosenberg, S. (1979) *Land Use and the States* (2nd edn), The Johns Hopkins University Press, Baltimore.
Hepner, G., Lewis, D. W. and Muraco, W. A. (1976) *Locational Factors and the Demand for Land on the Rural–Urban Fringe*, Regional Research Report 10, Business Research Center, College of Business Administration, University of Toledo, Toledo, Ohio.
Hilchey, J. D. (1970) *Soil Capability Analysis for Agriculture in Nova Scotia*, Canada Land Inventory Report 8, Department of Regional Economic Expansion, Ottawa.
Hirschmann, A. O. (1958) *The Strategy of Economic Development*, Yale University Press, New Haven.
Hoch, W. A. (1974) *Commuting Patterns of the Rural Non-Farm Resident: a Case Study of Nassagaweya Township*, BA thesis, Department of Geography, Wilfrid Laurier University, Waterloo, Ontario.
Hodge, G. (1965) The prediction of trade centre viability in the Great Plains, *Papers and Proceedings of the Regional Science Association*, **15**, 87–118.
Hodge, G. (1974) The city in the periphery, pp. 281–300 in Bourne, L. S. *et al.* (eds), *Urban Futures for Central Canada: Perspectives on Forecasting Urban Growth and Form*, University of Toronto Press, Department of Geography Publications, Toronto.
Honsberger, B. A. (1979) *Political Responses to Rural–Urban Planning Problems*, MA thesis, School of Urban and Regional Planning, University of Wateloo, Waterloo, Ontario.
Hoover, E. M. (1971) *An Introduction to Regional Economics* (1st edn), A. A. Knopf, New York.
Hoover, E. M. and Vernon, R. (1962) *Anatomy of a Metropolis*, Anchor Books, Doubleday and Co., Garden City, New York.
Howard, J. F. (1972) *The Impact of Urbanisation on the Prime Agricultural Lands of Southern Ontario*, MA thesis, Department of Geography, University of Waterloo, Waterloo, Ontario.
Hudson, J. (1973) Density and pattern in suburban fringes, *Annals of the*

Association of American Geographers, **63**(1), 28–39.

Hushak, L. J. and Bovard, D. N. (1975) *The Demand for Land in the Urban–Rural Fringe*, Research Bulletin 1076, Ohio Agricultural and Development Center, Wooster.

Hyslop, J. and Russwurm, L. H. (1981) Characteristics of farm holding types: Glanbrook Township, Hamilton rural–urban fringe, pp. 257–67 in Beesley, K. B. and Russwurm, L. H. (eds), *The Rural-Urban Fringe: Canadian Perspectives*, Monograph Series, Department of Geography, Atkinson College, York University, Toronto.

IAURIF (Institut d'Aménagement et d'Urbanisme de la Région d'Ile-de-France) (1976) *Schéma Directeur d'Aménagement et d'Urbanisme de la Région d'Ile-de-France*, Préfecture de la Région d'Ile-de-France, Paris.

IAURIP (Institut d'Aménagement et d'Urbanisme de la Région Parisienne) (1972) Choix entre transports publics et transports individuels en région parisienne, *Cahiers de l'IAURIP*, 26.

INRS (Institut National de la Recherche Scientifique) (1973) *Région Sud: l'Agriculture*, Office de planification et de développement du Québec and Université du Québec, Montréal.

INSEE (Institut National de la Statistique et des Etudes Economiques) (1976) *Resultats Provisiores du Recensement de la Population de 1975*, INSEE, Paris.

Ironside, R. G. (1971) Agricultural and recreational land use in Canada: the potential for conflict or benefit, *Canadian Journal of Agricultural Economics*, **19**(2), 1–11.

Ironside, R. G. and Williams, A. G. (1980) The spread effects of a spontaneous growth centre: commuter expenditure patterns in the Edmonton Metropolitan Region, Canada, *Regional Studies*, **14**, 313–32.

James, F. J. and Gale, D. E. (1977) *Zoning for Sale, a Critical Analysis of Transferable Development Rights Programs*, The Urban Institute, Washington.

Johnson, J. H. (1974) Geographical processes at the edge of the city, Ch. 1, pp. 1–16 in Johnson, J. H. (ed.), *Suburban Growth*, John Wiley and Sons, London.

Jung, J. (1971) *L'Aménagement de l'Espace Rural: une Illusion Economique*, Calmann Levy, Perspective de l'économique: économie contemporaine , Paris.

Kaiser, E. J., Massie, R. W., Weiss, S. F., and Smith, J. E. (1968) Predicting the behavior of pre-development landowners on the urban fringe, *Journal of the American Institute of Planners*, **34** (5), 328–33.

Kearns, J. (1974) *The Middle-Class Housing Crisis: Land Costs and the Land Development Process in the Toronto Metropolitan Area*, MA thesis, School of Urban and Regional Planning, University of Waterloo, Waterloo, Ontario.

Keeble, D. (1976) *Industrial Location and Planning in the United Kingdom*, Methuen, London.

Kehm, W. H. (1977) Near-urban parks – what are they? *Park News: Journal of the National and Provincial Parks Association of Canada*, **13** (1), 8–16.

Kitchen, C. M. (1976) Ecology and urban development: the theory and practice of ecoplanning in Canada, pp. 217–40 in McBoyle, G. P. and Sommerville, E. (eds), *Canada's Natural Environment: Essays on Applied Geography*, Methuen, Toronto.

Krueger, R. R. (1957) The rural–urban fringe taxation problem: a case study of Louth Township, *Land Economics*, **33**, 264–9.

Krueger, R. R. (1959) Changing land use patterns in the Niagara fruit belt, *Transactions of the Royal Canadian Institute*, **32**, Part 2 (67), 39–140.

Krueger, R. R. (1978) Urbanization of the Niagara fruit belt, *The Canadian Geographer*, **22**, 179–94.

References

Lakehead Planning Board (1974) *Rural Residential Report*, Lakehead Planning Board, Thunder Bay, Ontario.

Lambden, D. W. (1975) Public rights, private lands, pp. 40–44 in *Private Land, Public Recreation and the Law: Seminar Proceedings*, Conservation Council of Ontario, Toronto.

Latarjet, B. (1972) Les espaces naturels en région parisienne, *Cahiers de l'IAURIP*, **27**.

Lessinger, J. (1958) Exclusive agricultural zoning: an appraisal – agricultural shortages, *Land Economics*, **34**, 149–60.

Lewis, G. J. and Maund, D. J. (1976) The urbanization of the countryside: a framework for analyses, *Geografiska Annaler*, **58**,B (1), 17–27.

Lindeman, B. (1976) Anatomy of land speculation, *Journal of the American Institute of Planners*, **42**, 142–52.

Listokin, D. (ed.) (1974) *Land Use Controls: Present Problems and Future Reform*, Center for Urban Policy Research, Rutgers University and State University of New Jersey, NJ.

Little, C. E. (1974) *The New Oregon Trail*, The Conservation Foundation, Washington.

Lonsdale, R. E. and Seyler, H. L. (eds) (1979) *Nonmetropolitan Industrialization*, Scipta Series in Geography, V. H. Winston, Washington, DC, distributed by Halsted Press, New York.

Lorimer, J. (1979) *The Developers*, James Lorimer, Toronto.

Lowe, P. *et al.* (1977) *Land-Use Conflicts in the Urban Fringe: a Case Study of Aggregate Extraction in the London Borough of Havering*, Town Planning Discussion Paper 26, Bartlett School, University College, London.

Lower Mainland Regional Planning Board (1956) *Urban Sprawl in the Lower Mainland of BC*, Technical Report, Lower Mainland Regional Planning Board, New Westminster, British Columbia.

McHarg, I. L. (1969) *Design with Nature*, Doubleday, Garden City, NY.

McKay, R. D. (1976) *The Land Use Characteristics and Implications of Hobby Farming: a Case Study in the Town of Caledon, Regional Municipality of Peel*, BES thesis, School of Urban and Regional Planning, University of Waterloo, Waterloo, Ontario.

McKeague, J. A. (1975) Canada Land Inventory: How much land do we have?, *Agrologist*, **4** (4), 10–12.

McLellan, A. G. (1979) Aggregate mining and rehabilitation, *Minerals and the Environment*, **1** (1), 31–35, J. W. Larman, Cambridge.

McLellan, A. G., Yundt, S. E. and Dorfman, M. L. (1979) *Abandoned Pits and Quarries in Ontario*, Ontario Geological Survey Miscellaneous Paper 79, Ontario Ministry of Natural Resources, Toronto.

McQuinn, P. (1978) *Rural Retreating: a Review and an Australian Case Study*, Department of Geography, University of New England, Armidale.

Mage, J. A. (1974) *Part-Time Farming in Southern Ontario with Specific Reference to Waterloo County*, PhD thesis, Department of Geography, University of Waterloo, Waterloo, Ontario.

Maguire, G. (1979) The urban fringe: perspectives on land use in the North Okanagan, pp. 11–20 in *The Urban Fringe in the Western Provinces*, ICURR Occasional Paper, Intergovernmental Committee on Urban and Regional Research, Toronto.

Manitoba Municipal Planning Branch (1974) *Demand Analysis, Winnipeg Region Planning Study*, Municipal Planning Branch, Department of Municipal Affairs, Winnipeg.

Manitoba Municipal Planning Branch and University of Manitoba (1974) *The Nature of Demand for Exurbia Living*, Winnipeg Region Study, Department of City Planning, University of Manitoba, Winnipeg, Manitoba.

Manning, E. W. and McCuaig, J. D. (1977) *Agricultural Land and Urban Centres: an Overview of the Significance of Urban Centres to Canada's Quality Agricultural Land*, Report 11, Lands Directorate, Environment Canada, Ottawa.

Marsh, J. (1977) Near-urban parks, *Parks News: Journal of the National and Provincial Parks Association of Canada*, **13** (1), 2–7.

Martin, L. R. G. (1974) Problems and policies associated with high land costs on the urban fringe, in *The Management of Land for Urban Development*, Canadian Council on Urban and Regional Research, Ottawa.

Martin, L. R. G. (1975a) *A Comparative Urban Fringe Study Methodology*, Occasional Paper 6, Lands Directorate, Environment Canada, Ottawa.

Martin, L. R. G. (1975b) *Land Use Dynamics on the Toronto Urban Fringe*, Information Canada for Environment Canada, Ottawa.

Martin, L. R. G. (1976) Land dealer behaviour on the Toronto urban fringe, *Ontario Geography*, **10**, 4–10.

Martin, L. R. G. (1977a) The impact of government policies on the supply and price of land for urban development, pp. 40–71 in Smith, L. B. and Walker, M. (eds), *Public Property? The Habitat Debate Continued: Essays on the Price, Ownership and Government of Land*, The Fraser Institute, Vancouver.

Martin, L. R. G. (1977b) Land dealer and land developer behaviour on the rural–urban fringe of Toronto, pp. 289–376 in Russwurm, L., Preston, R. E. and Martin, L. R. G. (eds), *Essays on Canadian Urban Process and Form*, Publication Series 10, Department of Geography, University of Waterloo, Waterloo, Ontario.

Martin, W. T. (1953) *The Rural Urban Fringe: a Study of Adjustment to Residential Location*, Studies in Sociology 1, University of Oregon Press, Eugene, Oregon.

Massie, R. W. (1969) *A System of Linked Models for Forecasting Urban Residential Growth*, University of North Carolina, Chapel Hill.

Mayo, H. B. (1976) *Report of the Ottawa-Carleton Review Commission*, Ontario Ministry of Treasury, Economics and Intergovernmental Affairs, Eastern Ontario Region, Ottawa.

MEAR (Mission d'Etude d'Aménagement Rural) (1971) *Eléments pour un Schéma d'Aménagement Rural de la Région Parisienne*, France Ministry of Agriculture, Paris.

Metro (1980) *The First Year*, Metropolitan Service District, Portland, Oregon.

Metro Portland Metropolitan Service District (1979) *Urban Growth Boundary Findings*, Metropolitan Service District, Portland, Oregon.

Metropolitan Council of the Twin Cities (1975) *Development Framework Policy, Plan, Program*, Metropolitan Council of the Twin Cities Area, St Paul, Minn.

Metropolitan Council of the Twin Cities Area (1979a) *Rural Area Task Force Report to the Metropolitan Council*, Metropolitan Council of the Twin Cities Area, St Paul, Minn.

Metropolitan Council of the Twin Cities Area (1979b) *Citizens Guide to the Metropolitan Council*, Metropolitan Council of the Twin Cities Area, St Paul, Minn.

Moran, W. (1978) Land value, distance, and productivity on the Auckland urban periphery, *New Zealand Geographer*, **34** (2), 85–96.

Moran, W. (1980) Planning property tax and positive attitudes, pp. 68–89 in New Zealand Land Use Advisory Council, *Proceedings of the Seminar on Peri-Urban Land Use, Dec. 1979*, Department of Lands and Survey, University of Waikato, Wellington, New Zealand.

Morgan, J. B. (1978) *The Urban Fringe Taxation Problem: a Case Study of Glanbrook Township*, BES thesis, Department of Geography, University of Waterloo, Ontario.

Mumford, L. (1961) *The City in History*, Harcourt, Brace and World, New York.

Munson, M. (1980) Twin Cities Metropolitan Area land inventory and analysis, Paper for ULI-HUD *Seminar on Land Process and Public Policy, Feb 1980, Washington*, Metropolitan Council of the Twin Cities Area, St Paul, Minn.

Munton, R. J. C. (1973) Recent trends in farmland prices in England and Wales, *The Estates Gazette*, **227**, 2159–65.

Munton, R. J. C. (1974) Farming on the urban fringe, Ch. 10, pp. 201–23 in Johnson, J. H. (ed.), *Suburban Growth*, John Wiley and Sons, London.

Munton, R. J. C. (1975) The state of the agricultural land market in England, 1971–73: a survey of auctioneers' property transactions, *Oxford Agrarian Studies*, **4** (2), 111–30.

Munton, R. J. C. (1976a) An analysis of price trends in the agricultural land market of England and Wales, *Tijdschrift voor economische en sociale geografie*, **67**(4), 202–12.

Munton, R. J. C. (1976b) Agricultural land prices in 1974: some observations, *Chartered Surveyor, Rural Quarterly*, **3**, 14–16.

Munton, R. J. C. (1979) *London's Green Belt: Restraint and the Management of Agricultural Land*, Report to the Department of the Environment, London.

Muth, R. F. (1961) Economic change and rural–urban land use conversions, *Econometrica*, **29** (1), 1–23.

Myrdal, G. M. (1963) *Economic Theory and Underdeveloped Regions*, Methuen, London.

Myers, P. (1976) *Zoning Hawaii, an Analysis of the Passage and Implementation of Hawaii's Land Classification Law*, The Conservation Foundation, Washington.

National and Provincial Parks Association of Canada (1977) Near-urban parks, *Park News: Journal of the National and Provincial Parks Association of Canada*, **13** (1).

Nature Conservancy Council (1977) *Nature Conservation and Agriculture*, Nature Conservancy Council, London, England.

Neice, P. C. (1977) *Planning for Rural Areas: Rural Non-Farm Development in Central Perth, a Case Study in Perth County*, BES thesis, School of Urban and Regional Planning, University of Waterloo, Waterloo, Ontario.

Nelson, R. H. (1977) *Zoning and Property Rights: an Analysis of the American System of Land Use Regulation*, MIT Press, Cambridge, Mass.

Neutze, M. (1977) *Urban Development in Australia*, George Allen and Unwin, Sydney.

New Zealand Land Use Advisory Council (1980), Bishop, W. J. F. (ed.), *Proceedings of the Seminar on Peri-Urban Land Use*, University of Waikato, December 1979, Department of Lands and Survey, Wellington, New Zealand.

Norcliffe, G. B. (1975) A theory of manufacturing places, pp. 19–57 in Collins, L. and Walker, D. F. (eds), *Locational Dynamics of Manufacturing Activity*, John Wiley and Sons, London.

Nova Scotia Community Planning Division (1976) *Region of the Metro Influence Study for Area Surrounding Halifax–Dartmouth*, Department of Municipal Affairs, Halifax.

Odum, E. P. (1972) Ecosystem theory in relation to man. pp. 11–23 in Wiens, J. A. (ed.), *Ecosystem Structure and Function*, Oregon State University Press, Corvallis, **Okanagan–Similkameen Regional District** (1974) *Rural Residential Development*, Planning Department, Regional District of Okanagan–Similkameen, British Columbia.

Ontario (1971) *The Pits and Quarries Control Act 1971*, Ch. 96. Statutes of Ontario, Toronto.

Ontario Department of Treasury and Economics (1972) *Niagara Escarpment Study: Fruit Belt Report*, The Queen's Printer, Toronto.

Ontario Ministries of the Environment and Agriculture and Food (1973) *Agriculture Code of Practice for Ontario*, Ministries of the Environment and Agriculture and Food, Toronto.

Ontario Ministry of the Attorney General (1979) *Discussion Paper on Occupiers' Liability and Trespass to Property*, Communications Office, Ministry of the Attorney General, Toronto.

Ontario Ministry of the Attorney General (1980) *Property Protection and Outdoor Opportunities*, Communications Office, Ministry of the Attorney General, Toronto.

Ontario Ministry of Housing (1976) *Land Severance: Planning Guidelines for Land Division Committees and Committees of Adjustment*, Operations Control Branch, Plans Administration Branch, Ministry of Housing, Toronto.

Ontario Ministry of Housing and County of Huron, MacLaren and Associates, Consultants (1976) *Countryside Planning*, Local Policy Planning Branch, Ministry of Housing, Toronto.

Ontario Ministry of Natural Resources (1972) *Bronte Creek Provincial Park Advisory Committee Policy Recommendation Report*, Parks Branch, Ministry of Natural Resources, Toronto.

Oregon Land Conservation and Development Commission (1978) *Statewide Planning Goals and Guidelines*, Oregon Land Conservation and Development Commission, Salem, Oregon.

Owen, W. (1972) *The Accessible City*, The Brookings Institution. Washington.

Pahl, R. E. (1965) *Urbs in Rure: the Metropolitan Fringe in Hertfordshire*, Geography Paper 2, London School of Economics, University of London, London.

Parenteau, R. (1981) Is Canada going back to the land?, pp. 53–70 in Beesley, K. B. and Russwurm, L. H. (eds), *The Rural–Urban Fringe: Canadian Perspectives*, Monograph Series, Department of Geography, Atkinson College, York University, Toronto.

Parry, C. (1963) Une exemple de décentralisation industrielle: la dispersion des usines de 'La Radiotechnique' à l'ouest de Paris, *Annales de Géographie*, **72**, 148–61.

Parsons, J. J. (1972) Slicing up the open space: subdivisions without homes in Northern California, *Erdkunde*, **26**, 1–8.

Paton, Smith and Gram Ltd. (1973) *A Subjective Report on the Viability of Agriculture in Certain Sections of Delta Muncipality*, Greater Vancouver Regional District, Vancouver.

Pattee, H. H. (ed.) (1973) *Hierarchy Theory*, Braziller, New York.

Patterson, H. L. (1968) Ontario's disappearing agricultural land, *Agricultural Institute Review*, **23** (2), 7–10.

Pautard, J. (1965) *Les Disparités Régionales dans la Croissance de l'Agriculture Française*, Serie Espace Economique, Gauthier–Villars, Paris.

Pease, J. R. and Morgan, M. (1979) *Community Growth Management, Performance Zoning*, Extension Circular 963, Oregon State University Extension Service, Corvallis.

Pédelaborde, P. (1961) *L'Agriculture dans les Plaines Alluviales de la Presqu'ile de Saint-Germaine-en-Laye: le Contact des Structures Rurale et Urbain*, A. Colin, Ecole Pratique de Hautes Etudes, Paris.

Petersen, G. E. and Yampolsky, H. (1975) *Urban Development and the Protection of Metropolitan Farmland*, Urban Institute, Washington.

References

Philbrick, A. K. (1961) *Analyses of the Geographical Patterns of Gross Land Uses and Changes in Numbers of Structures in Relation to Major Highways in the Lower Half of the Lower Peninsula of Michigan*, Highway Traffic Safety Center, Michigan State University, East Lansing.

Phillips, P. D. (1977) *Exurban Commuters in the Kentucky Bluegrass Region*, Monograph 5, Centre for Real Estate and Land Use Analysis, University of Kentucky, Lexington, Kentucky.

Platt, R. H. (1972) *The Open Space Decision Process*, Research Paper 142, Department of Geography, University of Chicago, Chicago.

Porter, A. (1977) *Land Use*, Issue Paper 5, Royal Commission on Electric Power Planning, Toronto.

Poupardin, D., Meynard, C., Wolfer, B. and Ringwald, P. M. (1971) *L'Evolution des Modes d'Occupation du Sol dans le Départment des Yvelines*, France Ministry of Agriculture and Rural Development and the Institut National de la Recherche Agronomique, Paris.

Préfecture de la Région d'Ile-de-France (1976a) *Les Z. N. E. de la Région d'Ile-de-France: les plateaux de sud*, Préfecture de la Région d'Ile-de-France, Paris.

Préfecture de la Région d'Ile-de-France (1976b) *Les Z. N. E. de la Région d'Ile-de-France: le Hurepoix*, Préfecture de la Région d'Ile-de-France, Paris.

Priddle, G. *et al* (1976) *The Long-term Socio-economic Impact of an Electrical Power Transmission Corridor on the Rural Environment: Perception and Reality*, Submission to the Royal Commission on Electric Power Planning, Toronto.

Proctor and Redfern (1974) *Mineral Aggregate Study: Central Ontario Planning Region*, Report, Ontario Ministry of Natural Resources, Toronto.

Pryor, R. J. (1968) Defining the rural–urban fringe, *Social Forces*, **47**, 202–15.

Punter, J. V. (1974) *The Impact of Exurban Development on Land and Landscape in the Toronto-Centred Region 1954–1971*, Report to Policy Planning Division, Central Mortgage and Housing Corporation, Ottawa.

Raup, P. M. (1975) Urban threats to rural lands: background and beginnings, *Journal of the American Institute of Planners*, **41**, 371–8.

Rawson, M. (1976) *Ill Fares the Land*, Urban Prospects, Ministry of State for Urban Affairs, Ottawa.

Real Estate Research Corporation (1974) *The Costs of Sprawl – Detailed Cost Analysis*, US Government Printing Office for the Council of Environmental Quality, Washington.

Reeder, L. (1954) Industrial location trends in Chicago in relation to population growth, *Land Economics*, **30**, 177–82.

Reeder, L. (1955) Industrial decentralization as a factor in rural–urban fringe development, *Land Economics*, **31**, 275–80.

Reeds, L. G. (1969) *Niagara Region: Agricultural Research Report*, Ontario Department of Economics, Treasury and Intergovernment Affairs, Toronto.

Reilly, W. (ed.) (1973) *The Use of Land: a Citizen's Guide to Urban Growth*, Crowell, New York, for the Rockefeller Brothers Fund.

Ricour-Singh, F. (1979) *Poles and Zones of Attraction*, Statistics Canada Census Analytical Study, Ministry of Supply and Services, Ottawa.

Roberts, N. A. and Brown, H. J. (1980) *Property Tax Preferences for Agricultural Land*, Landmark Studies, Lincoln Institute of Land Policy, Allanheld, Osmun and Co., Montclair, NJ.

Rodd, R. S. (1976) The crisis of agricultural land in the Ontario countryside, *Plan Canada*, **16**, 160–70.

Rose, J. G. (1975) *Transfer of Development Rights: a New Technique of Land Use Regulation*, Center for Urban Policy Research, Rutgers University and State University of New Jersey, NJ.

Roskill Commission (1970) *Commission on the Third London Airport*, Paper and Proceedings 7 and 8, HMSO, London.
Russwurm, L. H. (1967) Expanding urbanization and selected agricultural elements, a case study, Southwestern Ontario 1941–1961, *Land Economics*, **43**, 101–7.
Russwurm, L. H. (1970) *Development of an Urban Corridor System, Toronto to Stratford Area, 1941–1966*, Regional Development Branch Research Paper 3, The Queen's Printer, Toronto.
Russwurm, L. H. (1975a) Land policies across Canada: thoughts and viewpoints, pp. 25–9 in *Battle for Land Conference Report*, Community Planning Association of Canada, Ottawa.
Russwurm, L. H. (1975b) Urban fringe and urban shadow, pp. 148–64 in Bryfogle, R. C. and Krueger, R. R. (eds), *Urban Problems* (rev. edn), Holt, Rinehart and Winston, Toronto.
Russwurm, L. H. (1976) Country residential development and the regional city form in Canada, *Ontario Geography*, **10**, 79–96.
Russwurm, L. H. (1977a) *The Surroundings of Our Cities*, Community Planning Press, Ottawa.
Russwurm, L. H. (1977b) The urban fringe as a regional environment, pp. 181–280 in Russwurm, L. H., Preston, R. E., and Martin, L. R. G. (eds), *Essays in Canadian Urban Process and Form I*, Publications Series 10, Department of Geography, University of Waterloo, Waterloo, Ontario.
Russwurm, L. H. (1980a) Land in the urban fringe: conflicts and their policy implications, pp. 454–96 in Preston, R. E. and Russwurm, L. H. (eds), , *Essays on Canadian Urban Process and Form II*, Publication Series 15, Department of Geography, University of Waterloo, Waterloo, Ontario.
Russwurm, L. H. (1980b) The developing spatial form of Canadian cities, pp. 273–361 in Preston, R. E. and Russwurm, L. H. (eds), *Essays on Canadian Urban Process and Form II*, Publication Series 15, Department of Geography, University of Waterloo, Waterloo, Ontario.
Russwurm, L. H. and Preston, R. E. (1980) Aspects of the spatial pattern of urban growth in Canada between 1966–1976, pp. 155–182 in Preston, R. E. and Russwurm, L. H. (eds), *Essays in Canadian Urban Process and Form II*, Publication Series 15, Department of Geography, University of Waterloo, Waterloo, Ontario.
Russwurm, L. H. and Sommerville, E. (eds) (1974) *Man's Natural Environment: a Systems Approach*, Duxbury Press, North Scituate Mass.
Sant, M. (1975) *Industrial Movement and Regional Development*, Urban and Regional Planning Series, Pergamon Press, London.
Schmid, A. A. (1968) *Converting Land from Rural to Urban Uses*, The Johns Hopkins Press, Baltimore, for Resources for the Future, Washington.
Schultz, T. W. (1953) *The Economic Organization of Agriculture*, McGraw-Hill, New York.
Seabrooke, A. K. (1981) Social and perceptual characteristics of urban fringe dwellers, Otonabee Township, Peterborough, pp. 244–56 in Beesley, K. B. and Russwurm, L. H. (eds), *The Rural–Urban Fringe: Canadian Perspectives*, Monograph Series, Department of Geography, Atkinson College, York University, Toronto.
SEGESA (Société d'Etudes Géographiques, Economiques et Sociologiques Appliquées) (1973) *L'Agriculture Spécialisée de la Région Parisienne face à la Croissance de l'Agglomération*, Report to the Ministry of Agriculture, Paris.
Sermonti, E. (1968) Agriculture in areas of urban expansion: an Italian study, *Journal of the Town Planning Institute*, **54**, 15–17.

Sévérac, G. (1963) Les prix de la terre et leurs components, *Revue Française de l'Agriculture*, summer 1963.
Shields, J. A. and Ferguson, W. S. (1975) Land resources, production possibilities and limitations for crop production in the Prairie Provinces, pp. 115–56 in *Oilseed and Pulse Crops in Western Canada*, Western Cooperative Fertilizers Ltd, Calgary.
Shively, R. W. (1974) Corporate and community decision-making to attract industry, pp. 89–93 in Whiting, L. R. (ed.), *Rural Industrialization: Problems and Potentials*, The Iowa State University Press, Ames, Iowa.
Shumway, C. R. (1971) *Urban Expansion on Agricultural Land in California*, Information Series 71–3, Giannini Foundation, University of California, Berkeley.
Sinclair, P. R. and Westhues, K. (1975) *Village in Crisis*, Holt, Rinehart and Winston, Toronto.
Sinclair, R. J. (1967) Von Thünen and urban sprawl, *Annals of the Association of American Geographers*, **57**, 72–87.
Smith, B. W. and Morganti, T. R. (1980) Rural residential development: a comparison of the costs of alternative forms, *Geographical Perspectives*, Department of Geography, University of Northern Iowa, **45**, 6–14.
Smith, C. R., Partain, L. E. and Champlain, J. R. (1966) *Rural Recreation for Profit*, Interstate Printers and Publishers, Danville, Ill.
Smith, D. L. (1966) Market gardening at Adelaide's urban fringe, *Economic Geography*, **42** (1), 19–36.
Smith, J. N. (1972) The gateways: parks for whom? Ch. 17, pp. 213–236 in *National Parks for the Future*, The Conservation Foundation, Washington, DC.
Snyder, J. H. (1966) A new programme for agricultural land use stabilisation: the California Land Conservation Act of 1965, *Land Economics*, **42**, 29–41.
Solberg, E. D. (1967) *The Why and How of Rural Zoning*, Agricultural Information Bulletin 196, Economic Research Service, US Department of Agriculture, Washington.
Spurr, P. (1976) Land and Urban Development, James Lorimer, Toronto.
Standing Conference (1976) *The Improvement of London's Green Belt*, Standing Conference on London and South-east Regional Planning, London.
Stevens Committee (1976) *Planning Control over Mineral Working*, HMSO, London.
Stockham, J. and Pease, J. R. (1974) *Performance Standards – A Technique for Controlling Land Use*, Special Report 424, Oregon State University Extension Service, Corvallis.
Stone, T. R. (1971) *Beyond the Automobile: Reshaping the Transportation Environment*, Prentice-Hall, Englewood Cliffs, NJ.
Strachan, A. (1974) The planning framework for modern urban growth: the example of Great Britain, Ch. 4, pp. 53–76 in Johnson, J. H. (ed.), *Suburban Growth*, John Wiley and Sons, London.
Struyk, R. J. and James, F. J. (1975) *Intrametropolitan Industrial Location*, Lexington Books, D. C. Heath and Co., Lexington, Mass.
Summers, G. F. and Selvik, A. (eds) (1979) *Nonmetropolitan Industrial Growth and Community Change*, Lexington Books, Mass.
Swan, H. M. (1975) *Land Market Control Strategy in France: the Case of the ZAD*, B.75.4 Discussion Paper, Ministry of State for Urban Affairs, Ottawa.
Taafe, E. J., Gauthier, H. L. and Maraffa, T. A. (1980) Extended commuting and the intermetropolitan periphery, *Annals of the Association of American Geographers*, **70**, 313–29.
Task Force (1969) *Report of the Federal Task Force on Housing and Urban Development*, The Queen's Printer, Ottawa.

Thomas, D. (1970) *London's Green Belt*, Faber and Faber, London.

Thompson, K. J. (1978) *Agricultural Change and Conservation in the Urban Fringe*, Report to the Countryside Commission, University of Newcastle-upon-Tyne.

Tisdale, H. (1942) The process of urbanization, *Social Forces*, **20**, 311–16.

Travis, A. S. (1976) Urban fringe recreation in other countries – some examples, pp. 31–41 in Travis, A. S. and Veal, A. J. (eds) *Recreation and the Urban Fringe: Conference Proceedings*, Centre for Urban and Regional Studies, University of Birmingham, England.

Travis, A. S. and Veal, A. J. (eds.) (1976) *Recreation and the Urban Fringe: Conference Proceedings*, Centre for Urban and Regional Studies, University of Birmingham, England.

Tricart, J. (1948) *La Culture Fruitière dans la Région Parisienne*, Etudes et Mémoires, II, Centre National de la Recherche Scientifique, Paris.

Troughton, M. J. (1976) *Landholding in a Rural–Urban Fringe Environment: the Case of London, Ontario*, Occasional Paper 11, Lands Directorate, Environment Canada, Ottawa.

Troughton, M. J. (1981) Aspects of employment and commuting in the fringe zone of London, Ontario, pp. 144–78 in Beesley, K. B. and Russwurm, L. H. (eds), *The Rural–Urban Fringe: Canadian Perpectives*, Monograph Series, Department of Geography, Atkinson College, York University, Toronto.

UK (HMSO) (1942) *Report of the Commission on Land Utilisation in Rural Areas*, Cmd. 6378, HMSO, London.

UK Government White Paper (1976) Regulating land development in the United Kingdom, *Ekistics*, **41** (244), 168–72.

UK Ministry of Agriculture, Fisheries and Food (1977) Peri-urban agriculture in the Slough-Hillingdon area (region of London), *Conference: Peri-Urban Agriculture*, OECD, Paris.

UK Ministry of Housing and Local Government (1955) *Green Belts*, Circular 42/55, HMSO.

University of Missouri (1972) *Recreation Needs of Inner City Residents in Missouri*, Missouri State Interagency Council for Outdoor Recreation, Columbia.

US Bureau of the Census (1970) *Statistical Abstract of the United States: 1970 (91st edn)*, US Bureau of the Census, Department of Commerce, Washington, DC.

US Council of Environmental Quality (1976) *Subdividing Rural America: Impacts of Recreational Lot and Second Home Development*, US Government Printing Office, Washington.

US Department of Housing and Development (1965) *Open Space for Urban America*, U S Department of Housing and Urban Development, Washington.

US Department of the Interior (1967) *Surface Mining and Our Environment*, US Government Printing Office, Washington.

US National Academy of Sciences and National Academy of Engineering (1972) *Urban Growth and Land Development*, National Academy of Sciences, Washington.

Vaux, H. J., Jr. (1977) Rural land subdividing: a lesson from the southern California desert, *Journal of the American Institute of Planners*, **43**, 271–8.

Verney Committee (1976) *Aggregates: the Way Ahead*, Report of the Advisory Committee on Aggregates, HMSO, London.

Vining, D. R., Jr., Plaut, T. and Bieri, K. (1977) Urban encroachment on prime agricultural land in the United States, *International Regional Science Review*, 2, 143–56.

Wager, J. (1967) Outdoor recreation on commonland, *Journal of the Town Planning Institute*, **53** (9), 398–403.

Walker, G. (1975) Social networks in rural space: a comparison of two Ontario localities, *East Lakes Geographer*, **10**, 68–77.
Walker, G. (1976) Social perspectives on the countryside: reflections on territorial form north of Toronto, *Ontario Geography*, **10**, 54–63.
Walker, G. (1977) Social networks and territory in a commuter village, Bond Head, Ontario, *The Canadian Geographer*, **21**(4), 329–50.
Wall, G. and Sinott, J. (1980) Urban recreational and cultural facilities as tourist attractions, *The Canadian Geographer*, **24**(1), 50–9.
Walrath, A. J. (1957) Equalization of property taxes in an urban–rural area, *Land Economics*, **33**(1), 47–54.
Wehrwein, G. S. (1942) The rural–urban fringe, *Economic Geography*, 8, 217–28.
Westmacott, R. and Worthington, T. (1974) *New Agricultural Landscapes: a Report*, Countryside Commission, Cheltenham, England.
Whitby, M. C., Robins, D. L. J., Tansey, A. W. and Willis, K. G. (1974) *Rural Resource Development*, Methuen, London.
Whitehead, J. C. (1969) *The Country Residential Survey*, Prepared for the Zoning Committee, Calgary Regional Planning Commission, Calgary, Alberta.
Whyte, L. L., Wilson, A. G. and Wilson, D. (eds) (1969) *Hierarchical Structures*, American Elsevier Pub. Co., New York.
Whyte, W. H. (1968) *The Last Landscape*, Doubleday and Co., Garden City, New York.
Wibberley, G. P. (1954) The challenge of rural land losses, *Journal of the Royal Society of Arts*, **102**, 650–70.
Wibberley, G. P. (1959) *Agriculture and Urban Growth: a Study of the Competition for Rural Land*, Michael Joseph, London.
Wibberley, G. P. (1972) Conflicts in the countryside, *Town and Country Planning*, **40**, 259–64.
Wibberley, G. P. (1974) Development in the countryside, *Journal of Environmental management*, 2, 199–214.
Williams, E. A. (1969) *Open Space: the Choices before California*, Report to the California State Office of Planning, Diablo Press, San Francisco.
Williams, G. D. V., Pocock, N. J., and Russwurm, L. H. (1978) The spatial association of agroclimatic resources and urban population in Canada, pp. 165–79 in Irving, R. M. (ed.), *Readings in Canadian Geography* (3rd edn), Holt, Rinehart and Winston, Toronto.
Wilson, L. P. (1979) The Knos model as applied to land values in Carbondale, Illinois, pp. 59–88 in Christensen, D. E. (ed.), *Papers on Planning and Land Value Analysis*, Occasional Papers in Geography 6, Department of Geography, Southern Illinois University at Carbondale, Ill.
Winnipeg City Planning Division (1973) *Draft Report on the Areas of No Urban Expansion*, City of Winnipeg Planning Division, Winnipeg, Manitoba.
Wolfe, R. I. (1964) Effect of ribbon development on traffice flow, *Traffic Quarterly*, Jan. 1964, 105–17.
Wood, P. A. (1974) Urban manufacturing: a view from the fringe, Ch. 7, pp. 129–54 in Johnson, J. H. (ed.), *Suburban Growth*, John Wiley and Sons, London.
Wurster, C. B. (1963) The form and structure of the future urban complex, pp. 73–101 in Wingo, L. (ed.), *Cities and Space*, The Johns Hopkins Press, Baltimore.
Yeates, M. (1975) *Main Street: Windsor to Quebec City*, MacMillan of Canada, Toronto.
Yundt, S. E. (1973) *Marketing and Transportation in the Sand and Gravel Industry in Waterloo and Wellington Counties*, M A thesis, Department of Geography, University of Waterloo, Waterloo, Ontario.

Yundt, S. E. and Augaitis, D. (1979) *From Pits to Playgrounds: Aggregate Extraction and Pit Rehabilitation in Toronto: a Historical Review*, Ontario Ministry of Natural Resources, Toronto.

Ziemetz, K. A., Dillon, E., Hardy, E. E. and Otte, R. C. (1976) *Dynamics of Land Use in Fast Growth Areas*, Agricultural Economics Report 325, Economic Research Service, US Department of Agriculture, Washington.

Zimmerman, C. C. and Moneo, G. W. (1972) *The Prairie Community System*, Agricultural Economics Research Council, Ottawa.

Zipf, G. K. (1949) *Human Behavior and the Principle of Least Effort: an Introduction to Human Ecology*, Addison-Wesley, Cambridge, Mass.

Index